A LIFE ON THE EDGE

JIM WHITTAKER

A LIFE ON THE EDGE

MEMOIRS OF EVEREST AND BEYOND

To Warren—

Jim Whittaker

THE
MOUNTAINEERS

Published by
The Mountaineers
1001 SW Klickitat Way, Suite 201
Seattle, WA 98134

Published simultaneously in Great Britain by Cordee, 3a DeMontfort Street, Leicester, England, LE1 7HD

Manufactured in the United States of America

Edited by Paula Thurman
Cover and book design by Ani Rucki
Layout by Ani Rucki

Cover photograph: *Jim Whittaker on the summit of Mount Everest, May 1, 1963. Photo: Nawang Gombu/National Geographic Society*

Frontispiece: *Jim Whittaker, 1978. Photo: Dianne Roberts*

Library of Congress Cataloging-in-Publication Data
Whittaker, Jim, 1929–
    A life on the edge : memoirs of Everest and beyond / Jim Whittaker ;
    forewords by Edward M. Kennedy and John Glenn ; introduction by Tom
    Hornbein. — 1st ed.
        p.   cm.
    Published simultaneously in Great Britain.
    Includes index.
    ISBN 0-89886-540-9 (cloth)
    ISBN 0-89886-754-1 (paper)
    1. Whittaker, Jim 1929–   2. Mountaineers—United States Biography.
    3. Mountaineering accidents—Everest, Mount (Nepal and China)
    4. Everest, Mount (China and Nepal) I. Title.
    GV199.92.W464 A3 1999
    796.52'2'092—dc21
    [B]   99–6453
                                                                  CIP

To Dad, Mom, Dianne, Carl, Scott, Bobby, Joss, and Leif

He who moves not forward goes backward.

—*Goethe*

CONTENTS

Forewords by Edward M. Kennedy and John Glenn   9

Preface by Jim Whittaker   12

Acknowledgments   14

Introduction by Tom Hornbein   15

Chapter One: EXPOSURE   19

Chapter Two: RISK   33

Chapter Three: APPRENTICESHIP   51

Chapter Four: BIGGER, FASTER, HIGHER   63

Chapter Five: FALLING   75

Chapter Six: EVEREST   87

Chapter Seven: CLIMBING WITH THE KENNEDYS   121

Chapter Eight: ROLLER COASTER   141

Chapter Nine: NEW HEIGHTS   155

Chapter Ten: REPRISE   177

Chapter Eleven: CUTTING LOOSE   203

Chapter Twelve: ROCK BOTTOM   215

Chapter Thirteen: THE SUMMIT ON THE SUMMIT   233

Chapter Fourteen: LIFE WELL LIVED   261

Index   267

FOREWORDS

Jim Whittaker was the first American to stand atop Mount Everest in 1963—and those of us who are privileged to call him a friend know he stands equally tall at sea level.

President Kennedy met Jim in 1963 when he honored him and his Mount Everest team at the White House. Other members of the Kennedy family met Jim in 1965 when he agreed to lead a National Geographic and Boston Museum of Science survey expedition up the tallest unclimbed mountain in North America, which had recently been named in honor of President Kennedy by the Canadian government. Robert Kennedy was part of the team that climbed Mount Kennedy with Jim, and Jim and Bobby knelt at the summit in memory of my brother. I had intended to make the climb too, but was unable to do so in the wake of the plane crash that nearly took my life in June of 1964. Bobby was fascinated by Jim's leadership, good humor, and courage on that expedition, and by the time they descended they had become friends.

Jim and his family were wonderful company on Christmas ski trips and river-rafting summer vacations, and Jim was a terrific organizer during Bobby's 1968 presidential campaign. I saw an example of Jim's courage and concern for others first-hand during a ski holiday in Sun Valley. One snowy day he was riding up in the chair lift and saw a fallen skier at the foot of the chair tower

Jim Whittaker on the summit of Mount Everest, May 1, 1963. Photo: Nawang Gombu/National Geographic Society

9

ahead of him, who looked shaken up. As he got closer he suddenly realized that it was my son Teddy. Without a thought about his own safety, he immediately slid off the chair, hung by his hands for a second and let go. He fell twenty feet and his skis were knocked off, but fortunately he was not hurt. Jim then skied down to Teddy, made sure he was not injured, and helped him get back down to the Roundhouse. In a sense, I inherited Jim from Bobby, and we have been great friends ever since.

Jim's extraordinary life has been filled with many significant milestones, and this memoir lets the world relive the amazing adventures that have shaped this remarkable man. He vividly describes the awe, terror, and exhilaration of climbing the highest mountains in the world and gives us insight into the unique physical and organizational skills that make these ascents successful. As a young man, he started climbing with his brothers in the pristine beauty of the Pacific Northwest. His inner compass—an awareness of the beauty and the power of nature and a visceral realization of the importance of preserving the environment—led him ever upward to the roof of the world. As his skiing and mountaineering abilities grew, he also took on the responsibility of a mountain rescue service with his twin brother, Louie. He had numerous harrowing moments, and readers are likely to come away feeling it is a miracle Jim Whittaker is still alive. For many others, Jim was himself the miracle who kept them alive.

As a family man, Jim has made his wife Dianne a partner in his endeavors and has also supported her as she reached for her own goals. He has encouraged his children to explore and appreciate the diversity of the world. As a businessman, Jim has devoted his life to introducing people to the wonders of nature and providing the equipment to enjoy it. As a mountaineer, he also reached out in inspiring ways, such as leading an expedition of people with disabilities to the top of his beloved Mount Rainier and the achievement of their dream, and persuading the Soviet and Chinese governments to allow their climbers to join Americans on a successful Mount Everest Peace Climb. He knew that the fellowship and trust developed on the steep face of a glacier could lead to closer ties between nations, and it did. He was our first high-altitude diplomat.

Jim has always been determined to succeed at what was thought to be impossible. In fact, that is what he named his sailboat—*Impossible*. The rugged individualist is alive and well in Jim Whittaker. The life story well told in these pages is a reminder of all the enduring virtues of our time and all time. He is himself a profile in courage—an Everest of integrity, determination, and loyalty.

—*Edward M. Kennedy*

Mountain climbing, real top-of-the-world high-altitude mountain climbing—not the more familiar hill and trail hiking—seems to have a way of generating polarities of passion. Rallied around the plus pole are those who see it as one of the noblest of human expressions, as setting high goals that require physical and mental toughness, then organizing all of one's resources and senses to accomplish that goal against whatever environmental odds there may be. At the negative pole are those who see climbing as the unnecessary risk of life and limb for, at best, vague personal satisfaction.

Whichever pole you find yourself drawn to, *A Life on the Edge: Memoirs of Everest and Beyond* will prove to be of tremendous interest. Jim Whittaker's vivid description of the "whys" of mountain climbing go far beyond "because it's there." He takes us past mental "exposure," as climbers call it—that sudden pit-of-the-stomach sensation that comes from looking down from hundreds of feet up on a precarious ledge—to explore the realities of "objective danger," another climber's term that is essentially a nice way of saying that unforeseen hazards, such as rock slides, avalanches, or lightning, can too often fatally override even the best planning and execution.

Jim's pursuit of "the highest," both as the first American to climb Mount Everest and the country's foremost mountain climber, makes for fascinating reading. As a friend of his for some thirty-five years, I believe he has written a landmark book, the most lucid account yet—one might almost call it a textbook—of the whys and hows of mountain climbing. Whether you are a "couch potato" or a mountaineer thoroughly experienced in the highest of the world's high countries, you will enjoy going along with him on this true-life climb.

—*John Glenn*

PREFACE

At 6:00 A.M. on May 1, 1963, after a miserable night in a tent hammered by hurricane-force winds, I crawled out into a maelstrom of swirling snow, strapped on crampons, shouldered my pack, roped up with my Sherpa friend Nawang Gombu, and took the first step on the last leg of a two-month struggle to climb the world's highest mountain.

Gasping for breath in the thin, cold air and wind at 27,450 feet and struggling to remain upright, it did not occur to me that this was an historic moment. It did not occur to me, despite the conditions on the mountain, that it was a particularly risky moment or that I might not return. It certainly did not occur to me that this was the moment around which the rest of my life would pivot.

It was, in fact, all these things. But at the time, only one thought was in my oxygen-starved mind: put one foot in front of the other. Climb. So that's what I did. And exactly seven hours later, at 1:00 P.M., I became the first American to reach the summit of Mount Everest.

■

In a lifetime of adventures, I've often felt blessed by fortune. But I believe that to a considerable extent luck is something you *make* happen—by extending yourself into situations of risk but also by preparing yourself to succeed under those risky conditions.

Not that success has always been the outcome, of course. My life has been a long series of planned ascents and unplanned falls, of surprise successes and abysses narrowly avoided, of moments of high triumph and plunging disappointment—on mountains, on the high seas, in business, and in my personal life.

Amid all these ups and downs, however, there has been one constant—my inspiration, my comfort, my compass and rudder: the beauty and richness of nature. Throughout my life I have been drawn forcefully to the outdoors, to forests and mountains, seacoasts and oceans, drawn by both a conscious delight in the grandeur and diversity of the planet and an unconscious spiritual yearning to be in the natural world. It is in the wild places—in the damp, clean air of an ancient forest, on a heaving ocean in unpredictable winds, on a snowy summit at the top of the world—that I enter my own personal cathedral and know where I fit in the vastness of creation.

■

I heard a phrase not too long ago that pretty well captures my philosophy of life: "If you aren't living on the edge, you're taking up too much space." It has nothing to do with thrill-seeking. It's about making the most of every moment, about stretching your own boundaries, about being willing to learn constantly, and putting yourself in situations where learning is possible—sometimes even critical to your survival. Being out on the edge, with everything at risk, is where you learn—and grow—the most.

This is a memoir of a life lived on the edge and some of the things I have learned out there.

ACKNOWLEDGMENTS

I am deeply grateful to The Mountaineers Club members for teaching me at an early age how to climb, and I thank The Mountaineers Books for publishing my autobiography.

Editor Margaret Foster was an excellent guide, and I felt comfortable roping up with her for this literary adventure. Bill Nothdurft taught me to move rhythmically and cohesively as I traversed each sentence and chapter. Jake and Susanne Page were pure inspiration, both in my life and with this book. Tom Hornbein, friend and philosopher, kept my eye on the goal and helped me avoid the chasms. Ani Rucki, with the heart and soul of an artist, did the visuals. Barney and Louie kept me from stepping over the edge. Dianne belayed, pushed, and pulled me up.

A thank you to the many friends and lifetime companions who gave me encouragement throughout this entire process. Not only has this memoir been made better by you, but so has my life.

INTRODUCTION

Between the bookends, life is a journey. For a few the journey becomes an odyssey of adventure. Jim Whittaker is clearly among the adventurers of the world, and not just in having climbed Mount Everest back in the days when it was still a full-bore adventure. At the age of seventy, he continues to live his life listening to that same restless inner spirit. You will see what I mean when you join him in this tale of his peripatetic quest.

Jim's life and mine first intersected when we were chosen to be among the nineteen Americans attempting to climb Mount Everest in 1963. I suspect most of us had dreamt of climbing to the highest point on earth during our teen years, at a time before Everest's first ascent by Edmund Hillary and Tenzing Norgay in 1953. Jim and I shared a common goal, although we chose different routes to achieve it.

Thirty-six years ago today, on May 1, 1963, while those of us watching from below assumed the swirling cloud cap creaming the summit meant no one would be moving up high, Jim and his Sherpa companion, Nawang Gombu, stepped from the tenuous security of their tent at 27,500 feet hell-bound for the summit. At 1:00 P.M. that afternoon, Big Jim Whittaker became the first American to reach the highest point on earth.

It's easy to view this first American ascent in 1963 through 1999 glasses and forget that when Jim and Gombu set foot on the top of the world, scarcely more than a handful of others had been there before them. Though a big unknown disappeared with the ascent by Hillary and Tenzing a decade earlier, plenty of uncertainty remained regarding the capacity of human beings to function not only at such high altitude, but especially under such bitter conditions. That Jim

15

and Gombu pulled it off was a major mountaineering achievement, one that gave those of us still seeking to climb the mountain a bit more confidence in our quest. Three weeks later, Barry C. Bishop and Lute Jerstad reached Everest's summit, following in Jim and Gombu's footsteps, and just before sunset that same day, Willi Unsoeld and I followed suit by way of the previously unclimbed West Ridge.

Jim's being the first American to reach the highest point on earth captured our country's imagination. He came home from Everest a hero. He had beaten the odds and pulled it off. Being a hero is not an easy role. For Jim, as for most of us, recognition for accomplishment was not unwelcome; it feels good to know that you and what you have done can make a difference to the lives of others. I think Jim understood that what he had achieved on Everest was a gift with strings attached. Over the years he has given much in return to stir the dreams of others. This book is but one more example of how the gift of having climbed Everest keeps on giving.

Reading Jim's account of his life rekindled in me questions that had been simmering for some time. For those of us who were part of this climb on Everest in 1963, how did having been there change our lives? To what extent was this experience a pivotal event, that is, a moment that impels a major alteration in the course of a life? When Jim and Gombu together walked those final feet to the summit of the world, the direction of Jim's life was altered in ways beyond imagination.

How Everest changed Jim's life is compellingly set forth in the pages that follow. He guided Bobby Kennedy on the first ascent of Canada's Mount Kennedy, named after Bobby's older brother, who was president at the time we climbed Everest. He became part of the Kennedy "family," along with a panoply of well-known public figures from many walks of life, a heady experience for a kid who grew up climbing and skiing in the mountains of the Pacific Northwest. He ran Bobby Kennedy's presidential campaign in Washington State; he was devastated by the terrible loss not only to himself but also to the world when Bobby was assassinated. He helped grow REI from a one-employee business to a multi-million dollar corporation, the nation's largest member-owned cooperative. He had one marriage dissolve and, later, began another with Dianne Roberts, who would become his partner in many adventures to come. Together they went to K2, the second highest mountain on earth, in 1975 and 1978. The lasting achievement of the first American ascent of this magnificent mountain in 1978 overshadowed the difficulties experienced in attempting to create a harmonious orchestra from a small cadre of virtuoso soloists. Shortly after returning from that second K2 trip, bringing home a great success, Jim and REI parted company; the timing seemed right for both. Jim was ready for new challenges off the mountains, but what he got in this new venture into the rugged ranges of the business world was near bankruptcy. Through this, I watched Jim and Dianne doing what had to be done to survive and not forget what they were surviving for.

I cannot help but wonder, though, whether all steps in the journey weren't part of some grand design destined to take Jim back to Everest. In 1990 Jim organized and led an expedition that placed a team of climbers from the world's most dangerously opposed superpowers—the United States, the Soviet Union, and China—on the summit of the world's highest mountain. With characteristically straightforward reasoning, Jim felt that if these three nations could summit together on Everest, their leaders might be inspired to master the other challenges facing them as well. When the first team of climbers from all three nations stood atop Everest together, this dream took at least a small step towards reality. What Jim pulled off in bringing about the International Peace Climb has to be one of his greatest accomplishments.

There is a difference between autobiography and biography. This is Jim's story. He has chosen to emphasize grand themes and tangible accomplishments, and also some cliff-hanging moments, both on mountains and off. We see the Jim he aspires to be; those parts of his personality that make him more like the rest of us don't take center stage. Indeed, Jim's purpose in writing this book was not just to talk about his life. He seeks to communicate his reverence for the natural world, what it has given to him and can give to others. He also wants to remind us that we have a responsibility to provide caring stewardship for our world and the peoples on it in return.

And the odyssey continues. As I write this, Jim and Dianne and their two sons are sailing around the world in their 54-foot ketch, *Impossible,* named for the craft that carried other adventurers searching for the mythical Mount Analogue in René Daumal's novel of the same name. If you ask Jim what makes him tick, what comes back is apt to be, "I don't reflect much. I just do it." Well, maybe. But perhaps this is the rudder to the *Impossible.*

Tom Hornbein
Bellevue, Washington
May 1, 1999

*(Left to right) Louie, Barney, and Jim with a neighbor's car, about 1935.
Photo: Whittaker family collection*

Chapter One

EXPOSURE

"The Tooth" is a 5,605-foot fang of rock that thrusts up from the jawbone of a ridge in the Cascade Mountains of western Washington State. The east face of the rock rises nearly 1,000 feet above the ridge, the west side 300 feet, and the summit is a lovely smooth slab. One sunny morning in 1943, when I was four-teen years old, my brothers Barney and Louie and I set out to climb The Tooth with our climbing teacher, Tom Campbell.

Tom was an experienced mountaineer who had lost an arm while serving in the U.S. Army's famous Tenth Mountain Division and now climbed with a hook screwed into his prosthetic arm. He had taught us the basics on Monitor Rock, a thirty-foot-high artificial wall of rock and cement in West Seattle, not far from our home. But this would be our first "real" climb.

That morning we hiked up a trail from Denny Creek through old-growth forest, crossing and recrossing the snow-fed stream until, after about three miles, we reached a big rockslide. Leaping from one lichen-encrusted boulder to the next, we gradually picked our way up through the slide. At the top, we followed game trails across scree and low brush, rising through open alpine forests to the west face of the ridge. Next, we followed a trail north through fragrant scrub cedar and, when the going turned really steep, roped up: Tom leading, then Barney, me, and finally Louie—the order in which we were born. We wormed up through stunted trees and between huge boulders, carrying the rope in coils between us, until we arrived at a notch in the north ridge.

Above us, The Tooth rose skyward, still in morning shadow. Directly ahead was a short but nearly vertical wall of rock—the first pitch of the climb. Along the rock face I could see good footholds and handholds. This would be easy.

Tom hopped over a three-foot gap to the rock face, climbed up a ways, found a good belay position (a place where he could brace himself to support the next climber), took in the slack rope between himself and Barney, and then called down:

"On belay. Climb!"

"Climbing!" Barney called back, as we'd been taught, and started smartly across the gap.

As he did, I saw him look to his left and hesitate for a split second. Then his movements became slow and deliberate, as if he were climbing in molasses. I watched his moves, as I had been taught to, so I could use the same holds he used, but I was impatient, wondering what was taking him so long. Finally, he reached Tom and got into belay position. It was my turn.

"On belay. Climb!" Barney shouted.

"Climbing!" I yelled back.

The gap lay in shadow. I stepped up to its edge, began to move out over it to the cliff a few feet away, glanced down past my left foot . . . and froze solid. The cliff plunged straight down for what looked like a thousand feet. Everything below was so tiny, so far away. I was absolutely terrified.

More than a half-century later, I can still see clearly every detail of rock, lichen, and shadow in that fearsome void. Scrambling around on a thirty-foot artificial wall in West Seattle had taught me a lot about climbing technique, but very little about what climbers call "exposure"—that heart-in-your-mouth surge of sheer terror when you first look down from a great height.

I willed myself across the gap, struggling to resist the palpable gravitational pull of the abyss below. From that point on up the rock face, every move I made was measured, focused, deliberate. Moving only one limb at a time, maintaining what climbers call a three-point suspension, I crept ever so slowly upward toward Barney. When I finally reached him, my mouth was dry as dust. It took me a moment to compose myself into a sitting hip belay. Then I called down to Louie:

"On belay. Climb!" My voice was a croak.

"Climbing!" Louie signaled from below.

"Check out the view below your left foot," I added.

His eyes were as round as an owl's when he came up the rock wall to my belay spot.

That day, Barney, Louie, and I all made the same vow: "Dear God, if you get me down off this mountain alive, I promise I'll never climb another mountain again." Barney, the older and wiser brother, kept his promise. Louie and I have spent the rest of our lives breaking it. That day, only moments apart, we had each crossed a gap within ourselves and, in the process, been exposed not just to danger but to our own destinies.

■

I was born in Seattle, Washington, on February 10, 1929, a unique individual for only the first ten minutes of my life. Then my identical twin brother, Louie,

Flower children—Jim (left) and Louie (right), 1930. Photo: Whittaker family collection

21

followed me into the world. Technically, we were "mirror twins"— I turned out to be left-handed, Louie right-handed—but otherwise we were identical. We were also inseparable.

We were known collectively simply as "The Twins." We rode in a twin baby carriage and were dressed in the same clothes into our teens—"Like shopping for one person," my mother used to say. For a long time, our language consisted of grunts and gestures only we could understand. As we got older, we often didn't need to talk to each other at all; we almost always knew what the other was thinking.

Hortense Elizabeth Whittaker, 1921. Photo: Whittaker family collection

We grew up in Arbor Heights, a neighborhood of West Seattle. My parents had bought a one-hundred-by-one-hundred-foot piece of property there in 1931 for $500 and spent another $350 to build a little two-bedroom house with a grand view of Puget Sound and the snow-capped Olympic Mountains beyond. We had a fireplace for heat and a wood- and coal-burning stove for both cooking and heat. (We didn't get an electric range until 1950, after Louie and I were out of high school.) Louie and I and Barney, who was two and a half years older, slept in "the bunk room." Barney had his own single bed, Louie had the lower bunk, and I had the top one. I felt like the king of the hill.

My mother, Hortense Elizabeth Gant, met my father, Charles Bernard Whittaker, in 1924, while she and her mother were touring the United States (Mother's father had died when she was seventeen). They never got any farther than Seattle. Dad (whose father had died when he was only eight) was a traveling salesman, and his gracious manner and ease with people won over

Charles Bernard Whittaker in World
War I army uniform, 1918.
Photo: Whittaker family collection

both of them. He and Mother were married in 1925.

My dad's nickname was "C.B.," or sometimes "Cannonball," but it wasn't because he was short and round—far from it; he was six feet tall, and Mother was five-foot seven, both quite tall in those days. Mother said Dad was "dashing"; Mother herself was a knockout. Despite Dad's frequent travels for the Cannonball Alarm Company, which made burglar alarms, bank vaults, teller cages, and the like and eventually became the international firm, Diebold, they were almost as inseparable as Louie and I.

Wherever Louie and I went together, people did a double take. Wherever we went separately, we were forever being confused with the other. Even Mother occasionally mixed us up; I can remember having my face washed twice on more than one occasion or being blamed for something Louie had done.

When we both stepped into identical Boy Scout uniforms at the age of twelve, it didn't help the mix-up much. Back then there was hardly a better place in the country to be a Boy Scout than Seattle. Out the front door we had the Olympic Mountains, and out the back door, the Cascades. Practically in our back yard was "The Mountain," as people in Seattle call Mount Rainier, the 14,410-foot dormant volcano that is so immense it sometimes looks like a fake painted backdrop in photographs of the city.

Frequent fishing trips and vacations at the ocean or in the mountains with Mother and Dad taught me to appreciate the wild, but scouting taught Louie and me both how to live in it and—in the days before the environmental movement—helped me develop an "outdoor ethic." In fact, that was something I had already begun to learn, the hard way, a couple of years earlier.

When I was ten, I got a bow and arrows and a target for Christmas. The target didn't last long, and I would wander around the vacant lots and woods in our neighborhood shooting at stumps, boxes, and the occasional bird. I was pretty good with stumps, but the birds all flew away unharmed. One day I was creeping through some woods near the house in my Indian Hunter mode, stepping soundlessly on rain-softened leaves so as not to break any twigs. I rounded a big fir, stood still, and listened to the silence around me. Something, a slight movement, caused me to look up, and there, on a branch about

Boy Scout hike, Vashon Island—(left to right) Louie, Doug Rickerson, Jim, Barney, an unidentified scout, Russ Casson. Photo: Whittaker family collection

forty feet directly above me, was an owl. Very slowly, I pulled back the bow-string, aimed, and let the arrow fly. To my amazement, the owl tumbled to the ground, dead.

Quickly, I gathered up my beautiful trophy and raced home. Mother took one look at it and said, in the saddest voice I had ever heard, "Oh, the poor thing." Suddenly, the full weight of what I'd done hit me: I had killed something that only a few minutes earlier had been as alive as I was. I burst into tears. I took the owl outside and buried it in our yard, sobbing my heart out the whole time. It was my first and last hunting experience. To this day, whenever I see or hear an owl, I think of that beautiful bird with its wise, round yellow eyes and wonder how many more owls it would have produced had I not killed it. The taking of a life is so easy, but the implications are so vast; it was a lesson I was to learn even more painfully years later.

Scouting, however, opened new worlds for me and developed what would later be called an "environmental consciousness." Our scoutmasters in West Seattle's Troop 272, Ray Meyers and Ed Ebert, took us camping on Vashon Island in the middle of Puget Sound, climbing on Mount Si in the Cascade foothills, and hiking deep into the Olympics. Along the way, I learned outdoor skills and values I would apply for the rest of my life.

■

Then a cloud moved in over our uncomplicated lives; my brothers and I were playing catch one day in 1941 when the ball went astray, landing in a fenced yard. As I climbed over the fence to get it, the owner came out and shouted at me to get out of his yard.

"And anyway," he yelled, "you should be at home. Don't you know we're at war?"

We ran home and turned on the radio. It was December 7—Pearl Harbor had just been bombed.

Within a few weeks we had blackout curtains on all our windows. A block captain patrolled our street to make sure no light was visible from any house. People in Seattle were anxious for good reason. We were closer to Japan than any other mainland city and home to the strategically important Boeing Aircraft Company. What's more, less than an hour away by ferry, right across

Puget Sound, was the Bremerton Naval Shipyard. Before long, Boeing completely disappeared under a camouflage screen of netting and fake houses. Large tethered dirigibles floated high in the air over Bremerton, with cables hanging from them to protect the shipyard from enemy bombing and strafing runs. Searchlights probed the night sky.

As the war progressed, it affected our lives more and more. It became harder to buy basic commodities: sugar and gasoline, among other things, were rationed. Worse, with such fear and uncertainty in the country, few new banks were opening or expanding, and that hurt Dad's income.

Then in 1944, Barney graduated from West Seattle High School and was drafted into the army and sent to fight the war in the Pacific. To help out at home, he sent us some of his pay. One day as I was sitting in front of our fireplace, my favorite spot in the house, the phone rang, and I could hear Mother talking quietly in the other room. When she hung up, she came into the living room in tears; one of Barney's best friends, Bill Amidon, was missing in action in Germany. All of a sudden the great, romantic drama of the war evaporated, and I realized that Barney, too, could be killed. Somehow that possibility had never quite registered on me before. With Bill Amidon's disappearance, however, the war moved much closer to home.

Throughout the war, and despite food shortages, Louie and I grew like crazy. Mother fed us everything she could get her hands on. We had milk and bread with Karo syrup before bed, and Ovaltine with milk between meals. We made trips to the "goat lady," a few blocks away, for goat's milk, which was supposed to be extra-nutritious but tasted awful.

The more we grew, the skinnier we got. The comic books we read had advertisements showing a skinny guy losing his girlfriend to a muscleman who kicks sand in his face. The skinny guy takes the amazing Charles Atlas Body-Building Course and, "after only two weeks of Dynamic Tension," turns into Superman in a bathing suit, decks the bully, and wins back the curvaceous girl. "Sure," I thought. But boy did I wish it could happen to me.

Instead, Louie and I kept getting taller. I could tell how tall I had gotten every time I rode the trolley to school. First my head hit the ceiling. Only a few months later I had to bend my neck to stand upright. Kids didn't grow that tall very often then, and I felt like I stuck out like a sore thumb.

■

Louie and I were used to drawing attention. The great Scottish poet Robert Burns once wrote, "Oh wad some power the giftie gie us, to see oursels as others see us." I had that power; I had an identical twin—a duplicate, a replica, a clone—a mirror of myself. I could see myself walk, talk, run, and jump. I could even hear myself on the other end of a telephone line. No one could ever tell our voices apart.

All this had been a lot of fun for many years, but in time it began to embarrass me. I started to yearn for a separate identity—no easy trick when you're a twin. By the time we reached our teens, we still looked the same, but inside we were changing. Gradually, Louie and I were becoming individuals—different from and increasingly independent of each other. Among other things, I became the introvert, Louie the extrovert.

Of course, we were still competitors—we were so closely matched we had to compete. Now, however, we were competing to distinguish ourselves from each other, to measure ourselves and learn who we were, to stand apart and be able to say, "This is who I am and what I can do, myself."

■

This having been said, the fact is we still did almost everything together. We both worked after school at the same neighborhood store to earn extra money for the family, and we both played church league basketball. At age fourteen, we both moved up in scouting and joined an Explorer Post, scouting's program for older teens. That's where we met Tom Campbell and, with him and his colleague Lloyd Anderson, began to learn mountaineering. Pretty soon we lost interest in almost everything else.

From Explorer scouting it was a short and natural step to joining The Mountaineers Club of Seattle. Formed in 1906 "to explore, study, preserve, and enjoy the natural beauty of the outdoors," the club was—and still is—arguably the premier mountaineering club in the country, if not the world. Its climbing courses were legendary, each one taught by previous course graduates who had perfected their technique in the mountains before ever being permitted to teach. Safety was the club's principal concern, and it had an outstanding record of accident-free climbs.

Classes were held first in the clubroom in downtown Seattle and then in the field, with climbs on nearly every mountain in the Cascade and Olympic Ranges. In winter we did classroom work; by spring we were out in the mountains. Gasoline was scarce, but by getting together climbers and instructors with cars, we could usually pool enough ration coupons to fill the tank, and we headed into the hills practically every weekend.

Louie and I were in our element. Not only was the out-of-doors where we felt most at ease, but we were increasingly up to the task physically, too. Actually, our conditioning probably started in grade school. We lived at the top of a very steep hill, a climb of at least 500 vertical feet from the bus stop. Every day, from grade school through junior-high and high school, we climbed that hill—twice a day in grade school when we came home for lunch! By the time we joined The Mountaineers in our midteens, we had strong legs and big lungs. And at six-foot five, we had legs that just ate up terrain.

Our first practice climbs were on the mountains close to Snoqualmie Pass, an hour or so east of Seattle, in the Cascades. On Red Mountain and Kendall Peak we learned glissading—a sitting or standing slide down a snow slope— and the ice ax self-arrest—a technique to stop a slide by quickly turning and plunging an ice ax into the snow. On Guye Peak and Snoqualmie Mountain we learned the kick-step in snow, different kinds of belays, and, over and over, the rest step—a slow but steady climbing technique in which you lock your downhill knee for a second or two and rest while placing the uphill foot securely for the next step up. The rest step, we learned, was the answer to climbing almost any mountain—especially higher ones where the air is thin and you need to take a breath or two (or three or four) with every step.

Soon we went farther afield, climbing Chair Peak, the south face of The Tooth, Mount Thompson, The Brothers, Cruiser Peak, and enough other Washington summits to earn The Mountaineers Club's Ten Peak pin.

One winter we signed up for a climb of Washington's Mount Margaret— on skis. Louie and I had both learned the rudiments of skiing; we could do snowplow turns on hard-packed ski slopes. But on Mount Margaret we were up to our knees in loose powder snow, and trouble. With mohair climbers attached to our skis, we were strong enough to bull our way up. Coming down, however, was another matter entirely.

Sam Eskanazi was the leader of our small party that day. A superb skier, he had fled Germany just before the war and settled in the Seattle area. After a nice lunch on the summit, we removed the mohair climbers from our skis and prepared for the downhill run. I watched Sam push off and carve three elegant, graceful turns through the snow-covered trees, the picture of grace in motion. Then he stopped and waited for the rest of the party. They skied down to him, if not quite as gracefully, at least in well-executed, controlled turns. Louie and I were still on top of the hill.

"Let's go!" Sam shouted.

"Dear God," I thought. "This is going to be so embarrassing."

Even though the snow seemed light and powdery and the track lay before me as an example of how it should be done, I knew in my heart of hearts I could not turn like that. So I did the only thing I could: I pushed off, aiming for the spot where he had made his first turn, gained speed, reached his turning point, and sat down in a spray of snow crystals. Then I got up, aimed for the place where he had made his second turn, and did the same thing all over again. Finally, I did it a third time, falling down just before I hit him. Louie was right behind me, using the "Whittaker Technique."

Sam showed us how to turn, and we tried to do it, but it was hopeless. In the end, it was easier just to aim for a route through as many trees as I could, then fall before I hit one. Sam and the rest of the party executed graceful linked turns all the way down to the parking lot. Louie and I crashed down the mountain, grabbing branches, doing a series of linked falls. It was humiliating. A few days later, my body covered with bruises, I swore I would learn how to ski before I tackled another snowy mountain. I decided to try on-the-job training and joined the Snoqualmie Pass Ski Patrol. The main qualification seemed to be having the strength to hold on to a heavy wooden toboggan while being hauled up the mountain on a rope tow. I wore holes in the armpits of my ski jackets and lost some hair as well, but this was a small price to pay for the free lift tickets offered to members of the patrol. Once I got hired, I figured, I could learn the finer points of downhill skiing. Fortunately, there were plenty of willing instructors, and by winter's end I had gone a long way toward meeting my goal.

We kept climbing through the spring and summer of that year and, in

August, joined a group of Mountaineers for a trip to the Olympic Peninsula to climb Mount Olympus. At 7,965 feet, it is the highest summit in the Olympic Range, and it was the first mountain with major glaciers that Louie and I had ever attempted. The trail began in the Hoh River rain forest and was almost flat for the first thirteen miles. Then it rose in switchbacks for two more miles to the lateral moraine at the edge of Blue Glacier, where we camped for the night. The next morning we rose just at daybreak and, after a light breakfast, tied on our crampons, roped up, and stepped out onto the ice. It took only a few hours to traverse the glacier, and afterwards, in sparkling sunlight, we climbed the final pitch of loose and rotten rock to the summit—and a sensational 360-degree view of Olympic National Park. After lunch we descended to Blue Glacier for another night and, the next morning, began the long hike back to civilization.

I thought that trail would never end. By the time we dropped our packs at the trailhead, I had bleeding blisters on both heels. But from the ankles up, I was euphoric: I had stood on top of the Olympics!

The euphoria rose beyond Olympic heights, however, when we reached the town of Port Angeles on our way back to Seattle. Horns were honking and people were shouting and waving in the streets. It was August 14, 1945. World War II had ended.

When we stepped off the ferry in downtown Seattle, the city was going wild. We stood on the sidewalk in our dirty clothes, carrying packs with ice axes and crampons strapped on the outside, but people hugged and kissed us anyway. It was every teenage climber's dream: after days in the bush, gorgeous, perfumed, deliriously happy women ran up and threw their arms around our necks. It was the first time ever that I came back from a climb covered with lipstick.

Even better, a few months later Barney came home safe and sound, though a more reserved and worldly man than when he had left us.

■

Looking back, I realize Louie and I were incredibly lucky. During and just after the war we were taken under the wings of some of the leading climbers and skiers in the Northwest. Besides Lloyd Anderson, Tom Campbell, and Sam Eskanazi, there were Wolf Bauer, Ome Daiber, Max Eckenburg, Lyle St. Louis, and Otto Trott among others. It was Lyle who got us involved in the National Ski Patrol, and it was Wolf and Ome who enlisted us in the Mountain Rescue Council.

We were still beginners, but these pioneers made sure we began right.

Mountain rescue at Snoqualmie Pass—Back row: Chuck Welsh, Dee Molenaar, unnamed, Cornelius "K" Molenaar, Max Eckenburg, Ome Daiber, unnamed, John Thompson, Lou Whittaker. Front row: Wolf Bauer, unnamed, Jim Whittaker, unnamed. Photo: Dee Molenaar collection

Chapter Two

RISK

"Louie!" I shouted down the smooth rock face, "I'm stuck!"

"It's okay," my brother called back, "I've got you!"

"The hell you do," I thought to myself. "I've got both of us—in big trouble." I was high above my brother on the vertical east face of Mount Index in the North Cascades, a mountain the famous climber Fred Beckey once described simply as "evil." Between us was about fifty feet of rope, none of which I'd anchored to the rock face. Louie had me in a hip belay, with the rope wrapped around him, but not pitoned in. Beneath me, the cliff dropped nearly straight down for a thousand feet. If I came off the wall—which I would do any moment now—I would fall more than a hundred feet—past the overhang and past him—before I hit his belay. Then, having gained so much momentum, I would either pull him off with me or the rope would break. Those were the only possible outcomes.

I had no business being in this kind of situation. I knew better. But I had made a couple of small mistakes on my way up this pitch, and with each mistake, I'd increased my risk. All of a sudden, unable to descend or ascend, hanging by one hand and a couple of toes, the mistakes totaled up to a sum that was about to become deadly.

I had marveled at 6,000-foot Mount Index every time Louie and I drove up U.S. Highway 2 on our way to Stevens Pass, where we worked for the ski patrol on winter weekends. The breathtaking east face is close to the highway and soars more than 3,000 feet above Lake Serene, which lies, blue and cold, at its base at an elevation of 2,800 feet. In the winter Mount Index wears a glittering mantle of snow; in the summer it is raw, bare rock, majestic and, with its north face perpetually in shadow, somehow ominous.

Louie and I and three companions had arrived the day before, on a warm afternoon in July 1949. After setting up camp at the bottom of a rockslide leading up to the face, Louie and I decided to reconnoiter the slopes above. We grabbed our climbing gear and headed up through fragrant scrub cedar trees and brush. At the first steep pitch, we roped up and began belaying and climbing, switching leads as we pushed higher. There was quite a bit of exposure, but now that we'd had a few years of climbing under our belts, we had become conditioned to it and felt comfortable. After an hour of scrambling and a few steep pitches, Louie stopped at a vertical wall. He belayed me up to him, but after looking over the next pitch, we decided to leave it for the next day. It looked like it would go, and we headed back down to camp.

At daybreak we were on our way back up again, Louie and I on one rope and our three companions on another. We moved rapidly up the route we had climbed the day before, switching leads again as we went. Leapfrogging this way, we didn't have to change belays as often, and we moved much faster than the three-man rope below us. The sun was up in a cloudless sky—it was going to be a perfect day.

Below the wall that had stopped us the previous afternoon, it was my turn to lead. I examined the severe pitch above us while Louie got into belay position on a narrow ledge. A few good holds led out to the left, to just above the overhang, and from there some smaller holds appeared to lead straight up the face to another narrow ledge—a distance of about sixty feet. Above that ledge, there appeared to be several less technical routes toward the summit. With Louie on belay, I took a few good breaths and started up.

At first the going was good. I felt strong and moved easily up the face. A soft breeze was blowing. The rock was solid and warm from the sun, and I could look down and see Lake Serene shimmering far below. Pushing the route higher, I noticed a crack I could use to put in a piton, but things were going so well that I didn't bother. Pitons cost thirty-five cents each, and I didn't want to waste any— mistake number one. I had moved around and above the overhang and was about four feet below the ledge when I completely ran out of holds. There simply wasn't anything else to grab. My right foot was on a small projection and my right hand was high above my shoulder, gripping a small hold. My left foot dangled in the air while my left hand searched for a hold that did not exist—mistake number two: always have three solid points of contact. What's more, with nothing else to hold on to, I couldn't let go of my right handhold to climb back down. Below me, Louie was in an unanchored hip belay—mistake number three: if I fell, he wouldn't be able to stop me, nor would he be able to stop me from pulling him off the rock as well. My muscles were tiring fast. My right leg was trembling from exertion, and the fingers of my right hand ached for release.

There is a condition that climbers sometimes reach—and other athletes as well—a moment of supreme stress when everything becomes crystal clear and remarkable feats of strength are possible. As I clung to the rock face, moments from falling, I reached that point.

"I'm gonna have to jump for a hold," I shouted down to Louie.

It was a desperate move, and I would have only one chance. With everything I had left, I pushed off the foothold, pulled on the handhold, and flung myself upward. The fingertips of my left hand hooked the ledge. Pulling for all I was worth, kicking against the wall, I hauled myself up and twisted into a sitting position, soaked in sweat, my heart hammering in my chest. The ledge was only twelve inches wide, but it seemed as wide as a street. God, it felt good. I drove in a piton, snapped into it, guzzled the entire contents of my quart water bottle, and belayed Louie up. When he reached me, he just looked at me and lifted his eyebrows; he didn't have to say anything.

We reached the summit of the North Tower of Mount Index that day early enough to have plenty of light for a careful and uneventful descent. Over the years I have forgotten the names of our three climbing companions, but the memory of that near-fall is clear enough to have happened last week. It was as close as I had ever come to checking out. It was as close as I ever wanted to come again.

I have lost more friends to the mountains than I care to count. Some have died from what climbers call objective dangers—rockslides, avalanches, lightning—dangers that exist outside oneself. Others have died as a result of what might best be called subjective risks—that is, a failure to recognize that an event, or series of events, has pushed the real level of risk higher than the climber perceives it to be. Often, as in my Mount Index scare, it's not one massive incident of poor judgment but the cumulative effect of small decisions, which in themselves appear insignificant, but when taken together turn lethal.

I think Louie and I are alive today in part because of that incident on Mount Index. We are both extraordinarily careful climbers. Another reason is that almost from the beginning of our climbing careers, Louie and I were involved in rescue missions to save other climbers—or, just as often, to retrieve their bodies.

■

A year before the Mount Index incident, Louie and I became charter members of the Mountain Rescue Council. Formed by Wolf Bauer, Ome Daiber, and Otto Trott, the council was an extension of the National Ski Patrol on which Louie and I already served. The idea, modeled after similar organizations in Europe, was to create a cadre of skilled mountaineers who could be mobilized quickly to aid climbers and others in trouble in the mountains.

We were busy almost from the moment the council was established. One of our first rescue calls came from the U.S. government. Not far from Mount Rainier are Fort Lewis, an army installation, and McChord Air Force Base. On the night of April 21, 1948, a military aircraft flying near the mountain was hit by severe turbulence, and the pilot could not control the plane. As he struggled to keep his craft aloft, the rest of the crew—eight men in all—parachuted into the darkness. The pilot stayed with his aircraft, managed to get it under control, and shortly thereafter landed safely. The crew was spread out somewhere on Mount Rainier.

We were on the mountain first thing the next morning. The only information we had was that the crew had probably landed on the forested slopes on the north side of the mountain, near the Carbon River entrance to the national park. It would almost have been better if they'd landed higher up, above the tree line. Finding them in the dense forest would be practically impossible.

We left our vehicles where the road ended, hiked in a few miles, and set up camp. Then we split into groups and fanned out to cover as much of the area as we could before dark. Louie was delegated to remain in camp and keep the fire going. Mount Rainier gets a tremendous amount of snow during the winter and even at that time, despite spring rains and thawing, it was still ten or twelve feet deep. What's more, new wet snow had fallen several days before and still clung in thick clumps to many of the trees, making it virtually impossible to detect a white parachute. To make matters worse, the temperature was near freezing, a steady drizzle was falling, and big clumps of snow would occasionally slip off the limbs above us and shower us with heavy, wet bombs.

Soaked from the drizzle, we struggled across the soft, compacted snow, continually breaking through the crust and sinking up to our knees, especially near trees, where the snow was less firm. Moving kept us warm, but we began shivering the moment we stopped. I much preferred the dry, below-zero cold of the heights to the bone-chilling damp cold of these lower slopes. We searched fruitlessly throughout the day but saw no sign of the crew members—no parachutes, no footprints, nothing. It was as if they'd simply vanished.

At dusk we returned to camp, thoroughly bedraggled and discouraged. What we found there lightened the mood. The whole campsite looked different and was illuminated by a weird, indirect light. Louie was nowhere to be seen. Approaching the light, I stepped to the edge of a circular bank of snow, looked down, and there he was, eight feet below the surface, sitting on bare ground before a blazing bonfire, wearing a big grin. Over the course of the day, he had kept the fire going, and it had melted its way down through the snow until it finally reached the ground. Then the heat gradually pushed back the walls of the hole, creating a sort of vertical cave. It was a good thing too—we needed that heat to warm up and dry out.

Our rescue party never did find the crew members. We later learned that six had walked out on their own, and a seventh was carried out with a broken back. The eighth crewman, Lieutenant Carl Schmitt, had apparently struck his head while leaping from the plane and, either dazed or unconscious, had been unable to open his parachute.

I didn't have to be mobilized to rush to another of my rescues that year; I was part of the event itself. It was in the summer of 1948, on a Mountaineers Club climb of Chair Peak in the Cascades. Fifteen of us had summited the peak and were beginning the second stage of our descent. We had completed our climb back down the rock cliff below the summit and had unroped to descend the steep snow slope that dropped to the valley floor.

On the ascent earlier in the day, in the sun, the slope had been soft, and we had no problem kicking steps with our Tricouni-nailed boots. But now the slope was in shadow and frozen hard. At the outset, we encountered a five-foot-wide bergschrund—a crevasse that forms between a bank of snow and an adjacent rock face. It was about twenty feet deep. The first climber jumped over the 'schrund and immediately began sliding down the snow slope on the other side. Climbing with a long alpenstock, or walking stick, instead of an ice ax, he couldn't self-arrest and quickly gained speed and lost control. About a hundred feet down the slope, he hit some boulders sticking up through the snow and somersaulted through them, finally coming to a stop, unconscious, in the valley below. Cautiously, I jumped the 'schrund myself and began glissading after him, using my ice ax to control and slow my slide. When I reached him, I found his head and face were badly cut. He also had a dislocated shoulder and a broken ankle. Though he regained consciousness, he couldn't walk. Luckily, someone else in the party was also climbing with an alpenstock, and using climbing ropes, we fashioned a stretcher from the two of them. Just as luckily, there were plenty of us to take turns with the stretcher; it was almost six miles to where we'd left our cars.

■

After becoming skilled climbers and then seasoned rescuers, it was a natural step for Louie and me to become mountain guides. In the winter of 1949, Bil Dunaway, an experienced climber and skier who operated a guide service on Mount Rainier, asked us if we'd be interested in guiding clients to the summit and to an area of ice caves that then existed on the mountain. It seemed almost too good to be true: getting paid to do what we loved! We started late that next spring, in May 1950, and I spent the next four summers on the mountain, leading dozens of climbing parties. For Louie, who later founded Rainier Mountaineering, Inc., and built it into a thriving business, guiding became a lifelong occupation.

Bil Dunaway taught us the crucial difference between being climbers and being guides. As climbers, we were always looking for the next big challenge;

Mount Rainier guides—(left to right) Bil Dunaway, Jim, Louie, 1950.
Photo: Ira Spring

as guides, our job was to make the climb as safe and routine as possible, while still ensuring a worthwhile experience for our clients. Good guides develop a sensitivity to the capabilities and ongoing condition of their clients, a kind of sixth sense that helps them monitor each individual. They also learn to monitor the mountain itself, to watch and listen for the often subtle messages it sends about its own condition. That doesn't mean there aren't surprises, however, as

I learned the next summer while leading a routine Mount Rainier climb on a routine June day.

The weather was clear and perfect for climbing. My three clients and I left the guide shack near Paradise Inn, at 5,400 feet on the southwest side of the mountain, at 11:00 A.M. A storm the previous week had dumped new snow on the mountain, but since then it had firmed up, and we had a good walking surface. We took the usual route, hiking on soft spring snow up to the ridge near a spot called Alta Vista, and then continuing up past Panorama Point to Pebble Creek, where we stopped for lunch, filled our water bottles, and slapped on more sun lotion. It had taken one hour to ascend 1,500 vertical feet—good time considering that my clients were novices and we were carrying heavy packs. Ahead of us was the broad, uphill expanse of the Muir Snowfield. Using a slow, steady guide pace, I kicked steps in the snow, and we climbed onto and up the snowfield. Judging from the condition of my climbers, I felt confident that as long as the weather held we would make the summit the next day. It was getting colder, but it was still clear; there were no cloud caps on Mount Adams, Mount Hood, or Mount Rainier.

At 9,000 feet, across from a formation called Anvil Rock, the footing on the snowfield became firmer and my steps shallower. But there were still a couple of inches of soft snow and the going was easy. We were moving at a good pace.

At 10,000 feet, just below the stone hut at Camp Muir, the traditional campsite for the night before the summit climb, there is a flat snowfield. As the four of us crossed it, I heard a *WHUMP!* and I stopped abruptly. "Hmmmm. Unusual," I thought. Apparently, the snowfall from the week before had not bonded to the old snow, and we were walking on a hard crust or "wind slab" that was fracturing under our weight. We broke a few more slabs, then walked on hard snow into Camp Muir. The mountain was talking to me, and I should have been paying closer attention.

It was now 4:00 P.M. It had taken us five hours to climb from Paradise to Camp Muir, about average for a guided party. I opened the hut, lit the lantern and stoves, and started to cook dinner. I melted snow from outside to make water, and while my clients rested, I made sure they drank plenty of liquids to help them overcome dehydration and to ease their altitude acclimatization.

After dinner they crawled into their sleeping bags. Outside, I uncoiled our rope—120 feet of 7⁄16-inch goldline—tied two middleman knots into it, and stretched it out on the snow. Back inside, I prepared more water for our breakfast, set the alarm for midnight, opened the door a crack, turned out the lantern, and hit the sack. It was 7:00 P.M. "A routine climb," I thought.

Sleeping can be difficult at Camp Muir. For clients who aren't used to the altitude, headaches, cramps, even a little nausea are common. Then too, the wind often rattles rocks across the roof. I always try to doze a little, but before I can, I have work to do: in my mind, I visualize taking each client up the route to the summit, worrying each one over every obstacle. The night brings out my deepest worries. I suppose it's an instinct, or fear, left over from the days of our earliest ancestors when real threats prowled around outside in the dark. I once found a bit of poetry Shakespeare had written that captured it perfectly:

> *Comfort-killing night, image of Hell;*
> *Dim register and notary of shame;*
> *Black stage for tragedies and murders fell;*
> *Vast sin concealing chaos, nurse of blame.*

I knew exactly what he meant. In the dark of night, especially before a climb, there is always something to worry about; everything seems more dangerous, more difficult.

But I had guided many clients to the summit by this time and knew the drill well: up at midnight, get dressed, light the lantern and stove, give the clients a cup of coffee before they get up. Serve oatmeal with lots of sugar, a slice of bread, more coffee, hot chocolate, tea. Pack up a summit lunch, two quart water bottles, extra clothing, camera, first-aid kit, compass, and a sleeping bag to keep a client warm if he can't make it to the summit and has to wait for the rest of us. Strap on the crampons, adjust the headlamps, and step outside. I tied the strongest client to the tail end of the rope, the weakest forty feet behind the lead, the third between those two, and then tied myself into the lead.

By 1:00 A.M. we were ready to go. Stars filled the sky, and a soft breeze was blowing. It would be another beautiful climb. Five thousand feet below us, the lights of Paradise flickered in the darkness. We would be climbing along a route that guided parties had taken throughout the 1930s and 1940s: it led north from Camp Muir beneath the Beehive near the Cowlitz Glacier, then turned up the glacier on a convex, forty-degree slope before traversing up to the shoulder of Gibraltar, a huge outcrop of rotten volcanic rock that sits on the southeast shoulder of Mount Rainier at 12,000 feet.

The morning was very cold. Picking our way up the Cowlitz, our crampons barely marked the hard snow. Our ice axes no more than nicked the surface. Using their headlamps in the dark, my clients followed the rope in front of them more than they did my tracks. We climbed steadily, detoured around two big crevasses, reached a notch below Gibraltar Rock, and then took a short break to watch the snow-clad summits of Mount Adams, Mount St. Helens, and Mount Hood rise out of the dark valleys around them and glow pink in the rising sun.

This had been a fairly direct route in the past, but more recently a huge chunk of ledge had broken off Gibraltar and disappeared down the mountain. Now we had to negotiate a twenty-five-foot drop down to a new, narrower ledge of equally rotten rock, covered with loose boulders and scree. Not only was this ledge exposed to rapid-fire rock fall, especially when the sun hit the face above, but there were also twenty- to thirty-foot icicles hanging hundreds of feet above that threatened to impale the slow or unwary. It was not a safe route, but it would be another year before we established a better one via the Ingraham Glacier.

We crossed the ledge in a hurry, close together, with ropes coiled, going as fast as the slowest of us could go. Even with everything frozen solid, every now and then boulders would whistle down from above and explode below us, scattering scree like shrapnel. We reached the top of Gibraltar safely, however, stopped there for a longer break, and had a sandwich. The sun warmed us, and we relished our view of the gradually brightening world below. I even dozed a little. My clients were holding up well.

Above Gibraltar there are a number of dangerous crevasses, but on this morning, plenty of solid snow bridges crossed them. The route to the summit was straightforward, and at 9:00 A.M. we sat down on the crater rim. The temperature was below zero, but the morning was windless and the sun was warm. From there we strolled to the summit register at 14,410 feet, signed in, and took a short nap before starting down. This time, using normal descending technique, I had the strongest client lead the rope and I tied in last, as anchorman in case of falls.

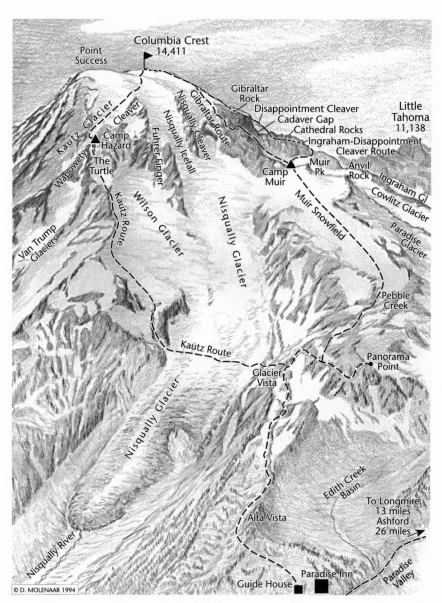

Mount Rainier, south side. Map: Dee Molenaar

I was anxious to get back across Gibraltar before the sun melted the ice and the bombardment really started, so we moved out quickly. Traveling close together with the rope coiled, we raced along the ledge and up the fixed rope I had placed there earlier. Small pebbles bounced around us as we gained the

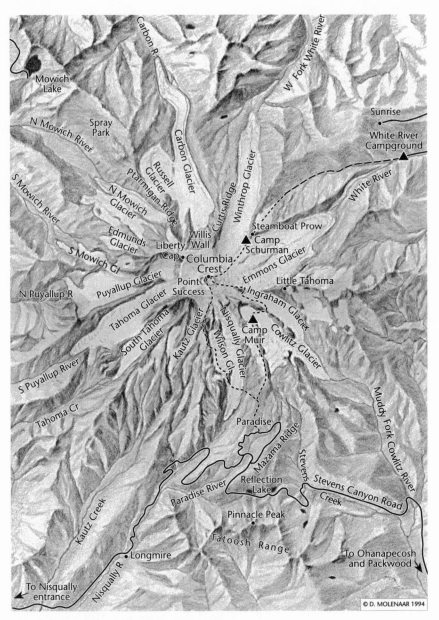

Mount Rainier, aerial view. Map: Dee Molenaar

upper ledge. We didn't rest until we had reached the notch leading onto the Cowlitz Glacier. It was noon, and we were just above 11,000 feet.

I breathed a sigh of relief. The most difficult part of the climb was over, and we now had an easy, 1,000-foot descent to Camp Muir. We took a long break and shed our parkas in the warmer air and sunshine of the lower mountain.

I was anchorman again as we started down the Cowlitz. The snow had changed from rock-hard to soft since our ascent, and we slogged down the slope, plunging into the snow calf-deep. As the slope became steeper, I had my clients sit down and glissade, while I continued plunge-stepping and anchoring the rope. The Cowlitz Glacier is convex, so you can't see what's below you, but I remembered the two crevasses we would have to avoid.

The smooth slope we were on suddenly broke into slabs with a thunderous crunch. The fracture line was twenty feet above me, two- to three-feet deep, and fully a quarter-mile wide. The slabs started moving.

"AVALANCHE!" I screamed.

I spun into a self-arrest, driving my ice ax into the hard surface below. But it didn't hold—the combined weight of the sliding blocks and the three clients on my rope pulled me out and off and I fell backwards and upside down.

"God help us now," I prayed. We were going down.

As we fell, I somersaulted, slowed, then was jerked by the rope into another somersault. Straightening out, swimming in the loose snow and shoving at slabs, I saw my clients being tossed every which way as we tumbled down toward the two crevasses that cut deeply across the steep slope below us. Still roped together, we were headed straight for them.

We had gained so much momentum that when we reached the first crevasse we flew into the air off its upper lip and sailed right over it, then banged down hard and slid toward the second. I could see that the uphill edge of this next crevasse had a prominent, upward curve that was throwing the avalanching snow out from the slope like a huge waterfall. I was facing out, in a sitting position, and tried desperately to work sideways to avoid it. But I couldn't quite make it. Then I was airborne.

I flew up and out twenty feet, then tumbled, landing on my rear with a painful thud on the other side of the crevasse. I rolled and slid another thirty feet and then suddenly jerked to a stop while the avalanche poured by, leaving us uncovered and strung out on the ice. We'd fallen more than four hundred feet.

At first, I couldn't figure out why we'd stopped. Then I heard screaming. One of my clients had fallen into the second crevasse and, in the process, had stopped our rope. My back hurt, and I had trouble unroping, but I managed to crawl to the lip and look over the edge. He was buried up to his neck against the lower side of the crevasse, scared to death, but not badly hurt. It didn't take long for us to pull him out.

Limping and shaken, we made our way back to Camp Muir where I nursed our various cuts and bruises. As we descended the Muir Snowfield toward Paradise, I suddenly remembered that *WHUMP!* I'd heard the previous day. The mountain had been talking to me, telling me that some time earlier the sun had melted the surface of the snow. Later it had frozen solid. Still later, there had been another snowfall—this one very dry, cold, and deep. The sun had then melted the surface of this new snowfall and a hard crust had formed on it, too. But the new powder snow below that crust had not bonded with the hard surface of the earlier snowfall. When the temperature rose, the outer crust softened and the powder snow began to settle. The combination of that settling, our weight, and our deep tracks caused the softer upper layer to break free of the hard crust of the lower layer, setting off the avalanche. Quietly, I thanked God—and the mountain—for letting me learn another lesson and live to tell the story. The Buddhists have a saying: "All mountains are the temples of God and are places which destroy sin." I would try not to commit that "sin" again.

◾

Throughout this period Louie and I continued to work with the Mountain Rescue Council, and I learned repeatedly how dangerous, and often fatal, it could be to take a mountain for granted.

On May 19, 1952, Louie, Otto, Ome, and I were called to Mount St. Helens to rescue a climber named Art Jessett. He and three others had been descending unroped from the summit. Art, who was twenty-one years old, was last and carrying the group's only climbing rope around his shoulders when he suddenly dropped through the snow into a deep crevasse. While one of his companions went for help, the others crowded around the manhole-sized opening Art had fallen through, and they talked with him for hours until, eventually, his voice grew still. Without a rope, there was nothing they could do. They marked the spot with a pack and came off the mountain, praying he would live the night.

Mountain rescue party—(left to right) Ome Daiber, Otto Trott, Wolf Bauer, about 1947. Photo: Ira Spring

Our rescue party reached the Mount St. Helens Ranger Station at 6:30 the next morning. A snow cat took us three and a half miles to the Timberline Ski Hut at 5,500 feet, and we started climbing from there. Louie and I raced ahead, on the chance that the climber might still be alive.

Following the tracks from the previous day, Louie and I found the hole in the glacier with the pack beside it. We shouted down the opening but heard no reply. We flipped a coin to see who would go down first, and I won; Louie belayed me into the hole. The hole was in the middle of a snow bridge across the crevasse that was about eight feet across. My rope sawed into the overhang, so I was able to get my crampons against one of the ice walls and rappel down it. As the walls narrowed, the blue glacial ice darkened. In the dim light seventy-five feet down, I came to a small, two-foot-wide mound of snow bridging the crevasse. I stood on it to take my weight off the rope. Turning sideways, my shoulders touched both walls. I couldn't get much deeper. The only sound was my breathing.

"I don't see him," I shouted up to the surface.

"He's got to be there!" Louie yelled back.

True, but where? As my eyes adjusted to the darkness, I peered harder and saw black-gloved fingers sticking up through the snow right at my feet.

"Oh my God," I yelled, "I'm standing on top of him!"

I leaned over, looked under the mound, and saw the climber's feet dangling below me. He was wedged by his shoulders, frozen solid to the ice. His head was completely covered. There was no question in my mind that he had been dead for some time.

Soon the rest of the rescue team arrived, and we rigged ropes for a crevasse rescue. I started up the rope using Prusik rope slings—tools by which you can "walk" up a rope—to lift the body. Everything went smoothly until I was stopped by the overhanging lip of the crevasse: I couldn't get us out from under it. In the semi-darkness, I pushed hard on the body from below while those above pulled. Suddenly, there was a long low moan.

"Oooohh."

"Jeez, he's alive!" I shouted, scared witless and almost falling back into the crevasse.

It took a moment for me to realize that the sound I'd heard had only been air forced out of the dead climber's lungs and over his vocal cords when we bent his body to get him out of the hole. The rescuers above thought it was me groaning.

We strapped Art's body to a toboggan and made our way back down in a dreary, cold rain. Not for the first time I thought about how often it seemed that the most dangerous part of climbing is coming down, not going up. There are lots of reasons why. On the descent, the downward momentum of the climber's own weight and gravity combine to create shear forces that don't occur during ascent. What's more, people often let their guard down; they've summited, and they think, "Heck, it's all downhill from here." They're also tired, sometimes affected by the altitude, and simply not thinking as clearly as they might—and so ignore simple precautions like staying roped together. It's a dangerous combination, one that's all too often deadly.

When we reached the bottom of the mountain, Art's family was waiting. His father, a minister, performed last rites. It's hard to know which is more tragic, the loss of a young life or the effect of that loss on those who continue living.

Either way, it's heartbreaking.

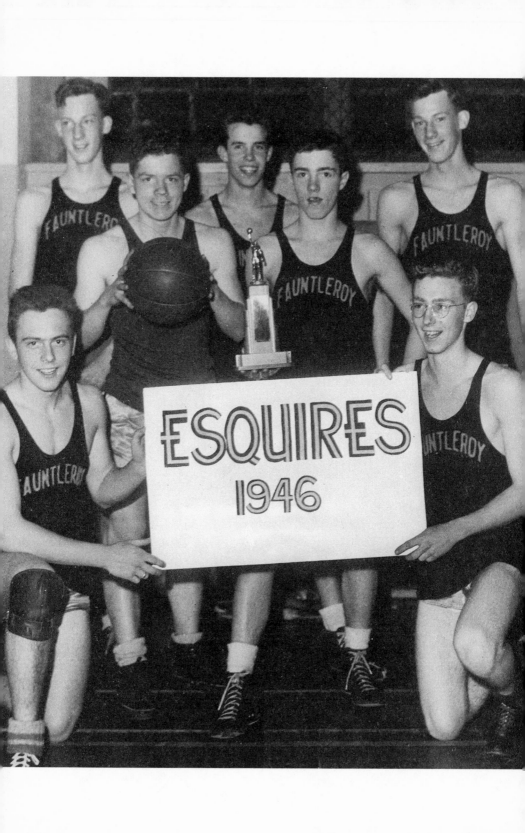

Chapter Three

APPRENTICESHIP

Louie and I got into college on basketball scholarships. The assistant coach of Seattle University's basketball team, Bill Fenton, went to our church, Fauntleroy Congregational, and saw the two of us playing in church league games. (We never played for our high school team because of our after-school jobs.) We weren't great players, but I guess the sight of six-foot-five twins who could handle the ball was irresistible; he recruited us, and we were incredibly grateful. Without those scholarships, we could never have afforded to go to college.

I'd been only an average student in high school, but college was a revelation for me. Seattle University is a Catholic institution, and the Jesuit order sets the educational and ethical standards for the school. Many of our teachers were Jesuit priests, and it was immediately clear that the years of study and discipline involved in preparing for the priesthood had also made them first-rate scholars and teachers. Every class opened a door to a whole new world of ideas.

I chose biology as my major because I wanted to deepen my understanding of the natural world I loved so much. I became particularly fond of the courses taught by Father Schmid, the head of the biology department. He was a brilliant lecturer, but it was his laboratory, with its Bunsen burners, beakers, and microscopes, that really captivated me. I particularly enjoyed his course

Fauntleroy Church basketball team, 1946—(front row, left to right) Mike Haskell, Bob Benson; (back row, left to right) Louie, Terry Mullin, Russ Casson, Warren Calvin, Jim. Photo: Whittaker family collection

on histology, the branch of anatomy that deals with the minute structure of animal and plant tissues. We studied single-celled amoebae and protozoans and dissected fish and frogs. Every time I put my eye to the microscope, I was simply awestruck: I couldn't get over the beauty and precision of what I saw and the amazing sameness in the structures and functions of individual living things.

"How can this little orifice in the jawbone of this frog be sculpted in precisely this way in every frog?" I asked Father Schmid at the lab table one day.

"That small orifice is necessary to accept the vessel that supplies blood to the mouth and jaw," he answered, matter-of-factly.

"I understand what it does," I said. "The real question is how did it come to be this way? What kind of genius conceived of this frog, designed it down to the most minute detail, had the power to create it, and has kept on creating it ever since?"

"Mr. Whittaker," he said, "the answer to *that* question lies in our theology department."

I was enthralled. How did the Creator come up with the plan? After designing the plan, how did the Great Architect manage the precision of its execution so that this one frog's medial subtrossa fossa was identical to every other's, every time, without error?

I added theology courses to my curriculum. I had already been certain that there was a Supreme Power, and not just because I'd gone to church all through my childhood. I simply couldn't conceive of our intricately functioning planet as an accident, any more than I could believe the components of the clocks my father loved to tinker with could fall together by chance to form a timepiece. But at Father Schmid's lab table I crossed a bridge between having a vague certainty that there was a Higher Power to understanding that there was an intricate Grand Plan. The natural next step was to seek an explanation of that Plan. In theology we studied all the major religions, but I found my answer, perhaps inevitably in a Catholic college, in the Catholic Church. I was baptized into the church in my sophomore year.

Seattle University was unique, I believe, in requiring candidates for a Bachelor of Science degree to earn a minor in philosophy. The Jesuits wanted us to understand not just the mechanisms of science but the ethical and philosophical issues that underlay them as well. We read Kant, Locke, Voltaire, Marx, and

Lenin, among others. We studied logic and epistemology, the theory of the nature and grounds of knowledge.

All this led to heated discussions in the Cave, the student restaurant, where we students expounded on subject after subject. I grew fond of debating these weighty intellectual questions with Theresa McKee, an attractive young woman who was studying nursing and doing her internship at nearby Providence Hospital. She was tall, slim, outspoken, swore occasionally, smoked like a furnace, and was completely different from anyone I'd ever met before. Not that I'd had all that much experience. Although Louie and I counted women among our friends, I had actually had only one formal date up to this point—at my high-school senior picnic.

Now another door was opening for me, and Theresa was holding it. Our playful debates quickly turned to infatuation and then to powerful physical attraction. This was, however, the late forties, and young people did not tumble lightly into intimate relationships in those days. Consequently, and without a great deal of deep thought, we became engaged.

It didn't last. We didn't so much fall out of love as fall into common sense. It wasn't long before we broke off our engagement and decided we were a lot more comfortable just being good friends.

My basketball scholarship didn't last either. The problem wasn't my basketball playing—I was the high point man in my freshman year—it was my climbing and skiing. The school was, in effect, paying me to attend so I would play basketball for them. The head coach had a hard-and-fast rule that his players were not permitted to ski during basketball season; he didn't want them to get injured and be unable to play. I had been breaking this rule regularly, but Coach Brightman didn't know about it. Until the avalanche that got me into the papers.

Each winter on weekends Louie and I and some of our friends worked for the Ski Patrol at Stevens Pass, high in the Cascades. On February 5, 1949, a group of us were driving toward the pass in a near-blizzard. Our cars were spread along the road, separated by others. I was in the lead car and was staring absent-mindedly out the window at the storm when I heard a low roar and our car skidded and swung sideways to an abrupt stop.

"Look at that!" the driver shouted.

An avalanche had swept down the mountainside and buried the road right in front of us. I yanked on my ski boots, not bothering to tie the laces, jumped out of the car, and climbed on top of the huge pile of snow, assuming other cars might be buried ahead of us. In the swirling snow, the visibility was terrible, but there didn't seem to be any cars on the road. Then I looked down the hillside and could just make out two tires sticking through the snow, about three hundred feet down in the valley.

"There's a car down there!" I shouted, and took off.

Plunging knee-deep in the soft snow, I lunged down the slope, stepping out of first one, then the other of my boots. Sock-footed, I heard muffled cries for help as I got nearer to the car.

"I'm coming! I'm coming!" I yelled, and when I reached the car I began digging furiously with my hands.

I dug down to the driver's side window and found it broken and the car full of snow. I pulled snow and glass from around the driver's face and then went to work on the passenger. More help arrived, and we managed to drag both occupants free of the car and up to the highway, where we put them into cars headed back to Seattle. I never did find my ski boots.

In the meantime, more snow had come down the mountainside and trapped the car in which I had been riding. I decided I might as well go on up to the ski area, rent some boots, and go to work. The weather cleared, and the skiing was fabulous that weekend. When I finally got back to Seattle, the newspapers were full of stories about my rescue effort, and I received the Purple Merit Star from the National Ski Patrol organization.

Coach Brightman, however, was not impressed. I had violated his hard-and-fast rule. My basketball career, and my basketball scholarship, were over. I didn't get my varsity letter, but my grades improved, and with more free time, I could continue to climb and ski on weekends.

Fortunately, I didn't need to worry about the tuition anyway; Louie and I both had part-time jobs at Osborn and Ulland, Inc., a downtown Seattle sporting goods store. During the war, Scott Osborn had been a member of the U.S. Army's crack alpine corps, the Tenth Mountain Division, renowned for its mountaineering and skiing skills. His partner, Olaf Ulland, was a world-champion ski jumper from Norway, the first man to soar three hundred feet on skis. Between working at Osborn and Ulland and guiding climbers, I was getting paid to do what I loved and covering college expenses in the bargain. It was perfect.

Seattle street photo, First Avenue—Jim (left) and Louie (right), 1949. Photo: Whittaker family collection

While neither my engagement nor my basketball scholarship lasted, my commitment to the church did. I enjoyed the litany of the Latin mass and the rich, elaborate traditions the Catholic Church had evolved over the centuries. I went to confession and mass regularly, but I still had questions, some spiritual, others practical—like how was I going to be in church every Sunday if I was climbing?

Out in the mountains, high on a summit ridge or deep in a cathedral of conifers, I often wondered about the significance of that human creation, the church. It didn't seem to me to take a building, or even a dogma, to make someone a believer; all you had to do was open your eyes, your ears, your heart. In the mountains, the "church" is all around you.

And gradually, over the years, my faith has deepened and broadened. You cannot travel the world and experience new customs and religions, as I have been privileged to do, without eventually concluding that there is no single, "true" path to God. There are as many paths as there are searchers for the way, and part of the essence of being a spiritual being lies in treating other travelers on that road as you would have them treat you—with an open mind and a compassionate heart. These days, all I know is that the more I explore the world and its faiths, the less anxious and the more humble I become.

■

In 1952 Louie and I graduated from Seattle University, earning both Bachelor of Science degrees—and draft notices. Uncle Sam wanted us to fight in Korea. We didn't.

The national park supervisor at Mount Rainier managed to get our college deferment extended a few months so we could run the guide service through the summer, but that fall we both went to Fort Lewis, almost in the shadow of the mountain, to be inducted for a two-year tour of duty in the army. In those days the army allowed twins to remain together, and we chose to do so.

As college graduates with minors in philosophy, it didn't take us long to figure out the philosophy of the military during the Korean War: forget thinking; learn to kill. We learned to shoot rifles, machine guns, and bazookas, and we were also taught the finer points of washing dishes, scrubbing floors, picking up cigarette butts, and doing push-ups in the mud. Unlike many of our fellow inductees, however, the physical side of basic training was a snap for us; the mountains had already trained us.

Next we were sent to a base in San Luis Obispo, California, to be "toughened up" by battle-hardened veterans just back from South Korea whose main purpose, it seemed, was to reduce "college punk assholes" to faceless serial numbers. At night, nursing our scorched egos, we vowed to "take 'em out behind the barracks and clean their clocks," but we knew better. It was a lot simpler to take the abuse for two months than to spend the war in the stockade. We'd be out of there by December, anyway. Meanwhile, when the army realized Louie and I could both type more than fifty words per minute, we were put in the U.S. Army Signal Corps.

During basic training, Louie and I learned that the famed Tenth Mountain Division had been succeeded by a unit called the Mountain and Cold Weather Training Command, located at Camp Hale, high in the Colorado Rockies. We knew we had to try to get assigned to it, but we also knew we'd get nowhere through the normal chain of command. I contacted a Tenth Mountain Division veteran: our boss at Osborn and Ulland, Scott Osborn, and enlisted his help.

It turned out he knew an officer at Camp Hale, Lieutenant Colonel Ed Link. Scott wrote Link a letter fulsome with praise for Louie and me and listed our qualifications: "(1) two seasons as professional guides at Mount Rainier; (2) four years as climbing instructors and climb leaders for the Seattle Mountaineers; (3) seven years as members of the National Ski Patrol; (4) charter members of the Northwest Mountain Rescue and Safety Council; (5) paid instructors at YMCA climbing classes and the Olympic Junior College in Bremerton." Then he laid on the sales pitch: "I don't think you could find two better men . . . they would be a definite asset to your organization and will probably be able to show you a few new wrinkles . . . They'll be worth twice what they're getting paid."

His letter did the trick. Two days before the end of basic training, Louie and I were in class breaking down and reassembling M-1 rifles when a master sergeant skidded a document across my desk. It was a transfer to the Mountain and Cold Weather Training Command in Colorado. Louie got one too. This was good news on two fronts. First, we wouldn't have to go to Korea after all. Second, I could get married.

■

Blanche Patterson, a tall and tan young woman from Seattle with a nifty figure and a warm, winning smile, worked at the soda fountain at Paradise Inn in Rainier National Park, just across the parking lot from where Louie and I ran the guide service. She was a student at the University of Washington and a member of the Seattle Tennis Club, and I liked a lot more about her than her vanilla shakes. We went for picnics in the hills near the lodge, and I invited her to parties at the guide house.

It was a classic whirlwind wartime romance. The fact that I was about to go off to war a virgin only added to the pressure. We became engaged but decided to wait on marriage until the war was over. When I got the news that I would become an instructor at Camp Hale, however, we changed our minds. As soon as basic training was over, we had a big wedding in the Catholic church in Laurelhurst, a neighborhood in Seattle.

I was actually "late to the altar," at least compared to my brother. Louie had already been married for a couple of years. He had met Pat Wales during his sophomore year at Seattle University, and they were married in 1950. Even though they lived only a few blocks from our house and I had known we would have to separate sometime, I still missed him. Now, however, I understood why he'd left. I was deliriously happy with Blanche and wanted to spend every free moment with her.

The day after our wedding, Blanche and I piled all our worldly possessions into the back of our car and headed for Colorado. Louie and Pat were right behind us in their car.

■

Early in January 1953, Camp Hale, Colorado, was an absolutely breathtaking winter wonderland, a world of brilliant sunshine and deep powder snow ringed with magnificent peaks. Not bad for the army. At 10,000 feet, Hale was at the same elevation as Mount Rainier's Camp Muir, and Louie and I felt right at home.

Our job was to train Special Forces soldiers in skiing, climbing, mountain maneuvers, and bivouacs. We dressed in "over-whites"—white pants and parkas that camouflaged our military olive drab. Even our skis, poles, and packs were white. In addition to skill training, we played war games, chasing and being chased by "enemy" patrols, "dynamiting" (with wooden blocks) the railroad tracks that ran over the pass, being "captured," and "escaping" into the woods for a week and building shelters out of fir trees and aspens. For the most part, it was a lot more like fun than work.

I can remember one still winter night in particular. A bright half-moon glowed in a deep, clear sky festooned with stars. I stood guard over a bivouac

Camp Hale ski troopers, Tennessee Pass, Colorado, 1953—Jim (second from left), Louie (fourth from left), Keith Wegeman (fifth from left). Photo: Whittaker family collection

site we had established above the highway. It was just after midnight. The temperature was twenty degrees below zero, a soft quilt of powder snow covered everything, and ice-dust sparkled in the moonlight. I sat in a small aspen grove blending into a snowbank, warm and comfortable in my over-whites and in awe of the beauty around me. Every once in a while a car, sometimes with skis on top, would come purring into the silence and then quietly disappear down the road. It was peaceful and beautiful, and although I wished I was in that car with the heater on, skis on top, heading for some ski lodge with a fireplace, I had to admit it was a lot better than being shot at.

What's more, I could go home to my wife. I was now a corporal, living off the post in nearby Colorado Springs. Considering how much of the time we were away working, Louie and I were lucky that Blanche and Pat had each other and got along so well. Life would have been pretty lonely for them had it been otherwise. On weekends, though, we tried to make up for our absences. A close camaraderie developed among the families of the married instructors, and we socialized together a lot. In addition, Louie and I and some of our fellow Mountain and Cold Weather instructors got weekend jobs teaching at a ski school located in the Arapahoe Basin and run by Willy Shaefler, coach of the U.S. Olympic Ski Team. Our wives often drove up to spend the weekend skiing with us. One of Willy's instructors was Keith Wegeman, a member of the U.S. Olympic Ski Team who had beat my old boss Olaf Ulland's ski-jumping record. Besides being an incredible athlete and a great guy, Keith was also good looking and had the body of a Greek god. Our wives fell into swoons whenever he came by to visit, and I could hardly blame them. He was a serious weight lifter who could do one-arm handstands with no apparent effort.

It was Keith who got Louie and me involved in weight training. We began to work out together three times a week and increased our protein intake. My weight in college had been a pretty steady 185 pounds, but with Keith's regime, it jumped to 205 rock-solid pounds. I thought about those comic book ads from my childhood; the 95-pound weakling was no more.

During the warmer months, the command operated out of Fort Carson near Colorado Springs, and we taught climbing and mountaineering in Cheyenne Canyon and on a rock formation called the Garden of the Gods. Five days a week we were up on the rocks first thing in the morning, teaching basic balance and rope techniques, sometimes putting on demonstrations for civilians. At noon we came down off the cliffs and were served a hot meal from insulated containers that had been trucked from the mess hall at camp. Then it was back to the rocks for more climbing instruction. In midsummer, thunderstorms often built up over the foothills in midafternoon, and we'd come down again to avoid the lightning danger. We'd sit around telling climbing stories, and the new recruits would hang on every word. When a climber confessed to me he was afraid of heights, I'd tell him, "Good! I wouldn't climb with you if you weren't; height demands respect." That seemed to help. It was really rewarding to see our students master the basics and become comfortable with the ropes. Once they got the hang of it, rappelling down the sheer face of a cliff was an especially good ego-builder.

And so the days passed. Louie and I would be high on the granite and limestone sun-warmed cliffs. The air was clean and crisp, tinged with the faint fragrance of evergreens. Our students' calls drifted across the rock faces: "On belay, climb! Climbing! Tension! Slack! Up rope! Falling! Rock!" And with each day, their skills and confidence grew. It was deeply rewarding work. At night in Colorado Springs, we would often see our trainees swaggering around in their uniforms with carabiners and pitons clipped to their belts like badges.

In the spring of 1954, Blanche announced we would be having a child in October, just before my scheduled discharge. She suggested she could return to Seattle and live with her mother during her pregnancy, but that started me thinking. I had heard a rumor that if you had "an important job of a seasonal nature" waiting for you, the army could discharge you in twenty-one months rather than twenty-four. It was time for another letter.

This time I wrote to Preston Macy, the superintendent of Mount Rainier National Park, whom I knew well from our guide service. I explained the situation and asked him to write to Colonel Shelor, then the commanding officer at Camp Hale, requesting our services on Mount Rainier that summer. Once again, it worked. Louie, Pat, and I were on our way back home to join Blanche.

We spent that summer guiding on Mount Rainier, and when the season ended, I returned to my old job at Osborn and Ulland. On October 3, 1954, Blanche and I welcomed our first child, Carl Bernard Whittaker, into the world. Carl was a lovely, healthy child, and I suddenly became more acutely aware of my responsibilities as an adult, husband, and father and began thinking about the future.

Later that fall, Scott Osborn asked me to take a friend of his from the East Coast to a few nearby ski areas. The friend's name was Howard Head, and he had just invented an all-aluminum ski that would revolutionize skiing. (He later revolutionized tennis with his Prince racquet and its giant "sweet spot.") We enjoyed each other immensely, and Howard offered to make me sales manager for Head Skis. Scott was none too happy to discover his friend was trying to steal away one of his employees, but he needn't have worried; I wasn't about to tear myself and my family from my beloved Northwest to work for Howard in Maryland.

It wasn't long, however, before another offer came along that would prove to be too good to turn down.

Louie (left) and John Day (right) in front of Mount Rainier, 1958.
Photo: Jim Whittaker

Chapter Four

BIGGER, FASTER, HIGHER

One evening in 1954 I found myself sitting in the living room at Lloyd and Mary Anderson's home in West Seattle. I was delighted to see them, but I wasn't sure why I was there. Lloyd had been one of my first climbing instructors. We had become friends and climbed a number of mountains together over the years. In fact, on the Fourth of July, 1950, we spent the night in the crater of Mount Rainier and set off fireworks that our friends saw all the way north in Seattle.

An engineer with the Seattle Transit System, Lloyd's real claim to fame in the climbing community was that he and his wife, Mary, had founded a little sideline business in 1939 called The Co-op, through which climbers in the Northwest could pool their resources to order hard-to-find mountaineering equipment from Europe. Membership cost one dollar for life, and by the mid-forties when Louie and I joined, there were more than six hundred members. (My membership card was number 647; Louie's was 648.) By the mid-fifties, despite the intervention of the war, during which time equipment imports stopped and he had to rely on army surplus, Lloyd had built up The Co-op to more than six thousand members, and annual sales had reached $80,000.

That was the problem, Lloyd explained to me that night; it had grown too big for him to manage on the side. He wanted me to run The Co-op for him. I was immensely flattered; any climber in the Northwest (and, increasingly, the nation) who was worth his or her salt was a member of The Co-op. It practically had cult status in the climbing world; people compared their membership numbers to see who had joined first.

The offer was exciting, but also risky. I was twenty-five years old and already had a family to support. I had a good, steady job at Osborn and Ulland, for whom I'd sold sporting goods all through college and who had taken me back again after my military service. Though The Co-op had grown steadily, it was still a "hole-in-the-wall" operation in a second-floor walk-up.

On the other hand, I was really attracted by the co-op ethic: the idea of a membership organization that not only acquired top-quality goods and sold them at fair prices but also paid back to its members an annual dividend usually equal to 10 percent of their total purchases—effectively giving them a 10 percent discount on everything they bought. It seemed to me to be a retailing concept that couldn't fail. When Lloyd offered me $400 a month and half a percent of gross sales, I decided to go for it.

My decision didn't go over very well with Scott Osborn and Olaf Ulland. By this time I was working in the retail store as well as making sales trips for them throughout the region. I stayed on with them for another six months to smooth the transition, then started at The Co-op on July 25, 1955. I had no way of knowing that I had just taken on a task that would keep me busy—and happy—for twenty-five years. Even in 1955, despite its growth, The Co-op wasn't much to write home about. Over the years the business had graduated first from Lloyd's basement to a former gas station and then to an accountant's office at Sixth Avenue and Pike Street in Seattle, up a flight of old linoleum stairs from the Green Apple Pie Restaurant. To buy something, you had to ring a little bell and the accountant, Adam Mayer (who was not a climber himself), would come out from behind his desk, begrudgingly, and ring up the purchase. When I took over, Mr. Mayer had moved on, and we had his entire space to ourselves: a whopping twenty by thirty feet. The location did have one significant advantage, however; the office of The Mountaineers Club was directly across the hall. Climbers and outdoor enthusiasts were coming and going all the time; it was a built-in clientele.

For seven months I was the only full-time employee. I unlocked the door in the morning, swept out the place, stocked shelves, talked with customers, wrote up sales, mailed price lists out to everyone I knew, ate lunch out of a brown bag, and locked the door when I had to run down the hall to the bathroom. When orders came from out of town, I packaged them up to be mailed. Locking up at the end of the day, I lugged packages down the stairs and out to my car, three blocks away. I stopped to deposit the day's receipts at the bank, went on to the post office to mail the packages, and then finally drove home. I was chief cook and bottle-washer all rolled into one, and I was enjoying myself thoroughly.

In the fall of that first year, with a budget of $5,000, I started a ski department. Soon The Co-op was as busy in the winter as it was in the summer, and

Original REI store above the Green Apple Pie Restaurant, 523 Pike Street, Seattle, 1960. Photo: REI collection

we were able to hire another full-time employee, Jeanette Lasher. We made a good team, and that first year, sales rose by 50 percent to $125,000. The Co-op had eight thousand members, and we paid out some $10,000 in dividends. I felt secure in this new job, and in my life as well. I had a wife and son whom I loved and a home on Mercer Island, only a few minutes from downtown.

With Jeanette around to share the workload, we decided to open the store on Saturday mornings so people could pick up gear they needed for weekend trips. Customers loved the idea, and Saturday morning business was brisk. On one Saturday, I locked up at noon as usual, walked to my car, set the packages on the ground, and tossed the bank deposit envelope on top of the roof of my convertible while I fished around in my pockets for the key. Then I loaded the packages into the car and drove off. At the bank, when I reached for the deposit envelope, it struck me that I didn't remember throwing it in the car with the packages. I jumped out and looked on the roof: nothing. There was more than a thousand dollars in that envelope! I drove madly back to the store, watching the road for the envelope, but I was pretty sure it had fallen off near the parking lot. As I swung the car into the alley where the lot was, I saw two men walking toward a white envelope that lay on the ground. Busy talking, they walked right past it. I stopped the car, jumped out and grabbed it, my heart racing like I had just speed-climbed Mount Rainier. It was unopened and full. Not for the first time it occurred to me that I might have been born more lucky than smart.

I guess I was also somewhat naïve. Quite a few folks from the waterfront— "street people," we'd call them today—came into our store to buy cans of Sterno, an alcohol-based cookstove fuel. It took me a while to realize that they were drinking it, not cooking with it, somewhere down by the docks. Hoping to discourage them, I raised the price by a quarter. The next Skid Road customer who came in brought his can of Sterno to the counter and counted out the correct change in quarters, dimes, and nickels—at the old price. When I told him the price was now twenty-five cents more, he never said a word. He just gave me a hurt and desperate look, gathered up his change, and left.

"I'm sorry," I said as he shuffled out the door and down the stairs. I meant it, too. But at least we wouldn't be poisoning him or his friends any more. That was the last of the Sterno drinkers.

In those early days, The Co-op sold mostly "hard goods." The floor was covered with crates filled with pitons, carabiners, Tricouni nails for boot soles, and more. Ropes hung from the walls. There were shelves of dried food and nuts for camping trips. We didn't even have a cash register, just a drawer that popped out when you hit a button on the counter. Service was personal and the atmosphere informal. Folks would come in and just stand around swapping stories about where they'd been that weekend. When they needed something we weren't carrying, we listened to them, and pretty soon it was on the shelf. That's how we got into our first "soft goods" products; somebody wanted reliable climbing and hiking socks, and soon we were stocking them. It wasn't long before we had sleeping bags, parkas, and tents as well.

We evolved a policy, which continues today, that we would focus only on "self-propelled" sports—no motorboat engines and water skis, for example. And despite the fact that some of our best customers were also hunters, we refused to carry guns and ammunition. (I never did forget that owl.) It was face-to-face, person-to-person retailing, and I loved it. Most of our customers were active professionals—lawyers, doctors, teachers, business people, and the like—who had the time and money to pursue a sport as arcane as climbing, and I got to know them all pretty well.

Sometimes that knowledge came in handy. One time, shortly after one of our customers had been killed in a climbing accident, his life insurance company sent an agent around to try to get me to say it might have been suicide, so they could avoid paying benefits to his family. I straightened him out pretty quickly about the fellow; these were kindred spirits, these climbers, and I understood them well: "He fell. His rope broke," I said. "Pay up."

My second year at The Co-op was even more fulfilling. Jeanette and I rang up $143,000 in sales, membership climbed to ninety-five hundred, and The Co-op paid out $13,000 in dividends. There were blessings at home, too; on September 6, 1956, Blanche gave birth to our second son, James Scott. My life was full, and Lloyd's "little sideline" was rapidly becoming a serious business.

When Lloyd took vacations, he often went climbing in Switzerland and Austria and bought equipment for the store while he was at it. Consequently, we always had the most up-to-date gear; what we didn't have was space for it. Pretty soon I was setting up tents and displaying them upside down from the ceiling so we could still have room to walk around. Often I'd be mounting ski bindings and Trima "uphill climbers" on skis on the mail-order wrapping bench at the same time Jeanette was trying to wrap packages. It was a good thing we got along so well. We gained a little extra storage space from The Mountaineers next door, but it still wasn't enough.

Finally, in 1959, we got a thousand square feet of warehouse space in the basement of a building a block away, beneath a restaurant. We kept our original retail space and stashed our excess inventory in the basement warehouse. We maintained a larger inventory than most retail businesses because it was often difficult to get timely deliveries from our various overseas suppliers. What's more, our product line had grown substantially, and we only had space in the store for display samples of many items. Month after month, the business grew and the warehouse filled.

■

At 1:00 A.M. on April 15, 1962, I was awakened abruptly by the phone.

"Mr. Whittaker?" a voice said. "This is the Seattle Fire Department. I'm afraid there's been a water main break, and your warehouse has seven feet of water in it. You'd better get down here."

I was still waking up as I sped across the Lake Washington floating bridge when the key item in the conversation finally registered.

"Seven *feet?*"

The scene at the warehouse was awesome. Huge spotlights illuminated the whole messy block. Massive hoses snaked around the pavement and down the stairs into the warehouse. Pumps throbbed and water and mud gushed over the sidewalk and into the street. Firemen were climbing up from the basement, wet and muddy. I went downstairs.

"Phew," I thought to myself, "it's only two feet deep."

Then I saw the muddy high watermark above my head.

It was a disaster. Everything we owned—sleeping bags, parkas, hats, gloves, socks, boxes of cookstoves, candle lanterns, canteens, fuel bottles, skis, snowshoes, ice axes, crampons, pitons, ropes, dehydrated food (now fully hydrated, no doubt)—lay floating in the two feet of water still remaining. I was in shock. We were also uninsured for this kind of loss.

As soon as daylight came, I got on the phone. Ray Morse, the superintendent of the Seattle Water Department, had been a neighbor of ours when I was
growing up. I told him The Co-op would very likely be put out of business by
this loss. He suggested that the city itself might be at fault and said he'd look
into it immediately. In the meantime, he promised to see what he could do to
help us clean up. The next day, the firemen returned and spent three full days
helping us wash mud off dirty clothes and sleeping bags, scrub hardware and
snowshoes, and empty and clean fuel bottles and other containers. We worked
like demons and, when we were done, had a pretty complete inventory of damaged goods to send to the Water Department.

After we cleaned out the space, we gathered up the salvageable gear and
ran an ad in the paper announcing a "Huge Co-op Water Damage Warehouse
Sale!" To our astonishment, hundreds of people showed up, and we recouped
a fair amount of our losses. Three weeks later, I got a letter from the Water
Department. Inside was a check for $61,419.02. I was ecstatic; it was a more
than fair settlement, and I rushed the check to the bank. This time I made sure
I didn't leave the deposit envelope on top of the car.

We survived the Great Flood (I think we actually made money on it) and
kept growing. We also kept adding small touches that made us different from
other stores. For example, for years we gave parents 50 percent trade-in discounts when their kids outgrew their boots. The parents loved it, and it helped
us develop long-term relationships with our customers. We were also one of
the first largely self-service retailers. We started that way in the early days by
necessity: I was the only employee, after all, and couldn't be everywhere at once.
But we continued it partly because it was efficient and partly because it gave
our customers a chance to browse on their own without pressure from a sales-
person. When you needed help, you got it; otherwise, you had pretty much
the run of the store.

Year after year, we kept setting records, and by 1960 our sales were triple
what they had been when I started in 1955. That same year, Lloyd was able to
retire from Seattle Transit and become our full-time general manager. I continued as store manager. For tax and legal reasons, we also changed the company's
name; though it remained a co-op, it was now called Recreational Equipment,
Incorporated—or simply REI.

But sales records weren't the only records I was setting in those days.

■

One day in midsummer 1959, a tall, tanned middle-aged gentleman wearing a cowboy hat walked through The Co-op door, introduced himself, and then said, "I want you to run me up a few mountains."

I told him I was really too busy and suggested he talk to Louie, who still worked at Osborn and Ulland. Louie told him he was busy too.

But the man was John Day, a millionaire rancher and businessman from Medford, Oregon, who was used to getting his way and wasn't about to take no for an answer. He was also very persuasive. Louie finally gave in, and not long afterward, I did too. For one thing, the money was good: $50 a day plus expenses—a lot in those days. For another, we were intrigued by his objective. It turned out he was speaking literally when he said, "I want you to run me up some mountains." He wanted to set new speed-climbing records on Washington State's six major peaks—Rainier, Adams, St. Helens, Glacier, Baker, and Olympus. And he wanted to do it immediately.

Over the next week, Louie took John up Mount Adams, Mount St. Helens, and Mount Rainier, setting records on the first two but getting snowed in on Mount Rainier. On their way north to Mount Baker, Louie called, bushed, and said he could use some help. I knew the store could do without me for a few days, so I agreed.

John was a fascinating fellow. Fifty-one years old and a former heavy smoker, he had become a fanatic about physical conditioning. He had laid out a series of trails on his big spread in Oregon and would go off running for hours—with his pet cheetah. He was nearly twice as old as Louie and I, but you'd never know it by his performance; he was tough as nails. An old back injury made it impossible for him to carry a pack, so Louie and I carried his gear. I didn't mind that so much as I minded his habit of unroping once we'd descended to a safe altitude and then running as hard as he could back down the mountain, all the way to the car. To make sure he didn't get lost or hurt, we'd have to run down too, and the pack would knock the stuffing out of me. Coming off Mount Baker, the pack hammered a bloody hole in my back. As soon as we got off Mount Baker, we headed across Puget Sound for Mount Olympus in Olympic National Park.

That summer, glaciologist Ed La Chapelle was doing research on Blue Glacier, at the foot of the mountain. He had permission from the National Park Service to support his research program by air and had arranged with Bill Fairchild, a local pilot, to make supply flights from the airport in nearby Port Angeles. With his usual determination, John had persuaded Bill to give us a lift to the glacier. Only twenty minutes after takeoff, Louie, John, and I were putting on our rucksacks and climbing equipment on top of the glacier. I didn't mind missing the usual fifteen-mile slog up from the Hoh River Ranger Station at all.

In high spirits, we roped up and took off up the mountain. Two hours later we were at the summit having a leisurely lunch. Then we raced back down to meet Bill, who said he'd be back by 3:00 P.M. True to his word, he came into sight shortly after we arrived, touched the plane down lightly in an uphill landing, gunned it around to face the opposite direction, and with engine still running, threw open the door. We had tossed in our packs and ice axes and started to climb aboard when he held up his hand and yelled above the engine whine:

"I can only take two of you right now. Too much turbulence. I'll come back for the third."

I stood aside and motioned for John and Louie to climb in.

"I'll be right back," Bill shouted.

"Okay, Bill," I yelled back. Then as an afterthought as he slammed the door, he said:

"If it gets too rough, I'll be back in the morning." Then he roared off down the glacier and lifted into the air.

I stood there on the glacier in light clothes, with no pack, food, or sleeping bag, and watched them disappear over the ridge.

"Nice going Whittaker, you jerk," I mumbled to myself.

I looked down the deeply crevassed glacier to the timberline, wondering how far I'd have to go before I found a sheltered spot and enough heather, leaves and fir boughs to cover me while I waited for morning. Meanwhile, I prayed for calm air.

About an hour later I heard the drone of an engine, and then Bill's little plane came into view, clearing the ridge crest and swooping in over the glacier. I was mighty glad to see him.

John had gotten his wish—or most of it. In the span of just over a week, he had "bagged" five of the six peaks, missing a record only on Mount Rainier.

As I came to know him better, and visited him in Oregon, I was happy he'd gotten interested in "peak-bagging." It sure beat his other hobby, which was bagging big game. A member of a prestigious hunting organization, John had a "living" room full of dead animals. There were glass-eyed trophies hanging from the walls and an enormous polar bear rug, complete with head, on the floor. Ever since my own childhood murder of that owl, I couldn't help being sickened by such displays. I thought it was a terrible shame that wealthy people, with their high-powered rifles, telescopic sights, and professional guides, could roam the world's wildernesses stalking the most magnificent animals, only to kill them. For sport. Natural selection takes the weakest of a species; big game hunters select only the finest, and then take them out of the gene pool forever. Privately, I hoped Louie and I could keep John busy mounting mountains instead of trophies.

The next summer we were at it again. At midnight on June 15, 1959, Louie, John, and I left the Paradise Ranger Station at 5,400 feet and headed for the 14,410-foot summit of Mount Rainier. John had missed his record the previous year, and he hadn't given up. The moon was full, the night magical, with diamonds glittering in the snow and twinkling in the sky. A light breeze kept us cool, and we traveled quickly on the hard-packed snow.

By 1:30 A.M. we had reached Camp Muir at 10,000 feet. After a swig of sugared water, we roped up, strapped on crampons, and moved rapidly up the Cowlitz Glacier, down onto Gibraltar Rock, then over to the Chute and up to the summit. We stood on top at 5:20 A.M. and took a twenty-minute break, watching the sunrise and catching our breath. Then we descended, rapidly but cautiously, to Camp Muir, where we removed our crampons. We passed the water bottles around and packed up our climbing gear. We were all feeling good.

"I'm going to run from here on down," John announced, characteristically.

Louie looked at me, and I nodded. We had expected this. In fact, this time we had cushioned our packs so they wouldn't dig into our backs. John sped away downhill. Without a word, we took off in pursuit. We caught up with him at Anvil Rock and ran along at his side for awhile, guiding him past Pebble Creek and Glacier Vista and then, after a quick glance at each other, we surged ahead of him, running, jumping, and bounding like scared deer. When John finally reached Paradise Ranger Station, we'd already been waiting for him for ten minutes.

"You two are the toughest, meanest sons of bitches I have ever met," he panted, a huge grin across his weathered face. It was 7:50 A.M., just in time for breakfast at Paradise Inn. At the age of fifty-two, John had another record: Mount Rainier in seven hours and fifty minutes.

But he wanted another one.

Camp below West Buttress at 14,500 feet, Mount McKinley, 1960—(left to right)
Jim, Louie, climber from a Japanese team, Pete Schoening. Photo: John Day

Chapter Five

FALLING

In 1960 Mount McKinley—called Denali by Native Alaskans—had been climbed by only a dozen or so expeditions. Rising to 20,300 feet, it had a reputation for being one of the coldest mountains in the world and normally took three weeks to climb. John Day was sure we could beat that handily. To help us meet that goal, Louie and I invited along our friend Pete Schoening, a legendarily strong climber.

On May 14, 1960, we flew to Talkeetna, a small airfield near the mountain. There John had arranged for the great Alaskan bush pilot Don Sheldon to fly us in his ski-equipped Cessna 180 to the 10,200-foot level of the Kahiltna Glacier, at the base of McKinley's West Buttress. This was 3,000 feet higher than where climbing parties were usually landed, but John, as usual, had made special arrangements with the National Park Service for a higher landing.

John and Don Sheldon were old friends. They'd known each other ever since, as Don put it, John had "spent a mountain of effort and a river of money trying to shoot a world-record Alaska brown bear."

"He failed," Don added.

Don himself was practically a legend in Alaska, landing and taking off in places no one else dared to, in his trademark shiny bare-metal planes. He ordered them that way from Cessna headquarters in Wichita, Kansas; without paint, the planes were 30 pounds lighter—which meant they flew faster and higher.

After he returned and air-dropped some supplies for us, we started climbing. Conditions were excellent. It was cold, but the sky was clear and the wind fairly calm. The plan was to race to the summit, Alpine-style, without acclimatization, and then descend just as rapidly. It was a risky strategy; the human body does not adapt well to rapid altitude changes. Starved of oxygen, the brain slows down and stops functioning rationally. The body slows down too, and sometimes simply fails. Pulmonary edema, in which the lungs fill quickly with fluid, is not uncommon and can be lethal. Cerebral edema, in which the same thing happens, but in the brain, is even more dangerous. But we were all seasoned climbers and felt the level of risk to be acceptable.

We made good progress. On the first day, we climbed from our Base Camp at 10,200 feet to 14,000 feet, where we established Camp II. Early the next morning we set off up the steep ice slope of the West Buttress. As usual, because of his back injury, John was carrying no pack. Louie, Pete, and I were carrying everything, in packs that weighed in excess of 70 pounds. By the time we established Camp III, at 17,200 feet, we were pretty well worn out. The next day, May 17, the climb to McKinley's summit was long, hard, and slow. Finally, after fourteen hours of climbing, we reached the top at 10:00 P.M., taking advantage of the bright twilight of early summer in the land of the midnight sun. At the summit, we met a climbing party from Anchorage led by Paul Crews, a local climber from the Mountaineering Club of Alaska. They began their descent shortly after we arrived.

We now stood a chance of setting an amazing record for McKinley—up and back in four days, rather than the normal three weeks. But we were paying a price. We were exhausted and oxygen-starved. What's more, the temperature was thirty degrees below zero. We didn't waste much time on the summit. We took a few pictures in the weak light, scraped the ice off the wolverine fur–trimmed hoods of our parkas, tied our two ropes together for extra safety in case of a fall, and began our own descent, eager to get down to thicker air and the protection of our tent. I led off, John was second, Louie was third, and Pete anchored the rear.

We had just picked our way down the steepest section of the summit dome and reached Denali Pass, at about 18,000 feet, when I stepped off a wind-hollowed ice block just as it broke beneath me, sat down hard on my butt, and started sliding. I twisted around and pressed my ice ax point into the face of

Summit of Mount McKinley—(left to right) Louie, John Day, Jim.
Photo: Pete Schoening

the ice slope beneath me, the way I'd taught others so many times, and made a quick self-arrest. That should have done it, but when I looked up, I saw John, airborne, above me. He had panicked, for some reason jumping out and down to avoid being jerked by the rope to which we were tied. It was a technically crazy, perfectly human, and potentially fatal thing to do. His lunge pulled Louie and Pete Schoening off the mountain, and me as well. Down we fell, through the shadows of the Alaskan twilight. We crashed into a small ledge, ricocheted off it, and tumbled down again, smashing into one ledge after another, falling upside-down, sideways, and backward down the steep ice slope of the Peters Glacier. Each time we hit a ledge, our momentum kept flinging us back out over the void. I couldn't get my breath; the body slams kept knocking it out of me. I smashed my head, hard, and still we fell.

After what seemed like forever, but could probably have been measured in seconds, we stopped with one final crash on a broad ledge or plateau some 500 feet down the face of the glacier. Beyond the ledge, the glacier fell away another 3,000 feet.

I became conscious of voices. John was groaning nearby. Louie was talking to Pete. I put out a feeler for pain; I didn't hurt any place in particular, I hurt everywhere. My vision was blurred, I was dizzy and nauseous. The world around me was spinning. I tried to stand up but fell over immediately. I tried

Below the accident site, Denali Pass, 18,000 feet, in the background—(left to right) Louie, Pete Schoening, Jim. Photo: John Day

again and fell again. It seemed like something was pushing me over to the left. It took three more tries before I finally managed to get to my feet and stagger to where John lay still, groaning.

"What's wrong, John?" I asked him.

"I think my ankles are broken."

It looked like he was right. Meanwhile, Louie, who seemed to be unhurt, was bending over Pete, who was dazed and uncommunicative. We were in big trouble. John was going nowhere anytime soon, and Pete looked questionable. Louie called down into the dim light, hoping the Anchorage climbers would hear him, and reported we had a casualty. We were still several hundred feet above our own High Camp, and there was no way we could get John down there, especially given the condition we were in. Louie and I chipped and scraped out a platform in the ice, bundled John into one of the sleeping bags we always carry, and anchored him to the slope. In the meantime, Pete had managed to get to his feet, though his speech was slow and slurred and he seemed disoriented.

We made John as comfortable as we could, told him we'd be back in a few hours with help, and then the three of us roped up and set off for our camp. Louie, who was in the best shape, anchored the rear, Pete was in the middle where we could keep track of him, and I took the lead. I was still having trouble staying upright, leaning and falling to the left, but I felt rational. Like a horse that can smell the barn, I started down the slope, going on instinct. Soon after we started, we met Paul Crews coming up toward us. Having heard our call for help, he had taken down our tent and carried it up toward us. When he saw the condition we were in, he took the tent all the way up to John, slit open the floor, and set it up around him.

The rest of us continued lurching downhill. Pete kept asking, in a strange, distant voice, "What happened?" No matter how many times Louie or I told him we'd fallen, he'd ask the same question again a few minutes later. At one point, he refused to go any farther, convinced I was leading us the wrong way. There's an old saying that climbers rope up so the smart ones can't leave. That may be, but I was at my limit, exhausted and in pain. After arguing with him for what seemed like forever, survival instinct took over, and I simply untied myself from the rope, stumbled down toward camp, and left Louie to persuade

Pete. Reaching camp, I got my crampons off and collapsed into my sleeping bag. It was soft, warm, fluffy, and wonderful. There was no tent, but there was also no wind. The stars were brilliant.

Back up the slope, Louie was in a dilemma. He knew I had been right about the route, but he was worried that in my unstable condition, I wouldn't make it to camp safely. Pete, confused but absolutely adamant, refused to follow, insisting instead the route lay in the opposite direction. Eventually, after more fruitless arguing, Louie untied as well and descended to the camp, telling Pete to do the same. His plan was to check on me and then make sure Pete had followed, but when he reached camp and lay down to rest briefly, he fell asleep.

Thankfully, he didn't sleep long. Awakening and realizing Pete had not yet arrived, Louie headed back up the slope to the point where he had left him, but Pete was gone. He set off in the direction Pete had wanted to go and, in a few minutes, found him sitting dazedly on a rock outcrop above a 3,000-foot drop, his legs dangling in space. One of his gloves was missing, and his hand was frozen white. He was still asking "What happened?" Carefully, Louie got him off the outcrop and coaxed him back to camp and safety.

The next morning we learned by radio that one of Paul Crews's climbers was in serious condition with cerebral edema and that he had called for an air evacuation of both his climber and John. A military helicopter was due the next day. Meanwhile, with help from the Anchorage team, we moved all our equipment up to where John waited.

John had spent a difficult but safe night. Although his toes were numb and his fingers had some minor frostbite, he wasn't in a lot of pain. Pete had recovered somewhat, though his hand was clearly damaged, and he was subdued and still had no memory of the fall. That afternoon the military helicopter flew by and looked us over. John, ever impatient, got on the radio and phoned a friend for assistance: former President Dwight Eisenhower. He also reached his son, John Day, Jr., and had him offer to pay the airfares for the first rescue team. Thanks, apparently, to Eisenhower, the military also provided transport planes.

We knew help was coming. What we didn't know was how massive the response would turn out to be. Thanks to Crews, the Alaska Rescue Group had been contacted first. The word went out to the Mountain Rescue Councils in

Bremerton, Everett, Portland, Seattle, Tacoma, and Vancouver. Pete, Louie, and I had been on countless rescues over the years and had made a lot of friends. Now they were mobilizing.

Up on the mountain, of course, we knew little of this. On the morning of May 19, the helicopter made several passes near us again, but the pilot decided it was too risky to land. I later learned that no plane or helicopter had ever landed at this altitude. After a time, a cargo plane dropped boxes of C-rations, stoves, fuel, and assorted supplies onto the ice—enough for a month. We wondered if the military was trying to send us a message.

At 5:00 A.M. on the following day, May 20, an air force helicopter dropped a toboggan to the Crews party below us. The weather was still perfect, with no wind. Their climber, Helga Bading, was now in critical condition and required immediate evacuation. Her companions lowered her down the steep ice slope of the West Buttress to a plateau at about 14,000 feet, near our Camp II. Don Sheldon piloted the plane that landed and flew her to a hospital in Anchorage, where she recovered. Louie and I were convinced we could haul John down to that plateau, but John was convinced a helicopter would reach him, so we stayed put.

Then disaster of a different sort: I was sitting outside our tent watching a Cessna 180 circling high overhead when it suddenly went into a nose dive and, with its engine revving, plummeted straight onto the ice only fifty feet away from me, bursting into flames on impact. I was horrified. Louie and I tried to get close enough to save the pilot and passenger, but the flames were too hot. There was nothing we could do but sit on the glacier in dreadful helplessness and wait for the wreckage to cool.

John was frantic that it might be his son scouting our location. It wasn't. As it turned out, the two in the plane had been warned to stay away from the mountain since a rescue was in progress. They must have thought they could help. That they had died was appalling, and we felt doubly miserable that we might have been an indirect cause of the crash. (In fact, the four of us were later sued by the flyers' next-of-kin for being an "attractive nuisance." John settled the case out of court.)

We were more determined than ever to haul John off the mountain. I had given up hope that any helicopter could land where we were. Then at about

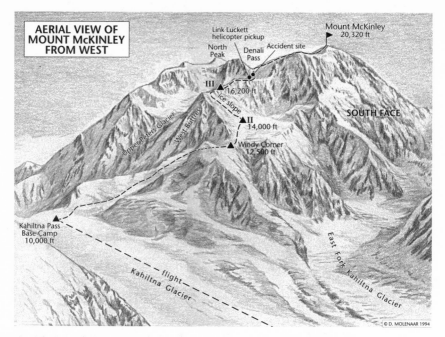

Aerial view of Mount McKinley from the West. Map: Dee Molenaar

five in the evening, I heard a *whup-whup-whup,* and a little two-seater Hiller helicopter appeared over the rock ridge, circled once, and landed thirty feet from our tent. Louie and I ran to the chopper, ducked under the whirling blades, and met pilot Link Luckett, sitting at the controls. He had drained most of the fuel out of the helicopter's tank, jettisoned the battery and other heavy items— including the doors and first-aid kit—and then guided his helicopter up along the rocky ridge toward us, using the rocks' thermal uplift. According to the manufacturer, the tiny chopper had an absolute operating ceiling of 16,000 feet; Luckett had just exceeded that by more than a thousand feet. It was the highest helicopter landing in the history of aviation.

Luckett wanted to know how many had been killed in the wrecked plane. Two, we told him.

"How many need help?" he shouted over the noise of his engine.

"Only one," I said, "John Day."

"I don't know if I'll be able to take off from here," he said, "but I'm going to try. If I make it, I'll come back in an hour for John. Try to light a fire so I can see wind direction from the smoke. Now back off, cross your fingers, and pray!"

As we backed away, bent over nearly double beneath the blades, he gunned the motor and lifted the fragile little chopper about ten feet off the ice. The craft tilted, flew over the ice to the edge of the ridge, and dropped out of sight. I held my breath, listening for the crash, but the Hiller came back into view, still airborne, and headed off down the mountain.

An hour later, we got John out of the tent and prepared him for evacuation. Two hours later, we moved him back in. Link hadn't come back. We didn't know what had happened and feared he had crashed. It turned out he had been flying without bottled oxygen and, in his oxygen-starved state, had forgotten everything he'd told us. Finally, at about nine in the evening, just as we were sliding John into the tent, we heard it: the faint *whup-whup-whup* of a chopper. Luckett was back.

I spilled some kerosene on the cardboard C-ration boxes that had been dropped to us and lit the pile. A ribbon of smoke stretched over the ice toward the west. Luckett brought the chopper in and landed close to the tent; we hauled John under the blades. This time Link had a black tube in his mouth and was sucking on an oxygen bottle.

"I just want one—no more—only one," he said.

We stuffed John into the seat next to Link, fastened his seat belt, exchanged thumbs-up signs, and backed away. Then Link Luckett entered the record books a second time with the highest helicopter evacuation in history, as he lifted John into the thin air at nearly 17,500 feet.

Pete, Louie, and I hollered and waved our thanks and began packing up all our gear. We were free, at last, to get off the mountain. We were about ready to leave camp when, once again, we heard the chopper. Link had returned to take Pete. Relieved, Louie and I thanked him again, but told him not to come back a third time—we could get down on our own. He said the weather was deteriorating anyway, and we bid him farewell. Afterwards, Luckett had a new business card printed: Link Luckett, Helicopter Pilot—Above The Best.

Luckett was right about the weather; as Louie and I started down the mountain, cirrus clouds began forming, and when we reached the Anchorage party at 16,400 feet, Rod Wilson, one of their leaders, said he'd received a radio report that an intense storm was coming. Inside one of their tents having tea, we learned more about the rescue effort going on below.

An astonishing thirty-six climbers were on the mountain at various elevations, all heading up toward us. Another twenty waited in Talkeetna. The various pilots and military personnel involved must have pushed the total number of people involved to nearly seventy-five. In addition to Don Sheldon flying people in and out of the 14,400-foot elevation, huge army air force "banana" helicopters were ferrying others to the 10,000-foot level. We couldn't believe so many people had come to our rescue. Certainly it was more than we thought we needed.

While we were talking, I heard a voice outside the tent that sounded familiar.

"Is The Co-op open?"

I looked out, and there was our old friend Dee Molenaar, roped to two members of the Anchorage team, having just come from the base of the West Buttress. It was a great reunion. Dee and the others had tea, and we prepared to descend by the route they had just come up. We roped up, this time with Louie first, me second, and Dee as anchor. Someone had taken Louie's pack, and I wished they'd taken mine. It seemed to get heavier with every step. Finally, I stopped, shrugged out of it, and just let it somersault all the way down the forty-degree ice slope of the West Buttress. The going was much easier after that. (The pack, a Kelty, was in perfect shape when I picked it up at the bottom.) Amid the shouts and cheers of friends, we walked into the 14,000-foot camp. After resting and rehydrating, we continued to descend.

By now, however, the wind had picked up and a light snow was falling. At about 12,000 feet, at a spot called Windy Corner, we ran into another old friend and Mountain Rescue teammate, Dr. Otto Trott. He and a group of other rescuers were acclimatizing and had set up a huge, floorless, army octagon tent, with smaller tents around it. It was snowing harder now, and the wind was rising rapidly, so we decided to wait out the storm there.

What a miserable night! The wind rose to hurricane levels and kept on rising. Eventually it knocked down and tore up the smaller tents, and everyone was forced to move into the big octagon. Though Otto did a great job of keeping the stove going to melt snow and warm the tent, the wind clearly wanted to take it down too. We all moved to the edges to sit on the tent fabric to keep it in place. Every once in a while, an enormous gust would whoosh under the walls, fill the inside with powder snow, and literally lift all 205 pounds of me up in the air and bang me painfully back down again.

Louie and I looked at each other. We shared the same thought: if this tent goes, there are people here who will die. The rescuers were suffering from their rapid ascent, and some seemed to be in a trance. Their equipment was scattered all over, inside and outside the tent—some did not even know where their boots were. After some thirty-six miserable hours, Louie and I decided it had to be better farther below—after all, this *was* called Windy Corner. While the others chose to stay put, six of us tied into two ropes of three each and left on snowshoes for the camp below.

As we'd guessed, within an hour we were out of the severe wind and plunging through two feet of drifting snow. We broke off a few small avalanches— they didn't go far—and groped our way through a virtual whiteout down to 10,000 feet, where more friends waited in what had become a small city of tents.

That afternoon, May 22, the sky cleared and Don Sheldon's ski plane flew in, followed by an army chopper. After a brief stop in Talkeetna, we were soon back in Anchorage, where we learned John had broken only one of his ankles, which would have to be fused; the other was all right. Pete lost parts of some fingers on his left hand to frostbite but otherwise recovered completely. Everyone else returned safely. We had learned, the hard way, the seriousness of speed-climbing into high altitude. The body needs time to adjust. Without acclimatization, thought processes and reactions are impaired and things can go wrong with a deadly suddenness.

In Anchorage, reporters wanted to know what we thought of this huge rescue. I told them I felt humbled. That two people had died in a plane crash, perhaps trying to help us, was terrible. But I was also overwhelmed by the sacrifices that so many people had made on our behalf. It dramatized for me the depth of loyalty and affection that had grown in the climbing community over the years. We had needed help, and our friends came from all points of the compass to assist us. I wished it had never happened, but I was deeply moved and grateful for those who risked their own lives in order to save ours.

Chapter Six

EVEREST

To the Nepalese, it is Sagarmantha. In Tibet, it's Chomolungma, "Goddess Mother of the Earth." Westerners call it Mount Everest. I first saw it on February 13, 1963, through the window of a Royal Nepalese Airlines DC-3 piloted by a man in a turban. I recognized it immediately; it had lived in my mind's eye now for nearly two years, ever since the mountaineer Norman Dyhrenfurth had invited me to become a member of the first team of Americans to attempt the summit.

Now here it was before me, towering above a snow-capped range of the highest peaks in the world, with its characteristic plume of windblown snow.

I looked at it for a long time . . . with the odd thought that I wanted to become its friend.

■

There had been twenty expeditions in the century or so since the British Survey of India discovered in 1852 that the mountain then known as Peak XV was the highest in the world (and named it, in true colonialist fashion, after the first surveyor general, Sir George Everest). But it wasn't until Edmund Hillary's and the Sherpa Tensing Norgay's triumph in 1953 that anyone had reached the summit. Only two other expeditions had succeeded by this approach since then,

Climbers move up the Khumbu Icefall. Photo: National Geographic Society

the Swiss, on their third attempt in 1956, while the Chinese are thought to have reached the summit in 1960 from the Tibetan side.

Dyhrenfurth, a Swiss filmmaker whose father, Günther, was then the world's leading expert on the Himalaya, had been to Everest as expedition photographer for the unsuccessful 1952 Swiss expedition, and he couldn't get the mountain out of his mind. A veteran of several Himalaya expeditions, he had written: " . . . there was always for me the strong feeling of having lived there before, in a previous incarnation . . . I knew I was leaving a part of myself behind, and that someday, somehow, I must return."

That someday came at last with a letter from the Nepalese Ministry of Foreign Affairs to the U.S. Embassy in Kathmandu, dated May 10, 1961, announcing " . . . His Majesty's Government's final approval of his [Dyhrenfurth's] proposed expedition to Mount Everest in 1963." In 1960, Norman, who was then living in Santa Monica, California, had applied to the Nepalese government for a first American attempt on the mountain in 1961. He got no answer. He knew that the narrow spring "weather window" during which Everest can be climbed had already been reserved for 1962 by an Indian expedition, so on his second try he applied for 1963. It was just as well; it had taken a year simply to get a response.

In the years since World War II, interest in climbing had grown significantly, but the number of experienced high-altitude climbers in America was still fairly small. Norman began scouring the country for capable climbers. For rock-climbing experts, he went to Yosemite and the Grand Tetons. For glacier-climbing experts, he came to the Northwest and Mount Rainier. So when the phone rang and Norman asked me—and later my brother Louie—to join the expedition, I was thrilled but, in retrospect, not all that surprised. Because of our climbing, rescuing, and guiding experience, we were among the best there was. And what could be more perfect for mountaineering twins than for the two of us to stand atop Everest!

People always wonder whether I ever had misgivings about joining the expedition, and I have to say I simply didn't. At thirty-four years of age, I already had a tremendous amount of experience at altitudes up to 20,000 feet and under extreme conditions. I had all the technical skills and was in peak physical condition. I could prone press 325 pounds, carry heavy packs for days, and had a seven-liter lung capacity—a full liter above normal.

That doesn't mean I didn't still have a lot of work to do to get ready. I knew it would be the most difficult climb of my life, and I immediately set about doing whatever I could think of to prepare myself. I continued weight training three days a week. I hiked as fast as I could up and down the hills around our Lake Sammamish home, carrying a 65-pound pack. I speed-climbed to Camp Muir on Mount Rainier several times. To get used to the heat we would encounter during the approach, I sat in a sauna until I couldn't stand it anymore. To condition myself for the cold we could expect on Everest, I swam in Lake Sammamish through the winter of 1962 and couldn't believe that members of the so-called Polar Bear Club did this sort of thing for fun. I got so numb the only way I could tell the temperature of the shower was by testing it with my tongue.

Because of my REI connection, Norman made me the expedition's equipment coordinator, and I set about the task of trying to figure out what we'd need. REI President Lloyd Anderson and I convinced the board to keep me on the payroll while I was in the Himalaya, for which I will always be grateful. With a wife and two young boys to support, I could not otherwise have afforded to go. "Now," I thought to myself, "I've got a four-month paid vacation!"

Meanwhile Norman was raising money and looking for sponsors. Our big break came when, after months of Norman's lobbying, the National Geographic Society decided not just to help sponsor the climb but to undertake scientific studies in glaciology and geology, and the sociological, physiological, and psychological effects of the expedition on the climbers. Now we had that most precious of commodities: scientific credibility. Gradually, the pieces were coming together.

Next we turned our attention to team building, and Mount Rainier was to be our proving ground. In mid-September 1962, the day before we were to start up Mount Rainier, we all gathered at my house for dinner. Norman had pulled together an amazing group of climbers and scientists. Nine had been professional climbing guides, and several had major expedition experience. Three of the expedition members had M.D.s, five had Ph.D.s, five had M.A. or M.S. degrees, and five more had bachelor's degrees.

Besides Louie and me, the original team included two other Northwesterners: our longtime Rainier guiding partner, twenty-six-year-old Lute Jerstad, and three-time Himalaya veteran Willi Unsoeld, age thirty-six. Willi couldn't join us on Mount Rainier—he was in the midst of Peace Corps training and would soon be serving, conveniently for us, in Nepal. Our rock-climbing experts included Al Auten, thirty-six, a magazine editor, and Dick Pownall, thirty-five, a teacher, both from Denver, as well as Barry Corbet, twenty-six, and Jake Breitenbach, twenty-seven, both guides and ski instructors and partners in an outdoor equipment store in Jackson, Wyoming.

Our M.D.s included Tom Hornbein, thirty-two, who, among other things, designed our oxygen masks; Gil Roberts, twenty-eight, a physician from Stanford released early from the air force to join us; and Dave Dingman, twenty-six, a surgeon from the University of Baltimore. All three were longtime climbers.

Among our scientists were noted Michigan State glaciologist Maynard Miller, forty-one; his young colleague Barry Prather, twenty-three; and Dick Emerson, thirty-eight, a sociologist from the University of Cincinnati—all three experienced climbers—and Jim Lester, a UCLA psychologist, who had no climbing experience.

Then there were our "documentarians": Dan Doody, twenty-nine, photographer, filmmaker, climber, and friend of Norman's; Barry C. Bishop, thirty-one, climber and *National Geographic* staffer; and Jim Ullman, fifty-five, author of many books on climbing and the outdoors.

Norman Dyhrenfurth, forty-four, was, of course, our leader. His second-in-command was Will Siri, also forty-four, a short but wiry pipe-smoking biophysicist/mountaineer from the University of California, who would coordinate the scientific projects.

Although Mount Rainier is only half as high as Mount Everest, altitude is all it lacks. Its glaciers and icefalls, its ferocious winds, and dangerous weather make it a near-perfect training ground for Himalaya expeditions, and it put us to the test. The first few days at Camp Muir were terrific; in fine weather we tested equipment, evaluated clothes and boots, honed skills, and gradually came together as a team. Norman's leadership skills were a pleasure to behold. Then the mountain decided to humble us. A storm closed in. The wind blew so hard one of the tents broke loose and, with Maynard Miller still in it, tumbled almost to the edge of a crevasse before we could grab it, and him. Twice we tried to reach the summit, and twice we were turned back, until the mountain blew us all the way back down to the inn at Paradise.

Louie missed most of this excitement. Though he visited Camp Muir once during the shakedown, he said he was too busy at work to be able to go through the whole thing. Knowing he was as skilled and capable as I was, I didn't give it a second thought. After our Mount Rainier training, we all went our separate ways to make our final preparations for the expedition, now only four months away.

Two months later, Louie and I and two of his friends, whom I did not know well, were out on the wild Washington coast, standing around a campfire. I was all pumped up, talking about our preparations for the trip. Out of the blue, one of Louie's friends said:

"Lou isn't going."

"What?" I asked, stunned.

"Uh, yeah. That's right, Jim," Louie stammered, "I can't go."

It was like the earth had opened up beneath my feet, like I had fallen into a bottomless crevasse.

Here he was—my twin brother, my other half, my best friend with whom I had shared virtually every major event of my life, with whom I had climbed all my life—telling me he wasn't going to Everest with me. Actually, it was worse than that because he didn't tell me. He let a stranger do it, instead of breaking the news to me himself when the two of us were alone. I learned that his friends had, unbeknownst to me, just invested in a sporting goods store in Tacoma with Louie as partner and proprietor. They were to finance the operation, which would be known as Whittaker's Chalet, and not surprisingly, they wanted him around. I started to argue. Then I got mad. We had been planning this for almost two years. The team was in place. Now when we were about ready to leave, he was pulling out? But I got nowhere; it was a done deal.

I suppose at some level I understood that Louie simply couldn't afford to go. He had his wife and two young children to support, and there was no generous REI to cover the time he'd be in the Himalaya. Still, I felt betrayed.

I understood that our lives had actually separated thirteen years earlier, when Louie married. But his decision about Everest—an historic event I expected to share with him—was a stunning blow, and after that evening, things were never quite the same between Louie and me. It took a long time to get over it. Years.

In time, I managed to convince myself that my dream of the two of us reaching the summit together would never have been a reality for very practical reasons. Louie and I were among the strongest team members; Norman would have wanted us to climb on alternate days, taking turns putting in the route, so our strength would not be concentrated on one rope. I would have fretted, while resting in Base Camp from the previous day's effort, while Louie was up there in danger, and I suspect Louie would have done the same. Some months later, I would learn that my fears had been justified.

In the winter of 1962, however, as our departure date approached, there wasn't much time to dwell on any of this. I was up to my ears in gear. We had amassed twenty-seven tons of food and equipment, everything from scientific instruments to long underwear, oxygen bottles to cases of Rainier beer. It was my job (with Dan Doody helping) to get it packed. We broke the tonnage down to 60-pound loads and packed them in cartons—eight hundred of them—catalogued every one, and sent them by ship to India.

Finally, on February 3, 1963, we left San Francisco for Japan, by way of Honolulu. (A few members had left earlier to collect our gear from the Calcutta docks and get it forwarded to Nepal.) After three days of sightseeing, steam baths, massages, and gorgeous hostesses in Tokyo, we headed south to Hong Kong for another three days. We spent two more days being tourists in Bangkok, then landed in Calcutta, where most of us received the shock of our lives.

We arrived just before dawn and took a bus from the airport to the Grand Hotel in the center of the city. Slumped in our seats, half-asleep, we watched the city waken.

"Look at all the junk on the sidewalks," someone said. The streets and alleys were littered with what looked like piles of trash and mounds of rags.

"Junk, hell, those are people," someone else replied.

There was shocked silence as we realized it was true. As the sky lightened, we could see men, women, and children huddled under the rags. When we got off the bus, a crowd of beggars blocked the entrance to the Grand Hotel. I saw old people, middle-aged people, youngsters, and babies, sick, crippled, and starving, many of whom I felt sure would be dead within a week. There were dozens of them. I thought, "My God, here we are spending hundreds of thousands of dollars to climb a mountain, and these people are starving to death." Sickened by the scene, there was nothing to do but go on into the hotel. I couldn't help but think how lucky, how damn lucky, I was to have been born where I was born.

I suspect Dyhrenfurth, a world traveler, wanted the team to experience the full panorama of the sights and sounds of Asia, but at least at that time, I could have done without the Calcutta chapter. We spent two days wandering through the noisy, crowded, desperate city, hounded by beggars, afraid even to carry a camera because Norman told us it could cost us our life. The "Grand Hotel" was as filthy as a Skid Road dive. Cockroaches and bedbugs kept us company at night, and the food, served to us by surly waiters in grimy uniforms, looked—and probably was—lethal. Terrified that we would be sick before the trek even began, all we could do was drink the bottled beer. I couldn't wait to leave.

A couple of days later, our Royal Nepalese Airlines DC-3 touched down in Kathmandu, 4,000 feet above sea level. Kathmandu was a place of mystery and magic, almost unimaginably exotic. Palaces shaped like elaborate wedding cakes lined the maze of narrow alleys. Ornate Hindu and Buddhist temples were at every turn. There were religious sculptures everywhere—goddesses with many arms, buddhas in many guises, amazing erotic carvings on the corners of buildings, prayer flags strung like festive telephone wires from house to house. Open-air bazaars blazed with color, in sharp contrast to the stone gray, two-story and four-story buildings that squeezed into every available space. Beyond the city itself, terrace upon terrace of lush green rice paddies and grainfields climbed the hillsides. Wherever we went, huge eyes painted along the rooftops watched our every move, as did the crowds of small, brown, smiling Nepalese for whom we were exotic.

We set up headquarters at the Hotel Royal—actually, a drafty old palace that had seen better days—and began sorting out our final arrangements while Norman did battle with the government bureaucracy. It was here that we met the last, and at this stage the most important, team member: forty-six-year-old Lieutenant Colonel James Owen M. Roberts—"Jimmy" to us—the former British military attaché, Himalayan expedition veteran, and all-around "fixer." Technically, he was our transport officer, but his knowledge of local languages, customs, and people smoothed our way over and over again.

Kathmandu was also where we first met the Sherpa. Of Tibetan descent, short of stature but big in heart and lung, the Sherpa were the backbone of our expedition. With homes at about 12,000 feet, they are born acclimatized to high altitude, and thus uniquely adapted to work on the mountain, helping to stock the camps. Our team respected them completely. We had a joke: "You don't notice them until they take a deep breath. Then their lungs fill up, and they block the view." They are wonderful people, both cheerful by nature and in tune with nature. In 1963 only a few had climbed high on Everest (Tenzing Norgay, of course, had summited with Hillary) because in those days most Sherpa lacked technical climbing skills. As more expeditions came to this highest of mountains, this situation changed; by 1970 Sherpa were guiding the sahibs (as they called Western expedition members), putting in routes, and installing fixed ropes. Even in 1963, however, we were immensely grateful to them; as it turned out, they would not only help us carry supplies up onto the mountain but would also carry three of us from Base Camp back down toward civilization. One would even go to the summit.

On February 20 we piled ourselves and all our gear into jeeps and trucks and left Kathmandu to begin the 185-mile journey to Everest Base Camp. After 15 miles, at the village of Banepa, the trucks stopped. End of the line. Today, climbers can helicopter most of the distance to Base Camp, but in 1963 we would make the rest of the journey on foot. Banepa was also where "we" became an entire army. On this day, as we climbed out of the jeeps, we met the nine hundred porters who would help us haul the hundreds of cartons we packed in Seattle to the foot of Everest. Before us was a vast, noisy, brown mass of humanity—men, women, children, young and old. Next morning, one by one, they signed up, shouldered a carton, and started uphill. Gradually, the huge, jostling crowd uncurled into an organized line of feet and boxes—a miles-long millipede.

At long last, we had truly begun.

◼

On the month-long approach march, I kept feeling as if I'd stepped into the middle of some wide-screen, epic film; the only thing missing was the swelling

Line of porters on Everest approach march. Photo: Willi Unsoeld/National Geographic Society

music of the soundtrack. The days took on a natural rhythm. Early each morning, the millipede would begin to stir. Nearly a thousand people would have breakfast, break camp, and then more than eighteen hundred feet would begin to move uphill. In the early days we rose through jungle in which bananas grew and monkeys scolded. The landscape changed slowly, giving way to forests of bamboo, then pine and rhododendrons with orchids in their branches. Each afternoon an amazing scene would unfold on the outskirts of some remote mountain village: hundreds upon hundreds of our porters, strung out along terraces stacked high up the hillsides, would hunch down in little groups, light small cooking fires from the brush they carried with them, and camp. At night we'd joke, swap stories, and sing songs. Often the Sherpa danced and sang as well.

The physicians among us worked overtime. At each stop they treated both our porters and local villagers for every imaginable ailment, from teeth that needed pulling to desperately severe burns to an outbreak of smallpox. They estimated that as many as 40 percent of our porters had tuberculosis, and the coughing often kept us awake at night.

In warm, dry weather, we wound our way eastward through small stone-built villages with exotic names: Panch-khal, Dolaghat, Chyaubas, Risingo, Chitare, Kirantichhap, Yersa. Nepal is a tiny country, barely five hundred miles east to west and one hundred miles north to south. But on foot it seems twice as big vertically as it is horizontally, like a very large piece of brown paper crumpled into a ball by some massive hand. In fact, what crumpled it—and continues to crumple it—was the Indian subcontinent which, riding northward on one of the earth's slowly moving tectonic plates over the span of millions of years, rode up over the Asian plate, buckling and creating what now are the highest mountains in the world.

Traveling across the grain of the mighty Himalaya, we climbed up hundreds of switchbacks to ridge tops, then descended to muddy rivers, only to climb more switchbacks, cross even higher ridges, and drop into narrower valleys cut by smaller, fast-flowing streams with clear water. As we rose, the path became more rugged, the stream crossings more primitive. The "bridges," such as they were, were little more than wire and narrow planks suspended on ancient chains. At one point, a chain broke, throwing several of our porters into the rocks and freezing water below. Luckily, the injuries were mostly minor. Soon, however, even the bridges disappeared, and there were only logs to cross.

On March 3 we topped our last ridge and descended into the valley of the Dudh Kosi, or "Milky River" (milky from all the glacial silt it carries). From now on we would head north, following the river deep into a region called Solu Khumbu—the Sherpa homeland, a Buddhist "world above the world." It was colder now, it rained from time to time, and at higher elevations we crossed patches of snow, but the barefoot porters didn't even seem to notice. On March 7 our millipede nosed into Namche Bazaar.

Full of bustle, barking dogs, and the smell of juniper smoke, Namche Bazaar is home and shopping center to most of the Sherpa people. Perched on a sloping terrace that drops off sharply to the river below, in 1963 it was a settlement of some 140 stone houses and perhaps 500 inhabitants. All of the houses seemed to have the same plan. The ground floor was for livestock. Steep stairs led to a living space with a fire but no chimney. The smoke rose, eventually, through holes in the roof. Consequently, the walls were blackened, but the rooms were often full of brightly colored fabrics. The day we arrived, the Sherpa had a major homecoming party involving, primarily, the drinking of large quantities of *chang*, a rice-based beer.

In Namche the weather cleared, and I found myself in the most beautiful mountain scenery I had ever seen. It was a mostly monochromatic world—hills, houses, walls, terraces, even the clothes people wore were a sandy grayish-brown. Here and there bare trees sported prayer flags for leaves. Jagged ridges and peaks spiked the sky, cloaked in snow. Once, just for a moment before clouds closed in again, we got a glimpse of our goal: Everest, looming just beyond the Nuptse Ridge.

On March 9 we reached the monastery of Thangboche and promptly got snowed in. There are worse places in the world to be delayed. Surrounded by the highest peaks on earth, it is one of the most stunning and remote outposts of humanity. The magic of the place is enhanced by the monks blowing on long Himalayan horns and chanting prayers in a mesmerizing monotone. On the second night there, unable to sleep, I stepped out into a moonlit wonderland. Silver-rimmed clouds drifted around the peaks, which glowed brightly. Below us the whole Dudh Kosi valley was illuminated, all the way down to Namche.

After several days of acclimatization and breaking out the cold-weather gear, we headed out of the Dudh Kosi valley for the last push. We were in a white-and-brown world now; it had snowed on and off for several days, and the only landmarks were the mountains themselves, the cairns along the trail, and the stone walls of springtime yak pastures. On the seventeenth we finally reached the great Khumbu Glacier—first the jumble of boulders of its terminal moraine and then the glacier itself. Everest had disappeared behind the hulking mass of Nuptse, soaring 25,790 feet above us to the east.

On March 21, Willi Unsoeld, Will Siri, Lute Jerstad, Norman, and I, along with our nineteen high-altitude Sherpa, picked our way along the edge of the glacier. Between the altitude and having to break trail through newly fallen knee-deep snow, the going was difficult and we were worn out. At last, at 17,800 feet and after a month on the trail, Norman picked a site for our Base Camp. Hemmed in by Everest, Lhotse, and Nuptse, it was a place of incredible beauty, awesome and humbling.

It would also be "home" for the next two and a half months. We built stone platforms for our tents and waited for the rest of the team, Sherpa, and porters to ferry up our gear, a process that would take several days. Gradually, the population rose, gear piled up, bright orange tents sprouted on the bleak white surface of the glacier, and pretty soon we had a full-scale community going. The site Norman selected was smack in the middle of the glacier, on a sort of hummock, safe from the avalanches that roared down off the heights with unnerving regularity.

But we soon learned that safety was a relative thing.

One of the strangest things about climbing Everest by this route is that perhaps the most dangerous spot of all is at the very beginning. This is the Khumbu Icefall, a 2,000-foot-high chaotic maze of constantly toppling blocks of broken glacial ice that are the size of buildings, an area cut with deep crevasses and smooth vertical walls topped by huge, precariously balanced towers of ice known as seracs. The Icefall is a living, moving, groaning, white-fanged, homicidal mass of glacial debris. All the hanging glaciers and icefalls on Mount Rainier put together don't begin to match the mass of the Khumbu Icefall. No experienced climber in his right mind would, by choice, go into this tumbling mess of ice. But we had no choice. There was no way around it.

Norman picked Willi, Lute, and me to be the first to tackle the Icefall, with the Sherpa Nawang Gombu, Nima Tenzing, and Pasang Temba to help. I felt comfortable climbing with Lute, who had worked with me as a Mount Rainier guide. His highest summit, like mine, was Mount McKinley. He was five feet eight inches tall and weighed 150 pounds. A complex and wonderfully interesting man with a Ph.D. in theater from the University of Oregon, Lute could recite from memory my favorite Robert W. Service poems about the cold, cold north. It was one of the things I liked best about him.

I had also been looking forward to roping up with Willi, whom I knew through friends, but with whom I had never climbed before. At five feet ten inches tall and a trim 160 pounds, he was far and away the most experienced climber of the whole team. A climbing guide in the Tetons for seven seasons, Willi had climbed in the Swiss Alps and was on the Garhwal Himalaya Expedition in 1949, the Himalaya Makalu Expedition in 1954, and the American-Pakistan Karakoram Expedition to 25,660-foot Masherbrum in 1960. Having just become the deputy director of the Peace Corps in Nepal, he was on leave for the climb.

The Sherpa were, by now, much more than mere porters; they were important, hard-working members of our team. Of the three on our rope this day, however, I had been drawn particularly to Gombu. Five feet three in his climbing boots, with a big chest, he weighed just 120 pounds and had a wonderful smile. The nephew of Tenzing Norgay, Gombu was already a veteran climber, with the 1953 British expedition and the unsuccessful 1960 Indian expedition under his belt. He had studied to become a Buddhist monk and spoke several languages well, including English. He had told me he switched to climbing for the money, but I could see something else in his eyes: that same burning desire to summit that I had. I was delighted to have him as my ropemate.

On the morning of March 22, equipped with willow wands to mark a path through the snow and around crevasses and ropes and ice screws for scaling ice walls, we left camp. On a ridge above Base Camp, Norman, Will Siri, and the Sherpa Ang Dawa, studying the Icefall through binoculars, helped guide us through the maze by sending suggestions by radio—at least for as long as they could see us.

At the beginning the going was good, with big ice blocks bridging yawning crevasses. But even though we were now at about 19,000 feet and surrounded by ice, the heat of the sun had raised the surface temperature far above freezing. We had stripped down and were struggling against dehydration. But dehydration was only one of our problems. We were approaching what climbers call the "Death Zone." Below about 18,000 feet, the human body can acclimatize to the relative scarcity of oxygen and, in time, function normally. But the higher you climb, the more difficult the business of being a living organism becomes. Metabolism—which is to say, life—requires oxygen; without it, cells die. Birds, butterflies, and spiders occasionally fly or get blown up this high by the wind, but since nothing grows here, they soon perish. The same goes for humans. Above 25,000 feet, in the heart of the Death Zone, systems just slowly shut down. Starved for oxygen, the brain stops functioning normally. Without adequate metabolism, the body can't keep ahead of the cold and pulls blood inward to vital organs, sacrificing extremities; the fire of life literally goes out. I was surprised to find that even in the Icefall, doing anything, just breathing, took extra effort.

After a few hours of route-setting, we reached a thirty-foot-high wall that stretched from one side of the Icefall to the other. We took a break. I didn't like the looks of the glistening wall of ice in front of us. It seemed too detached from the ice above, yet it wasn't a true serac. It was more like a wide, freestanding wall between two big crevasses. We looked for some way around it, but there was none.

Despite our misgivings, we climbed the wall and installed a fixed rope for the team to use, anchoring it with ice screws. Then, exhausted, we headed down. Back in Base Camp I drank three full quarts of water, coffee, tea, and juice before going to sleep but was still so dehydrated I didn't have to get up to pee all night long. The first real climb of the expedition was over, however, and we had already navigated two-thirds of the Icefall. It had been a good day.

The next day wouldn't be. As part of the scientific work of the expedition, each climber was required to make notes in a preprinted diary that was issued to us at the outset. Every day for the last month, we had each been recording how tired we felt, how dangerous conditions seemed, how optimistic or apprehensive we were, and what had happened during the day. My diary entry for March 23 stopped abruptly at about 3:00 P.M., when shouts drifted down from the Icefall.

■

Earlier that morning, while I had been relaxing in the sun, Jake Breitenbach, Dick Pownall, and Dr. Gil Roberts, along with the Sherpa Ang Pema and Ila

Tsering, had climbed into the Icefall to strengthen the route we had set and pick up where we had left off. Sometime around 2:00 P.M. they reached the ice wall and didn't like the looks of it any more than we had. Like us, though, they could see no other route. Using the rope we fixed the day before, Pownall began to climb with Jake and Ang Dawa behind him. It was hot, the sun was beating down, and there was no wind. The only noise was the occasional croaking of goraks, Tibetan ravens, as they soared overhead. Gil and Ila Tsering waited below.

Suddenly there was a loud crack, a rumble, and Pownall was falling. Later he would tell me only one thought passed through his mind: "So this is death."

Beneath them and just to one side, Gil and Ila Tsering heard the crack too. Then, Gil later said, the noise became a roar as "ice the size of two railroad cars" crashed over them. Gil was flipped over backward by the force and slid for thirty feet. He and Ila Tsering jumped back onto their feet and looked where the others had been, but all they could see was ice—the others had disappeared.

They found Dick Pownall first, his chest pinned by the edge of what Gil figured must have been a thousand-pound ice block. As they were digging Dick out, they heard a moan from under the rubble. They dug deeper and found Ang Pema, upside down but conscious, buried below Dick. The climbing rope led downward into the ice from Ang Pema who was roped to Jake. But the ice was solid and they could dig no farther. Gil cut Ang Pema loose from the rope.

When we heard the shouts for help floating down from the Icefall, those of us at Base Camp first tried to raise the climbing party on the radio but got no answer. The radio had been in Jake's pack, so I knew he, at least, was in trouble. Something was dreadfully wrong. Willi and I threw on our gear and shot up into the Icefall.

We found Dick badly bruised and shaken, but he could walk. Ang Pema had deep facial cuts—his teeth were exposed through his cheek—as well as a skull fracture and a dislocated shoulder. He couldn't walk. I hoisted him onto my back and carried him back through the steepest sections of the route. His blood dripped down my parka.

"Ang Pema finish, sahib. Pema finish," he kept saying.

"Pema be okay, Pema be okay," I kept telling him.

Eventually, we reached another group from Base Camp who had brought a stretcher. I left Ang Pema with them and headed back to the accident site.

For the next two hours, Willi, Lute, and I chopped doggedly at the ice looking for Jake's body. As darkness fell we had penetrated only four feet. It was hopeless.

As we came down the Icefall that night by the light of headlamps, the shadows from the broken blocks of ice danced around us like goblins, making it difficult to pick out the route. We turned off the lights and continued by the light of the stars toward the glow of the Base Camp tents far below. We were stunned and silent; the only sound was the squeak and crunch of our crampons on the ice. Walking in the darkness, I *Jake Breitenbach. Photo: Lila M. Bishop/National Geographic Society*

was torn between the terrible loss of Jake and the equally terrible realization that it could have been Louie. Had my brother come on the expedition after all, he would most certainly have been on that rope. And for the first time, I was truly glad Louie had dropped out.

That night Dick and Gil got drunk. The rest of us retreated to private thoughts. I remember thinking about how I had told everyone back home that Everest was not a difficult climb technically; the only problem was the lack of oxygen and the weather. Now it had killed one of us, and we'd only just begun.

The next day dawned bright and sunny; perfect climbing weather, but the team lay around Base Camp mourning Jake. No one ventured out on the mountain. Most of the Sherpa, who believe in reincarnation and are, perhaps, more accepting of death, wondered why we were making such a big deal of it. The exception was Jake's personal Sherpa, Nima Tenzing. "Nima," Dan Doody, would later write, "had known Jake for only about five weeks, but on the day after the accident we found Nima in Jake's sleeping bag crying his eyes out. He felt guilty that he had not been along up in the Icefall and was heartbroken at what had happened."

There was a lot of soul-searching going on. Each of us struggled with the question "Why Jake and not me?" We were all taking the chance that the Icefall could kill us. It was an objective danger—an unpredictable event in nature over which we had no control and from which no amount of skill or care could protect us. I hoped and prayed that the rest of us would get the breaks we needed to make it safely through the Icefall and up the mountain.

After a couple of days passed there was a new feeling among some members of the team. As Norman expressed it later, "The fun has gone out of the thing. There is a certain attitude of 'let's climb the damn mountain and get the hell out of here.'" Others of us had found a new motivation: doing it for Jake.

Starting over would be tough for all of us, but hardest of all for Jake's best friend, Barry Corbet. "The one thing that remains to determine if I ever climb again," he said one day, "is my ability to push a route over Jake's body in the Icefall." At his insistence, Barry was in the first party to reenter the Icefall and prepare the lower section for Sherpa carries.

◘

On March 27, Willi, Lute, Gombu, and I climbed past the accident site to push the route higher. By noon we were near the top of the Icefall, at almost 20,000 feet, when we encountered another vertical cliff of ice, this one 70 feet high—twice as high as the wall that had collapsed on Jake. Once again we searched for a route around either side, and once again we found none.

Finally, Willi turned to me and said, "Well, Jim, you're the ice climber."

There was a five-foot-wide crevasse between the wall and us. It looked bottomless. I stuck a bunch of ice screws on a carabiner, gulped, and took a flying leap. I cleared the crevasse and rammed my ice ax and the front points of my crampons into the face of the wall. I stuck like a fly on flypaper. I put in an ice screw, snapped in my rope, and called for tension. Then I climbed higher and did the same thing all over again. I continued this way for an hour. It was at this point that one of my theories about this climb began to break down. Months earlier, I had persuaded myself that climbing Everest would be just like Mount Rainier, only higher, with less oxygen. But on this hot afternoon, I was sure they could hear me gasping all the way down in Base Camp, 2,000 vertical feet below.

I was about halfway up the wall, sucking air, when Willi hollered, "Jim! You're turning blue! Come on down; it's my turn." Bushed, I rappelled off the wall and Willi replaced me. After another hour, it was Lute's turn. But by now Willi was very high, and he decided to finish it off himself. After another hour, he'd done it; it was a remarkable performance.

Over the next three days, while the four of us rested in Base Camp, the others improved our route and installed ladders to bridge crevasses and get up ice walls. On March 30, with the weather still excellent, we established Camp I, well above the Icefall, at 20,200 feet—2,400 feet above Base Camp.

■

We were now in the Western Cwm. *Cwm* is a Welsh word for a high, glacier-scooped valley; this one was surrounded by the mightiest walls on earth. To our left was Everest, 29,028 feet; ahead, Lhotse, 27,890 feet; and on our right, Nuptse, 25,790 feet.

The next day, Gil, Barry Prather, and I searched out a route to what would become Camp II, our Advance Base Camp. It was a bit like threading a needle; we had to find a route that would avoid as many of the huge transverse crevasses in the center of the glacier as possible (two would eventually have to be bridged) and, at the same time, steer clear of the avalanches sweeping down to the edge of the glacier from Nuptse and the west shoulder of Everest. Eventually, halfway up the Cwm at an altitude of 21,350 feet, we found a terrific site. This would be the second-largest camp on the mountain and our home for the next three weeks as we established camps on the upper slopes.

The process of scaling a mountain like Everest is not linear. The first job is scouting a route. After we found one, we would then install fixed rope on the steeper sections and ascend until we located a good site for the next camp. There we would dig platforms in the snow and ice, put up tents, and then descend to the previous camp and begin the laborious process of hauling up food and equipment—not just for that camp but for all the camps yet to be established. It was exhausting work, even with Sherpa help, and as the altitude increased, we could feel our bodies and brains rebelling. At this stage in the ascent, I hadn't yet experienced the altitude headaches and nausea that others had, but I was struggling with a hacking cough and chronic shortness of breath. I dreamed of lying on a warm beach somewhere.

Above Base Camp, Camp II would prove to be our most comfortable site, but it still had its thrills. Huge avalanches poured off the walls of Everest, Lhotse, and Nuptse toward our campsite. By the time they reached our tents, they were just blasts of wind and powder snow, but that didn't make them trouble-free. More than once, squatting over the pit toilet fifty feet from the nearest tent, we would hear the avalanche coming and, our pants at half mast, start running for the tents. Those who didn't make it would be blasted with snow and ice crystals. For those of us out of harm's way, of course, it was a source of great hilarity.

Back in the States, the team had debated how to make the final ascent and had planned to climb Lhotse and Nuptse as well. Norman was focused on summiting and was fine with following the route up the South Col that the British and Swiss expeditions had used. Instead of climbing Lhotse and Nuptse, Tom Hornbein and Willi Unsoeld were determined to create a new route up the West Ridge. The competition between the "West Ridgers" and the "South Colers" was pitched but remarkably friendly, although serious issues were at stake, including the distribution of oxygen tanks and Sherpa support. It was from Camp II that we planned to split into two smaller expeditions. The South Col team, spearheaded by Lute Jerstad, Dick Pownall, Gombu, and me, would follow the established route to the summit. The West Ridge team, which included Barry C. Bishop, Barry Corbet, Dave Dingman, Tom Hornbein, and Willi Unsoeld, aimed to push the new route. Most of the rest of our expedition group, including our scientists and Jimmy Roberts, our logistics coordinator, did not often go higher than the lower camps.

On April 3, Lute, Gombu, and I did a reconnaissance climb to locate a site for the South Col team's Camp III, and two days later we had put in a tent and cached oxygen bottles at 23,900 feet at the base of Lhotse. By now we were really struggling to breathe, and we finally began to use bottled oxygen.

A week later, thanks to bad weather and exhaustion, we still hadn't established Camp IV. Frustrated with being stuck at Camp III, I wrote in my diary on the twelfth, "I am leaving early tomorrow to put in the route to IV or know the reason why!" The next day, with the weather clear and windless, that's exactly what Gombu and I did, high on the Lhotse Face at 24,900 feet. The next step would be to cut across the face to Everest's South Col, but for the time being, we headed down again to Advance Base to rest.

At this point, the process of ferrying supplies from Advance Base to Camp IV began in earnest. Dozens of loads had to be shifted first to Camp III and then to Camp IV. The days dragged by—two weeks of days spent humping heavy loads from one camp to the next camp higher, descending to sleep, then getting up the next morning and doing the same thing all over again. And again. And again.

Finally, with all the camps to Camp IV stocked, Norman selected me, Gombu, Ang Dawa, and himself for the first assault team. As expedition leader, he hadn't originally planned to be in the first group, but we needed a photographer/film-maker. Dan Doody was laid up with a blood clot, and at least at that point, Barry C. Bishop was working with the West Ridge team members, who were still strug-gling to put in their own route. He had no choice. Meanwhile I had my own worries. I had shrunk from 200 pounds at Base Camp to a scrawny 175, and I hoped I had what it would take to reach the summit.

We left for Camp III on April 27 with thirteen Sherpa, carrying the gear for Camps V and VI on our backs. It had snowed in the interim and that meant breaking trail all over again. I kicked steps all the way up to Camp III. Then the next day, I kicked steps again, all the way up the Lhotse Face to Camp IV. And on April 29, with the weather deteriorating, I kicked steps across the Lhotse Face and up to the South Col, following a route Lute and Dick had set in a reconnaissance climb days earlier. There, at 26,200 feet and in rising wind, we set up Camp V. Norman, Ang Dawa, and a group of Sherpa carrying cam-eras and supplies followed soon after. Others had reached this point before; their trash littered the high plateau. But few had gotten much farther.

Finally, on April 30, eight Sherpa, Norman, Ang Dawa, Gombu, and I climbed to 27,450 feet, carrying on our backs everything needed for Camp VI— High Camp. Desperately slowly, not using oxygen in order to conserve it for the final summit push, we hacked a platform out of the ice and set up two tents. By radio, I advised Base Camp of our progress and learned that high winds were forecast. I cut our 120-foot climbing rope in half and, using pieces of it, pitoned the tents to a rock outcrop.

As the Sherpa turned to begin their descent, I was shocked to see them pick up oxygen bottles.

"No!" I shouted. "Those stay here. Sahibs and Sherpa both go down mountain *without* oxygen." But they continued as if they hadn't heard me.

"Gombu, explain to them!" I pleaded. It had always been the plan that we would conserve our oxygen for the ascent; we simply did not have enough. But they didn't listen to Gombu either. Only one relented; the other seven left with oxygen bottles.

Norman and Ang Dawa waged the same battle with them farther down the slope, but they had no more success than we had. Meanwhile the wind was gaining strength. Exhausted, brain-numb from the altitude, we crawled into our tents, the highest shelters on earth, melted snow, drank liquids, tried to force down some solid food, and waited for the storm we knew was coming.

The night was fierce. Sleep was impossible. Lightning flashed around us. The wind shrieked and howled and tore at the tents. Inside, Gombu and I lay breathing a thin half-liter flow of oxygen per minute. Moisture, condensed from my breath, trickled out of my mask, ran down my neck, and froze on the sleeping bag. As the storm intensified, I heard a whistling. Half-conscious, I imagined things. An Abominable Snowman? No, just the wind in the ropes. And still the wind intensified, gusting over eighty miles an hour. The temperature dropped to twenty below.

■

May 1, 4:00 A.M. I sat up. The storm outside raged on, the tent poles whistled, and the nylon walls hammered my head and shoulders. I turned to Gombu, pointed my forefinger up, and said, "We go up." He nodded. To the extent that I could think at all, what I was thinking was "Dammit, we've come this far, I'll crawl the rest of the way if I have to." On Mount Rainier, you always have a second chance; here, I knew there wasn't going to be one. With only two bottles of oxygen apiece, enough to last approximately seven hours, we couldn't wait another day for the weather to improve.

I lit the stove and started melting ice to fill our water bottles. Gombu protested; he was trained to do these housekeeping tasks. But as far as I was concerned, we were a team now, equals before the mountain. Many times in the past weeks, Gombu had made me think of the line from Kipling's poem, " . . . by the living God that made you, you're a better man than I am, Gunga Din." On this morning, I felt honored to make his breakfast. Without appetite, but knowing we'd need whatever fuel and liquid we could take in, we forced down freeze-dried crabmeat, tea, and two cups each of hot, sugary Jell-O, mixed double strength.

At 6:00 A.M. I yelled over to Norman that we were going up. He shouted back from his tent that they would follow soon. Then Gombu and I crawled out of our tent into a raging ground blizzard.

Overhead, the sun was brilliant. But from my chest down, it was a white-out. Snow and ice crystals were screaming past us at sixty miles an hour. Gombu was an eerie-looking goggled head sitting on top of this layer of blowing snow.

We set off anyway. Ahead, I could just make out the Southeast Ridge that was our first goal, but I couldn't see my feet. The howling wind cloaked the terrain in a four- to five-foot-deep cloud of swirling and drifting snow. The going was terribly slow. We kicked steps in the snow, alternating leads. Kick. Pause. Step. Rest. Suck oxygen. In two hours of climbing, we gained only about 700 vertical feet.

My pack, jammed with two oxygen bottles, two cameras, a radio (that never worked), two water bottles, a first-aid kit, food, extra clothing, a flashlight, a picket with the American flag attached, and a minus-thirty-degree sleeping bag (just in case we had to bivouac overnight), weighed 45 pounds but felt like a ton of bricks. High on the ridge, about 700 feet below the South Summit at what I estimated to be the halfway point to the summit, Gombu and I decided we would each cache our partly used bottle for the return and use the remaining bottle for the summit. At 13 pounds apiece, leaving one behind would make a huge difference.

Then we were off again. But now I had a new problem: the relentless wind and ice crystals blowing up under my goggles had frozen my left eyeball and I couldn't see clearly. Without binocular vision, it was hard to judge distances. In addition, I was terribly thirsty, but my water bottles were frozen solid. Stupid from lack of oxygen, I had put them in the outside pockets of my pack earlier and now they were completely useless. (Even stupider, it had not occurred to me to cache them with the spare oxygen bottle to lighten my pack.) The only liquid I'd had since Camp VI was the icicle that kept forming on the oxygen mask from my exhaled breath—periodically, I broke it off and slipped the ice behind the mask into my mouth. I was drinking my own breath.

Even on a two-liter-per-minute flow of oxygen, climbing just two hundred vertical feet an hour, we had to take five or six breaths with every step. In addition, we were continually being knocked over by the wind. The less steep the slope, the more we staggered; we came to prefer climbing to walking—at least we had something to hold on to. We kept plodding ahead, half-crawling, half-climbing, becoming more exhausted with each labored step. I felt like a tarantula in a ninety-mile-an-hour gale.

The ridge we were climbing had a heavy cornice of windblown snow and ice stretching out to the right over the void, and it was impossible to determine where the rock ended and the overhanging snow cornice began. If we went out on the cornice too far, we courted disaster; if we moved too far to the left, we faced difficult rock climbing. It was guesswork. Watching for signs in the texture of the snow, I chose the best route I could, hoping we were following the true ridge.

We crested the South Summit at about 11:30 A.M. and, for the first time, could see the true summit above us to the north. There was a sharp drop ahead of us and then a saddle between us and the next obstacle, a steep rock face that we'd have to climb. During the 1953 British expedition, Charles Evans and Tom Bourdillon had stood where we were now, looked at that pitch, then turned around and descended. The valves on their oxygen sets had frozen, and they couldn't go on. The following day, New Zealander Ed Hillary and Sherpa Tenzing Norgay scaled it, and ever since it had been known as "the Hillary Step."

We squatted on the South Summit and climbed the Step with our eyes. Then we descended to the saddle and crossed over to it. At the base of the Step, buffeted by the wind, we rested again. From here, it was practically straight up—rock on the left, snow cornice on the right. The cornice clung to the rock, but there were wind-cut cracks and hollows. Beneath the cornice, the Kangshung Face of Everest dropped thousands of feet into Tibet.

"If we fall," I thought to myself, "it'll be one hell of a border crossing. And I don't have my passport."

As Gombu belayed and anchored me, I wiggled and pried myself up through a slot between the lee side of the rock and the cornice, gasping for breath and cursing my pack for its weight and awkwardness. At last, I crawled out on top to a good belay spot, took in the slack, and jerked on the rope for Gombu to come up after me. Slowly, I coiled in the rope as he climbed up alongside me. We sprawled flat and took another break.

Finally, Gombu and I stood again and turned. Moving once more and near complete exhaustion, I suddenly realized I was sucking on an empty oxygen bottle. I had thought one bottle each would take us to the summit and back to our cache, but the ascent had taken longer—and taken more out of us—than I had expected. Gombu, smaller than I, used less oxygen and still had some left, but he would be out soon too. If my brain had been functioning normally, I probably would have been frightened. Instead, about the only thing that registered was "Keep moving." And we were close, with only a gentle slope ahead of us.

About fifty feet from the top, I coiled in the rope again, and Gombu came up beside me. I leaned toward him and shouted against the wind, "You first, Gombu!"

"You first, Big Jim!" he shouted back. Even with his oxygen mask I could see him grinning.

We compromised. Side by side, we staggered the last few feet until, at 1:00 P.M., we stood together at the highest point on earth—29,028 feet above the sea. The sky above us was that deep, dark blue you only see when you've climbed above most of the earth's atmosphere. We were on the edge of space.

Though the sky above was clear, the view was limited. Tibet was completely hidden by the plume of snow blowing past our feet to the north, but we could see into Nepal. Close by, Makalu, the world's fifth-highest mountain, and Lhotse, the fourth-highest, looked back at us.

We dropped our packs. I pulled out a four-foot aluminum picket, placed the point of the stake on the highest part of the summit, and drove it into the snow, pounding it in with my ice ax. At long last, the American flag, and the flag of the National Geographic Society, flew over Mount Everest. Gombu deposited a *kata*, a Buddhist friendship scarf, and held the flag of the Himalayan Mountaineering Institute as I snapped his picture. He snapped mine as well, stepping back and turning the camera sideways to fit me into the frame.

I looked around the summit for any sign of previous climbs. Deep down, I hoped to find some clue that Mallory and Irvine had, in their final effort, made it to the top in 1924. They had disappeared in the clouds at 28,000 feet, never to be seen again. But there was no trace of them or anyone else.

At this moment, I did not feel expansive or sublime; I felt only, as I said later, "like a frail human being." People—mostly nonclimbers—talk about "conquering" mountains. In my mind, nothing could be further from the truth. The mountain is so huge and powerful, and the climber so puny, exhausted, and powerless. The mountain is forever; Gombu and I, meanwhile, were dying every second we lingered.

And that thought brought me back to reality. The wind continued at hurricane force. The temperature was thirty below. We were out of oxygen, cold, exhausted, and in danger. Weeks later, at a press conference, Gombu was asked what he was thinking when he reached the summit. He got a big laugh when he said, slowly, "How . . . to . . . get . . . down." But at the summit of Everest, I was just responding automatically to my body, which was screaming, "Get down! Get off! Go lower now! Climb down to the oxygen!" So after more than two years of planning and more than two months of climbing, Gombu and I spent only twenty minutes on top before we began our descent—every bit as dangerous as the climb itself. What happened next was a bizarre combination of comedy and nightmare.

Gombu took the lead while I belayed and anchored him. Already, the roaring wind had almost filled our uphill tracks with snow. Gombu was sixty feet ahead of me. We had not gone far when, suddenly and without warning, the entire cornice directly before me simply dissolved and slid off into Tibet. There was no noise; the roaring wind drowned out any other sound. I stared dumbfounded at the gigantic hole in front of me. The fracture line began thirty feet to my left, ran up literally to my feet, and turned sharply down the slope, following our tracks for sixty feet or so. Then it cut back to the edge again. I looked up, and to my relief, Gombu stood safe on the other side of the void. Exhausted and oxygen-starved, this was my thoughtful reaction: "Gee. I guess I'd better move over a foot or two." And we continued our stumbling and lurching descent.

I belayed Gombu off the steep Hillary Step, then scrambled down myself. At the foot of the Step, in the saddle formed by the lower South Summit, Gombu led off again. As I watched him disappear over the rise of the South Summit, however, I was suddenly hit with an urgent need to . . . take a crap. There was nothing to do but stop, lay down a few coils of rope, throw off my pack, and drop my pants, answering what had to be the highest call of nature yet dictated to a human being. There I was, squatting bare-assed on the down slope to Nepal—in the Throne Room of the Mountain Gods—crampons flat on the surface and all points secured, with a ground blizzard freezing my private parts. It was a humbling—not to mention numbing—experience. I felt very mortal.

Dressing quickly, I grabbed my pack and struggled toward the South Summit. Gombu, who had no idea what was going on, had begun pulling on the now-taut rope, thinking it was snagged on a rock. A hard tug threw me off balance and turned me sideways. As I fell, my pack tipped and one of my cameras fell out, rolling about thirty feet down the West Face. "To hell with it," I thought to myself. Then I thought again; it was my old friend John Day's expensive Leica. I stared down at it for a few seconds, then changed my mind. As I started down the slope, Gombu felt the rope go taut again. This time, though, he backed up to give me some slack. I retrieved the camera, stuffed it in my pack, and climbed back up the slope. (Three weeks later, I realized how dangerous this gambit had been; on the second assault, Lute Jerstad followed the faint outline of my footprints heading down the West Face, thinking they must lead to the summit. He had gone a long and perilous way toward the edge before he realized the track went nowhere.)

Without oxygen and severely dehydrated because of my frozen water bottles, I barely managed the uphill stretch from the saddle to the South Summit. We rested briefly, then headed down toward our oxygen cache, hooked up the bottles, turned on a two-liter flow, took a few wonderful deep breaths, and continued our descent to High Camp. Even on oxygen, though, we moved slowly, placing our crampons carefully, thankful that we could see our feet now that the wind had at last lessened and the ground blizzard was gone. Three hours later, just before dark, we staggered into High Camp, where Norman and Ang Dawa awaited us, having themselves been frustrated from summiting because of oxygen problems. I was so wasted I almost crawled into my sleeping bag with my crampons on. We melted ice to make drinks, and Norman and Ang Dawa passed us hot Jell-O and more hot water—but I was still desperately thirsty when I finally fell asleep.

At midnight I ran out of oxygen again. Lying in my sleeping bag, I could feel the cold work its way up my extremities. My body was telling me it was slowly dying, and it was moving my blood to my vital organs. The cold crept toward my middle, and my feet and hands grew numb. I lay there, inert, waiting for daylight.

Sunrise. Thank God, the sun. The wind had died down, and the sky was clear all the way into Tibet. Norman wanted to stick around and do some filming, but I could think only of getting down to thicker atmosphere. Gombu and I descended to Camp V on the South Col, meeting the second assault team on their way up. Seeing the shape we were in, and recognizing the general shortage of oxygen, they abandoned their summit attempt, took us down, and cared for us at Camp V, doing the same for Norman and Ang Dawa when they caught up. After a couple of hours of rest, Gombu and I, with Dick Pownall roped in with us, headed down again, still without oxygen. Not long afterward, the rest of the team followed. We continued almost nonstop through Camps IV and III. As we descended, I could feel the air getting thicker and heavier, the breathing easier. The numbness in my extremities had started to dissipate by the time we reach Camp II—Advance Base—at 5:30 that evening. Ecstatic, we arrived to a great celebration.

■

It was a feeling that wouldn't last. Amid all the congratulations and backslapping, I was already worrying about the Khumbu Icefall.

I had stayed above the Icefall most of the expedition, working from Advance Base upward. In all I had spent thirty days at 21,350 feet and above, and had lost more than 25 pounds, my body deteriorating in the thin air. Now it suddenly hit me that perhaps we had committed a great transgression on that remote summit; we had stolen a jewel from the breast of the Goddess Mother of the Earth, and Chomolungma might strike back. What better place to bring us up short than at the very gate of escape, the Khumbu Icefall, before we could get the jewel to Base Camp. As I lay in my sleeping bag, my old night fears returned in earnest.

Gombu and I left early the next morning. It was now spring, and it would be hot by midafternoon. Eager to reach the Icefall before it began melting, we half-walked, half-ran as we entered the top of the labyrinth. We threaded our way down, listening for movement in the ice, running in some places and balancing precariously in others. But this time, the Icefall was quiet. Nothing

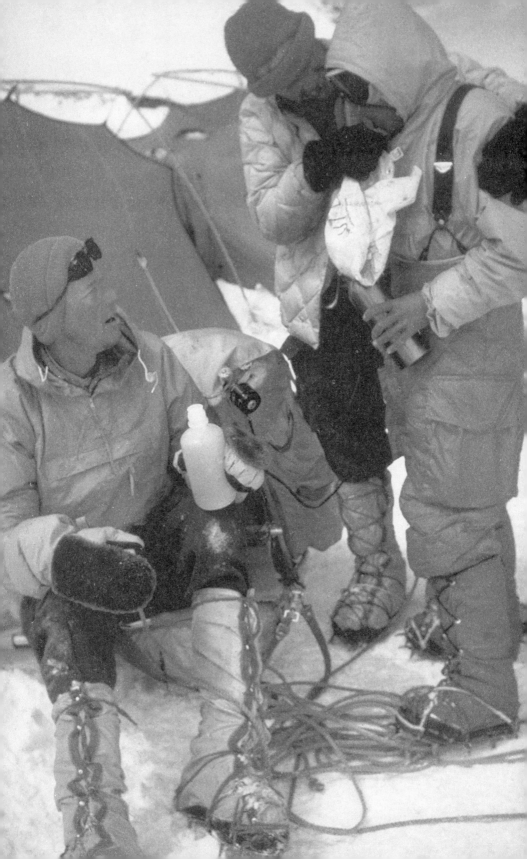

moved. The descent went smoothly and—with broad smiles and full lungs—we walked into Base Camp, our jewel in hand.

With the Icefall behind me, I finally relaxed. Dear God, it felt so good to take off my clothes and lie naked on a slab of rock in the warmth of the spring sun. The tips of the big toes and second toes on both my feet were black from frostbite, so I sat soaking them in a metal tub. I had frostbite scars on my face, where the mask and goggles had not covered my skin, and frostbite blisters on my left (Nepal side) wrist, where there had been a gap between my glove and parka. But all signs of frostbite would go away in a few weeks. It was the same with Gombu.

By now the entire team was down at Base Camp, and we were fielding congratulatory telegrams left and right. President Kennedy wrote:

> I am most pleased to learn of the success of the American Expedition on Mount Everest. These American climbers, pushing human endurance and experience to their farthest frontiers, join the distinguished group of Swiss and British mountaineers who have performed this feat. I know that all Americans will join me in saluting our gallant countrymen.

We had taken a vote and agreed no names would be released to the press until the other groups had had a shot at the summit, which we figured would be in another couple of days.

In the end, it took three weeks. (And in the meantime, the expedition had been pressured into revealing that it had been Gombu and me who had summited.) While the first summit team rested in Base Camp, the rest of our crew launched a two-pronged summit attempt, aiming for the record books a second time. The idea was for Tom Hornbein and Willi Unsoeld's West Ridge group to meet the second South Col group, led by Lute Jerstad and Barry C. Bishop, on the summit, then descend together down the South Col route. If they could pull it off, Tom and Willi would have to their credit not only the ascent of Everest by a new route but also an unprecedented traverse of an 8,000-meter peak.

Breathing oxygen at Camp V after descending from the summit—Jim, Lute Jerstad, Gombu. Photo: National Geographic Society

Lute and Barry found Camp VI—the High Camp on the South Col route—intact, with our two small Eureka tents still up in spite of storms and high winds during the three-week interval. On summit day, they got a late start—the result of trying to change butane gas canisters on one stove next to another stove that was burning. (They were spaced out at high altitude.) The resulting explosion forced them to dive out of the tent, almost down the Kangshung Face. They had toasted cheeks and singed eyebrows for breakfast and did not leave camp until 8:00 A.M.—two hours later than Gombu and I had left. It was perfect climbing weather, however, with no clouds and only a very light breeze.

On the same day, Tom and Willi, with the help of Barry Corbet, Al Auten, and five Sherpa, put in a new Camp VI on the West Ridge. They had been working on this route for weeks, repeatedly being driven back by bad weather and the sheer difficulty of the route. It was an incredible challenge—it had never even been attempted, much less climbed. Tom and Willi spent the night at their high camp alone, ready to make their final assault the following day.

With good weather, they set out at 5:00 A.M., first light, for the summit. As they worked their way up, I sat in the radio tent, well rested, waiting for a call in case they needed help. Rather late in the afternoon, around 2:00 P.M., they called. It had taken them hours to climb above the so-called Yellow Band—a crumbly layer of rock that was far more trouble on their side of the mountain than it had been for our first South Col team. The warmth of the sun had made the snow too unstable to risk retreating back down the forty-five-degree slope beneath them, and they had no idea what route would take them to the summit. Nonetheless, they decided it was safer to go up than down. A risky gamble.

On the opposite side of the mountain, Lute and Barry reached the summit at 3:30 P.M. Lute had been leading, and Barry was struggling to keep up. They looked and shouted down the West Face but saw no sign of Tom and Willi. Seeing and hearing nothing, they started their descent back to the South Col. It was 4:15 P.M. Late. Too late.

Meanwhile, as Lute and Barry descended, Tom and Willi, in an extraordinary feat of mountaineering, pushed their West Ridge route all the way to the summit, reaching the top at 6:15 P.M. A tattered American flag greeted them as they hugged each other and watched the setting sun. They had committed themselves to go all the way and risked everything in their summit bid. Now, however, they knew they would have to descend in the dark down a route they did not know—one of the worst situations a mountaineer can face. They rested only briefly before heading down toward the South Col, following Lute and Barry's footsteps. By 8:00 P.M., with dimming flashlights, they were groping their way down, hoping to make contact with their teammates.

Lute and Barry were having their own troubles. They were both exhausted, and Barry kept stumbling and collapsing in the snow. They were descending very slowly. Suddenly, out of the darkness, they heard shouting. At first they thought it was from Camp VI below them, then realized the sound was coming from above. Shouting back and forth, the four climbers finally joined forces and continued the descent. Barry could hardly walk and kept telling the others to leave him alone. Lute was hammered too, partly because he had burned up so much energy getting Barry to the summit and part way down. At midnight, after taking three hours to descend 400 feet, totally exhausted, out of

Below left: Willi Unsoeld, with frostbitten feet, being carried by Sherpa from Base Camp. Photo: National Geographic Society
Below right: Lute Jerstad, also with frostbitten feet, with Sherpani.
Photo: National Geographic Society

oxygen, and with flashlights dead, they had to stop. At 28,000 feet, they found a fairly flat rock outcrop and, without tent, sleeping bags, or oxygen, sprawled on the rocks to wait for dawn.

Down below in Camp VI, at about 9:00 P.M., Dave Dingman and Sherpa Girmi Dorje had thought they heard voices above their camp. They went out to look but found no one. The next morning, knowing the climbers above must be in serious trouble—and fearing they were dead—they headed up.

But it had been a rare night on Everest; there had been no wind. At the highest bivouac site in mountaineering history, the morning sun found Tom, Willi, Lute, and Barry alive, all but Tom with feet and hands numb from frostbite. They stumbled toward Camp VI and were met by Dave and Girmi, who gave them oxygen and liquids. Escorted from camp to camp, they reached Advance Base at 10:30 P.M. The next morning, walking painfully, they descended the Icefall into Base Camp.

Lute's feet recovered enough that he could complete the return march on foot. But Willi and Barry had to be carried from Base Camp, past a huge rock in which the Sherpa had carved "In memory of John E. Breitenbach," to a helicopter evacuation spot just above Namche Bazaar. Both had toes amputated, and Barry lost parts of some fingers as well. They had pulled off a breathtaking success, a shining victory. But they had paid a price.

The rest of us returned the way we came, on foot, and the descent from the frozen, sterile world of ice and snow and rock to the world of the Nepalese spring was almost too much for the senses. Warm, moist air caressed my chapped face. The thin, odorless air on the peak yielded to the rich smell of thawed earth and the pungent odor of animals. The first green plant was a jolt to the eyes. The first village overwhelmed me, and I stared at the men, women, children, chickens, dogs, and yaks and reveled in the juniper smoke from the cooking fires. At one point, I just sat hugging a warm, furry dog that licked me continuously, and I wept, thinking about Jake, buried in that Icefall, and about how lucky I was to be alive.

In the years to come a debate would ebb and flow: which was the "most important" accomplishment? Getting the first American to the summit or completing the West Ridge route? I suspect the climbers for whom this argument held the least meaning were those of us who had been on the team. We had done it—whatever "it" meant to each of us.

◾

On June 24, 1963, after a series of flights that seemed to take almost as long as the march from Everest, we finally reached the United States—only to be stunned by the attention we received. The press focused most of its attention on me because I was "first," all too often missing entirely the incredible achievement of Tom and Willi's West Ridge/South Col traverse. I kept thinking, "Look, all we did was climb this mountain!" But it was, I suppose, a more innocent era, in which an individual could somehow embody a sense of hope for a nation. At any rate, we had little say in the matter. Gradually, it began to dawn on me that my life had changed forever.

◾

On July 8 our entire Everest team, including five Sherpa, stood in the sun in the Rose Garden of the White House. President John F. Kennedy presented each of us with the Hubbard Medal of the National Geographic Society. Gombu, in turn, took a Buddhist friendship scarf, similar to the one he had left on the summit of Mount Everest, and draped it around the president's neck. Gombu was astonished when the president joked with him, squeezed his thigh muscles, and commented on his tremendous strength.

It was a great privilege for me to meet President Kennedy. Along with millions of other Americans, I admired him immensely. We shook hands, and he said, "Congratulations on your great ascent."

Five months later, he was gone.

Chapter Seven

CLIMBING WITH THE KENNEDYS

"Have you ever climbed a mountain before?" I asked the senator.

"No," said Bobby Kennedy, on the phone from Washington, D.C.

"What are you doing to get into shape for the climb?" I asked.

"Running up and down the stairs and practicing hollering *Help!*" he replied.

"Great," I thought to myself.

A year after John F. Kennedy was assassinated, the Canadian government named their nation's highest unclimbed mountain after the slain president. The peak rises in the glacier-clad St. Elias Mountains that form the border between the southwestern corner of the Yukon Territory and the panhandle of Alaska. The National Geographic Society and the Boston Museum of Science, along with the Canadian government, were cosponsoring a surveying expedition. Bradford Washburn, the director of the museum, knew the mountain better than any man alive; in 1935, when this region had been nothing but a blank spot on the map of Canada, he had been the first to explore it. Brad had described the peak now called Mount Kennedy as " . . . another giant that we judged to be 14,000 feet high. Unlike the rounded domes of its neighbors, this mountain had a sharp, almost Himalayan summit, flanked with staggering precipices of ice and granite."

Because I had summited Everest less than two years earlier, the Society

Senator Robert Kennedy and Barry Prather climbing to Camp II.
Photo: Whittaker family collection

asked me to lead the climb. Then they told me I would be leading the former president's brother, Senator Robert F. Kennedy, to the top. (In fact, the Society had invited Bobby's younger brother, Teddy, as well, but he was recuperating from an airplane accident and couldn't make it.) Other members of the team included another veteran of the 1963 Everest expedition, Barry Prather; three others, Dee Molenaar, William Prater, and George Senner; *National Geographic* magazine photographer William Allard; and a member of the Canadian Alpine Club, James Craig.

I first met the senator on March 21, 1965, when he arrived in Seattle from Washington, D.C. I was relieved; though he had slept on the flight and looked rumpled and weary, he also looked—at a wiry five-foot ten and about 165 pounds—to be in good physical condition. The next morning, he, Brad Washburn, and I flew to Juneau, Alaska, and from there chartered a plane to Whitehorse, in the Yukon, where our Canadian climber, James Craig, was waiting for us. The rest of the team had gone to the mountain earlier that week and had established Base Camp at 8,700 feet.

On the flights to Juneau and Whitehorse, Bobby and I sat together and talked. I found him somewhat shy but warm and personable, and intensely curious—about everything: me, our team, the mountain, and mountain climbing in general.

From Whitehorse, we had planned to charter a ski plane to Base Camp, but bad weather and deep snow canceled the flight. We stood around nonplused for a while, then learned that a big Royal Canadian Air Force helicopter had just set down to refuel. Casually, Brad asked the pilot if it could be made available to us—I was impressed that he had the nerve to ask. I was doubly impressed when, after consultations with Ottawa and a check on the weather at the mountain, the pilot agreed.

We choppered to Base Camp atop Cathedral Glacier, roughly a vertical mile beneath our goal. We dumped our packs, jumped out, said goodbye to Brad Washburn, who would stay in Whitehorse, and ate powder snow as the helicopter blasted off. I felt like a pampered kid as I walked into the six-man tent where dinner was waiting.

The next morning I showed Bobby how to walk in the snowshoes we'd be using for the first day's climb and tied him in as the middle man on our rope. At 10:00 A.M. we started up the snow-covered glacier. He seemed content to be guided rather than instructed; I got the feeling he was a "learn by doing" person. But his curiosity about mountaineering, and everything we had done as climbers, was insatiable. Each time we stopped for a rest break, he'd pepper me with questions about climbs I'd made, problems I'd encountered, and especially, the details of the Everest expedition. (He became so interested in the Sherpa and their problems that he sent the check he received for writing a *Life* magazine article on his climb to a fund to improve living conditions for them in Nepal.)

Despite the fact that he'd never worn snowshoes before, and that we were climbing a pretty steep slope, he had no trouble keeping up—in fact, he kept asking me to go faster. I was setting my normal "guide pace," learned from many years of experience with clients on Mount Rainier. Typically, novices climb too fast and burn themselves out before they ever reach High Camp. I told him to slow down.

Before long, however, I felt the rope between us go slack and heard him moving close behind me again. I stopped and explained that if I fell through a snow bridge into a crevasse and too much slack had developed, it would mean a long fall for me and one hell of a jerk for him. He might even follow me into an icy tomb.

"OK, Jim," he said, agreeably. "But could you pick up the pace a little?"

It had been a brilliant morning, with the temperature rising to twenty-five degrees above, but now it was beginning to snow. I began to move faster, convinced that any minute now I would feel the rope tighten as he began to poop out. He never did. I felt great knowing he was in such good shape—by now I was certain that if we got a break in the weather, he would get the mountain.

Five hours later, having gained 3,000 vertical feet in deepening snow, a cardboard sign loomed ahead in the gathering twilight: "High Camp—Three Miles." Mountain humor; in fact, it was just over the rise. The advance team— Dee, George, and Bill Prater—had already set up two tents and dug a beautiful snow cave with "Senate Chamber—Members Only" spray-painted on the ice walls. Inside the cave, completely comfortable and out of the wind, Bill had dinner going: soup, Alaskan crabmeat, chicken stew, strawberries, coffee, and tea. The guys had done a great job. All through dinner, Bobby kept asking the other members of our team questions about their climbing experiences—where had they gone, what had happened, what had they done? Finally, we headed off to the tents to sleep. During the night, however, the snowstorm turned into a raging blizzard, and our tent shuddered and flapped badly. I tossed and turned, worried that I'd have to call off the climb. In the darkness, all my usual night demons came to visit. I couldn't sleep. Restless and uncomfortable, I yanked on the parka I was using as a pillow and tried to stuff the hood—with its wolverine fur ruff—further under my head.

"Ouch!"

I had grabbed Bobby's hair instead.

The wind howled on, and my old nighttime companions, my demons of doubt, cramponed my consciousness. What a night.

By morning the wind still raged, and the temperature was close to zero. But when I peered through the tent flap the sky was clear! Though windy, it was a good summit day, and at 8:30 A.M. we were roped up and ready to go: Bobby, Barry, and I on the first rope; George, Bill Allard, and Dee on the second; and Bill Prater and Jim Craig on the third. We strapped on crampons and headed up the mountain in that order.

At one point I stepped over a fragile snow bridge and warned Bobby that there was a crevasse and to stay in my footprints. He did exactly as I'd told him. Suddenly my rope jerked, and Bobby yelled "Whoa!" as he dropped chest-deep into the crevasse, his feet dangling below in empty space. Pulling himself out, he looked down the hole and shook his head—he couldn't see the bottom.

On we went up the mountain until we reached the most difficult section, the sixty-five-degree ridge of the summit pyramid, one of the "staggering precipices of ice and granite" Brad Washburn had described thirty years earlier. On a small snow ledge, I coiled the rope as Bobby came up to me, then he brought in Barry. To my left was a drop of 6,000 feet; to the right a somewhat gentler 1,000-foot slope. Ice crystals sparkled in the sunlight, and the wind had stopped. We stood there, breathing hard in the thin, cold air, staring up.

"Can that be climbed?" Bobby asked skeptically.

"I think so," I said, and got ready to tackle the last obstacle. Barry went into belay position, and I plunged my ax into the face and kick-stepped sixty feet up the ridge to where it began to slope off to the summit. I drove my ax into the snow, looped the rope around it, and shouted to Bobby, "On belay! Climb!"

"Climbing!" he shouted back, and started up.

I expected him to fall. The slope was very steep—loose snow on top of hard-pack—and exposed. Beginning climbers tend to lean into a steep slope, to cling to it. It's a mistake; the force of gravity pushes their feet out from under them and down they go. I knew this is what Bobby would do; I was positive he would fall. But he didn't. I had forgotten Bobby was a good skier and knew about snow. He didn't lean into the slope. He just kick-stepped up to me, hauled himself over the lip of the ridge, and sat down, breathing hard, while I belayed Barry up.

We were now only a few hundred feet from the summit. I broke trail through soft snow and then stopped about a hundred feet from the summit. I coiled rope again, and Bobby came up, followed by Barry.

"It's all yours, Bobby," I said.

"Can I go the rest of the way now?" he asked.

"Yes," I answered, and Barry echoed, "It's okay now."

The two of us stood quietly while he trudged up the ridge, laying the first human tracks on the virgin summit. When the rope was fully uncoiled and he was sixty feet ahead of us, we followed. He stopped for a minute, catching his breath, and then walked to the highest point of Mount Kennedy, becoming the first human being to stand on the summit of the mountain named after his brother.

He stood alone, head bowed, and made the sign of the cross. Tears rolled down my cheeks and froze on my parka. From his pack he pulled out a pole and flag with the Kennedy crest, knelt down, and drove it into the snow. After a few moments, I joined him, knelt on one knee, put my arm around his shoulder, and congratulated him.

"This can never be taken away," I said. "There'll never be another who will be first on Mount Kennedy."

"Yes," he said quietly.

It was March 24, 1965. As the rest of the team reached the summit, we added the flags of the United States, Canada, and the National Geographic Society, along with an eight-foot-high surveying marker, and took pictures. The Canadian Yukon shone white and silent below us. For Bobby, it was the top of the world. He dug a little depression in the summit ice and left behind a copy of J.F.K.'s Inaugural Address, an inauguration medallion, and a couple of PT-109 tie clasps. Then we headed down.

Senator Robert Kennedy on the summit of Mount Kennedy. Photo: Whittaker family collection

Later, when the photos appeared, *Life* magazine was deluged with letters from Kennedy-haters that Bobby's Kennedy banner was bigger than the American flag. I had to write a response explaining that Bobby had not known the size of my flag in advance, and I had not known the size of his—the kind of adolescent detail I hadn't worried about since puberty. In addition, gossipmongers claimed Bobby was hauled up the mountain by the experienced climbers on the team. They couldn't have been more wrong. In fact, even though he was carrying a heavy pack, he seemed in better shape and moved better than some other members of the team. In the years to come, I would never cease to be amazed at the way the Kennedys brought out people's passions—both the best and the worst.

Later Bobby would write in *National Geographic* magazine:

> *President Kennedy loved the outdoors. He loved adventure. He admired courage more than any other human quality, and he was President of the United States, which is frequently and accurately called the loneliest job in the world. So I am sure he would be pleased that this lonely, beautiful mountain in the Yukon bears his name, and that in this way, at least, he has joined the fraternity of those who live outdoors, battle the elements, and climb mountains.*

It was also in this article that I learned for the first time that Bobby Kennedy was afraid of heights.

■

The climb of Mount Kennedy had done more than give me a new peak to add to my list; it had given me a new and dear friend. As often happens to people who face extreme conditions in the mountains, in only a matter of days Bobby and I had formed a deep and lasting friendship.

Despite his wealth and fame, I found Bobby to be a gentle, modest, informal man. He had a quick, wry sense of humor and seemed to me to be completely without ego, pretense, or cant. As shy as he was, he nonetheless wore his heart on his sleeve: he loved children and thought it obscene that they could go hungry in a country as rich as ours. He hurt for the disadvantaged and disenfranchised—and they knew it. He had an intense curiosity, absorbed information like a sponge, was passionate about fairness, and worked doggedly on the issues that mattered to him. He had the courage, rare among politicians, to seek the truth and stand up for it. People who didn't know him well sometimes took his passion and honesty as ruthlessness. It was a description that could hardly have been less appropriate and, to me, said much more about the people who used it than it did about Bobby himself. Those who know him well—and I became one of them—adored him.

Since I had to help write the *National Geographic* article on the climb, Bobby and I returned to Washington, D.C., together, and he invited me to stay at his home. There were two cars waiting for us at National Airport—a convertible full to overflowing with Bobby's wife, Ethel, and their mob of children, and a second car for all our luggage and gear. I started toward the second car, but Bobby and Ethel wouldn't hear of it. So I piled into the convertible with all of them, and away we went, packed in like circus clowns.

Bobby and Ethel's home, Hickory Hill, was one of the grand old houses of McLean, Virginia, just across the Potomac River from D.C. Outside, it had rolling lawns, a tennis court, a swimming pool, and a cabana. Inside, the house was crammed full of antiques and art. Countless silver-framed family photographs filled nearly every available surface. I never did figure out how many dogs and other animals lived there as well.

I went to the National Geographic Society's offices to work for a few hours each day, then returned to Hickory Hill to swim, play tennis (usually losing), or join in a game of touch football (barely holding my own). I began to understand

Lunch at the Seattle Tennis Club on Lake Washington—(standing, left to right), ?, Bobby Kennedy, Jr., Carl Whittaker, Joe Kennedy, Michael Kennedy, Anne Coffey, David Kennedy, Kathleen Kennedy (seated, left to right) Scott Whittaker, Blanche Whittaker, Jim Whittaker, Ethel Kennedy. Photo: Seattle Post Intelligencer Collection, Museum of History and Industry

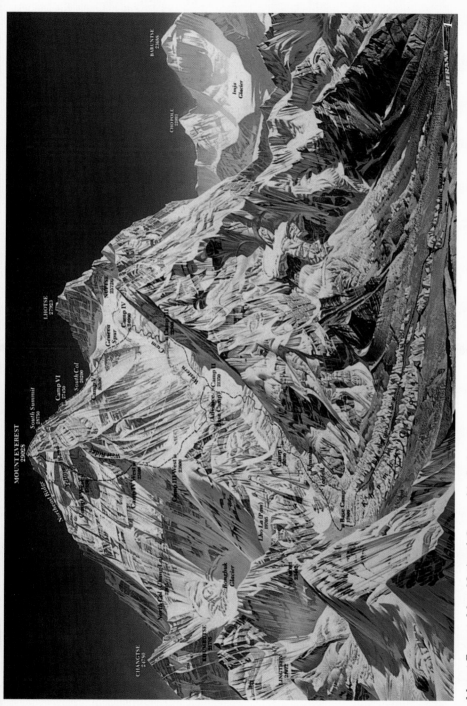

Mount Everest. Map: National Geographic Society

Gombu and Jim get ready to leave Camp II for the summit of Everest, April 27, 1963. Photo: Barry C. Bishop/National Geographic Society

Left: Camp II in the Western Cwm, Mount Everest expedition.
Photo: Barry C. Bishop/National Geographic Society

Helicopter evacuation from above Thangboche, Mount Everest, 1963—(front, left to right) Dingman, Siri, Dyhrenfurth, Prather, Gombu, Pownall; (seated) Bishop, Unsoeld, Hornbein, Jerstad; (standing) J. Roberts, G. Roberts, Miller, Whittaker, Lester, Auten, two Sherpa, Knut Solbakken (helicopter pilot), Emerson, Corbet, Doody. Photo: Thomas J. Abercrombie/National Geographic Society

6

East meets west—Jim and Gombu one month after the White House visit.
Photo: Seattle Post-Intelligencer Collection, Museum of History and Industry

Left: Receiving the Hubbard Medal of the National Geographic Society
from President Kennedy in the White House Rose Garden—(left to right)
Mel Grosvenor and Mel Payne of the National Geographic Society (with an
unknown person behind), Auten, Emerson, Pownall, Dyhrenfurth, Hornbein,
Prather, Bishop, Gombu, Jerstad, Whittaker, President Kennedy, Corbet,
G. Roberts, Sherpa. Photo: George Mobley/National Geographic Society

Ice cave on Mount Kennedy—(left to right) Jim Craig, Dee Molenaar, George Senner, Robert Kennedy, Jim Whittaker. Photo: William Albert Allard/National Geographic Society

Ski bums at the Roundhouse, Sun Valley, Idaho, December 1967—(left to right)
Willi Schaeffler, Ted Kennedy, John Glenn, Jim Whittaker, Bobby Kennedy.
Photo: Whittaker family collection

Left: Whittaker and Kennedy on the summit of Mount Kennedy. Photo: William
Albert Allard/National Geographic Society

Returning from Mount Kennedy, April 1965—(left to right) Blanche, Jim, Brad Washburn, Carl, Scott, Hortense and C.B. Whittaker. Photo: Phil Webber

Jim at the cabin on John's Island, with pet parrot and Josie the deer. Photo: Whittaker family collection

Porters gather outside the "Pay Tent" during the porter strike at Urdukas, K2 expedition, 1975. Photo: Dianne Roberts

The summit of Gasherbrum IV, by moonlight. Photo: Dianne Roberts

14

1975 K2 team with Vibram soles—(left to right) Galen Rowell, Rob Schaller, Leif Patterson, Jim Wickwire, Louie Whittaker, Dianne Roberts, Jim Whittaker, Fred Stanley, Fred Dunham, Steve Marts. Photo: Dianne Roberts

Leif Patterson. Photo: Dianne Roberts

15

Porters on the approach march near Lilliwa, with Trango towers in the background, K2 expedition, 1978. Photo: Dianne Roberts

Paiju Peak. Photo: Dianne Roberts

Porters negotiate the route over the upper Baltoro, near Urdukas. Photo: Dianne Roberts

Team members flake out at Camp I
after a day carrying loads to Camp II
—(left to right) Rick Ridgeway,
Skip Edmonds, Bill Sumner, Craig
Anderson. Photo: Dianne Roberts

Four climbers en route to Camp III, with the summit pyramid behind. The Abruzzi
ridge is the left skyline; the "Polish Route" is up the couloir to the left of the right
skyline. Photo: Dianne Roberts

Lou Reichardt anchoring Camp III tent in
windstorm. Photo: Dianne Roberts

22

Jim hangs his ax on the "gear wall," a serac at Camp III, 1978 K2 expedition. The knife ridge and the upper mountain are in the background. Photo: Dianne Roberts

The knife ridge between Camp III and Camp IV. The tents of Camp III are visible at the base of a serac in the upper right, and two climbers can be seen on the track leading from Camp III to the top of the ridge, where it crosses to the Tibetan side and continues to Camp IV, perched on the ridge crest in the lower left of the photo. Photo: Dianne Roberts

24

Rick Ridgeway and John Roskelley back at Camp III, exhausted after putting in the route to Camp IV. Photo: Dianne Roberts

Jim Wickwire and Craig Anderson leave Camp III for Camp IV. Photo: Dianne Roberts

Four climbers en route to Camp V, 1978 K2 expedition. Photo: Dianne Roberts

Camp V. Photo: Craig Anderson

Rick Ridgeway's frostbitten fingers.
Photo: Dianne Roberts

The 1978 K2 expedition team and high altitude porters at Base Camp, after the climb—(kneeling, left to right) Lou Reichardt, Tajiran Shah, John Roskelley, Jim Wickwire, Terry Bech, Dianne Roberts, Jim Whittaker, Liason Officer Mohammed Saleem Khan; (standing, left to right) Rob Schaller, Gohar Shah, Cherie Bech, Chris Chandler, Diana Jagersky, Sajeran Khan, Skip Edmonds, Craig Anderson, Rick Ridgeway, Bill Sumner, Honar Baig. Photo: Dianne Roberts

Pelion climbers cross debris from the icefall that had claimed eleven lives two weeks earlier, just above camp on the Ingraham Glacier, Mount Rainier. Photo: Dianne Roberts

Blind climber Kirk Adams practices a Tyrolean traverse on the Nisqually Glacier, Mount Rainier. Photo: Dianne Roberts

The crew of the first Impossible *on the Victoria to Maui Race, 1976—Alan Rutherford in front; Steve Marts, Jim, Kay Henshaw astern. Photo: Dianne Roberts*

The domes of St. Peter's Basilica, Moscow. Photo: Dianne Roberts

(Left to right) Steve Gall, Robert Link, and Ed Viesturs try on hats in a Russian village market. Photo: Dianne Roberts

The Peace Climb poster, with team members in front of Mount Everest—a photo composite done by a Seattle artist.

Some of the team in the "communication tent." Photo: John Yaeger

Climbers approach the summit of Mount Everest, where another climber waits.
Photo: Ian Wade

Steve Gall and Bud Krogh parade with the rest of the team toward the Potala, Lhasa.
Photo: Kurt Papenfus

Tibetan residents of Lhasa welcome the climbers back with a parade.
Photo: Kurt Papenfus

Tibetan schoolchildren in Lhasa welcome the climbers.
Photo: Kurt Papenfus

Joss, Dianne, Jim and Leif on the bow of the third Impossible, *Puerto Vallarta, Mexico; April 1997. Photo: Dianne Roberts*

why Bobby did so well on the mountain; Kennedy sports, like much else in their lives, were legendarily competitive, even for the littlest Kennedy in any game.

When I left for Seattle after that first of what would become many visits, *Sports Illustrated* wrote: "Mount Everest climber Jim Whittaker, upon leaving Senator Robert Kennedy's Hickory Hill home and limping onto the airplane said, 'It will be nice to get back home so I can rest up and recover from all that exercise.'"

The following winter, our families spent Christmas vacation together skiing in Sun Valley, Idaho. I knew how competitive the Kennedys were from the tennis and touch football games at Hickory Hill, and I expected they would ski the same way. But I was confident. Now they were on my turf—after all, I had been a ski instructor for years and was a member of the National Ski Patrol.

For our first run, Bobby and I took the chair lift to the top of Mount Baldy. I was enjoying the sunshine and the glittering snow diamonds in the air at the top when Bobby abruptly said, "I'll see you at the bottom," and took off straight down the fall line, going like a bat out of hell. I lunged after him, careening down Ridge Run, flying off moguls, gaining speed until I finally passed him, and barely reached the bottom first. We stood there panting.

"Jeez," I said, "where'd you learn to go so fast?"

"I love to ski fast. It takes your mind off other things, makes you focus. You have to concentrate on the here and now."

We skied with Bobby's family and their entourage for several winters in Sun Valley. You never knew who was going to turn up on these forays. On any given day I would find myself riding up a chair lift with Ethel or Jackie or Joan or Teddy Kennedy; John Glenn or his wife, Annie; the singer Andy Williams or his wife, Claudine; or Henry Mancini . . . it was, in a sense, an outdoor extension of Camelot.

Summers were much the same. We alternated between Hyannisport and Seattle. One summer, Ethel and her children stayed with Blanche and me and our boys at our Lake Sammamish home for a week. We water-skied on the lake and went up into the San Juan Islands to the summer cabin we had on John's Island. I took Ethel to Mount Rainier, and we hiked up to Camp Muir. I had arranged for Louie to hire and train her son Joe as a Mount Rainier guide, and she seemed to love the mountain wilderness as much as Joe did.

After she went back east, she sent a wry thank-you note:

> *Thank you for introducing me to the incredible beauty of Rainier—looming*
> *silently in the moonlight and radiating dazzling brilliance in the bright sun of*
> *high noon, a constant eloquent reminder of creation and the Creator . . . Now*
> *that I am back in the land of running water, light switches and blessed,*
> *beautiful, marvelous, wonderful plumbing, even John's Island looks pretty good.*
> *Hyannisport is no fun at all with all that clean, white, sandy beach and warm*
> *water. I sure do long for the sharp stones, slimy kelp and icy blast of the San*
> *Juans.*

In July of 1967 I helped organize a float trip down the Colorado River for our two families and a crowd of Bobby and Ethel's friends. In all, there were forty-two of us, including columnist Art Buchwald and his wife, Otis Chandler (the publisher of the *Los Angeles Times*), writer George Plimpton, Andy Williams, and many others, along with some fourteen children.

Guided by Hatch River Expeditions in Utah, we plummeted through foaming rapids, floated lazily through slack water, swam in pools and eddies, had gooey, sticky mud fights, and basked in the hot sun. River running was a new experience for me. At times the river would roar and other times be almost soundless. Above us, multicolored rock cliffs soared thousands of feet toward the sky. The warm, turbulent river was a brown, moving highway; we drifted through a canyon paradise. At lunchtime and at the end of the day, we'd pull up at a sandbar and Ted and Don Hatch would lay out a sumptuous spread for us. We'd stuff ourselves and just take in the scenery. One evening, though he hated to sing unaccompanied, we got Andy to do "Moon River" for us.

At the end of the trip, we had to climb up from the river to the rim of the canyon. It was a seven-mile hike and the temperature was 119 degrees, but I was raring to go, eager for the exercise after days in the raft. During the trip, I had especially enjoyed Art Buchwald, a man who had turned a childhood of physical limitations and desperate poverty into an adulthood as a charming raconteur through the power of his sharp but endearing wit. But Art was having none of the hike. He later wrote: "Bobby chose to climb up the seven miles, as did the Kennedy children, and when Ethel, mother of ten, said she would climb out too, the other members of the party were too embarrassed to say they would rather go by helicopter. Fearful that they would cancel the helicopter, I stopped breathing when Bobby and Jim Whittaker came up to me to see if they could persuade me to change my mind.

'Why don't you want to climb the mountain?' Bobby asked.

I just smiled weakly and replied, 'Because it's there.'"

■

I have to admit it was a hell of a lot of fun hobnobbing with folks like these, not to mention good for the ego of a scrawny kid from West Seattle. I remember one particularly shining moment when John Glenn, the first American to orbit the earth, stood up and proposed a toast:

"To Jim Whittaker," he said, "the first American to summit Everest. And a chimp didn't do it before him!" I was breathing rarified air of an entirely different sort than what I was used to.

But whenever I needed to be brought back down to earth, nothing did it more abruptly than dinner on any given night at Hickory Hill. It always seemed to me that the main course at dinner was political discourse. These were non-stop, free-flowing debates on history and current affairs, in which the children participated as avidly—and often as competently—as whichever network news broadcaster, head of state, or other luminary happened to be at the table.

All too often I felt I was in over my head. The Kennedy children already knew far more about national and world affairs than I did. The arguments and discussion would ebb and flow around me, and I often felt marooned. The children were expected to field questions from their parents—or, just as often, from Defense Secretary Robert McNamara or news anchor Tom Brokaw—and if one couldn't, it would be passed on to whomever was next. When that was me, I was often as not humbled to find I had little to add. I would joke and say, "Next question!" but inside I felt like a dumb hick, naïve and inadequate as hell. Like many Americans, I guess I hadn't really paid a lot of attention to what was going on in the world beyond the details of my own life. Now I did.

Those evenings around the Kennedy dinner table were the beginning of my political education. It wasn't long before my limited but growing political skills were put to the test.

■

It was the spring of 1968 and raining hard as Bobby and I rode through the center of Portland, Oregon, on a campaign swing during his run for the presidency. The sidewalks were lined with people who had come out to see him. We were in a convertible.

"Let's put the top down, Jim," Bobby said suddenly.

"Jeez, Bobby, it's pouring," I said.

"*They're* getting wet," he answered, pointing to the crowds.

Down the top went. Forty minutes later, the procession over and the top still down, we drove out of town. Soaking wet and utterly bedraggled, we picked at a chocolate cake an admirer had thrust into the car as we passed. Lunch. Bobby, drenched, gave me his trademark sheepish grin.

"Name something you have done," he challenged me, "that was more fun than this!"

Deciding to run for the presidency had been a painful process for Bobby. All through the winter of 1967 and early spring of 1968, arguments raged around the dinner table at Hickory Hill about the Vietnam War. Appalled at the violent social divisions the war was creating, Bobby had become convinced that the United States had to get out. But as only the junior senator from New York, he was virtually powerless to do anything about it. He knew that the decision-making authority lay in the Office of the President but, though there was no love lost between them, he felt it wrong to challenge Lyndon Johnson, a fellow Democrat. In any event, the election was less than a year away.

In February, Eugene McCarthy, the soft-spoken senator from Minnesota and peace candidate, defied the experts by defeating President Johnson in the New Hampshire primary. Bobby didn't think McCarthy could win the election even if he did get the party's nomination. At the end of March, Johnson stunned the nation by bowing out of the campaign entirely. The party was in turmoil. Vice President Hubert Humphrey was the favorite of old-line Democrats, but Bobby felt he was out of touch with the times. Then, on April 4, only a few days after Johnson's announcement, Martin Luther King, Jr., was shot and the nation was, once again, in shock. A pragmatist as well as an idealist, Bobby thought a Kennedy might have a better chance of reuniting the country, and so after weeks of agonizing, he finally made the decision to run.

I made a decision of my own. Even though I had no previous political experience, I would try to help Bobby climb this mountain by organizing the Washington State campaign. On Saturday, March 16, I stood in the Senate Caucus Room, where his brother had declared for the presidency only eight years before, as Senator Robert F. Kennedy announced his candidacy.

The night before, a great celebration had taken place at Hickory Hill. Although everyone knew it would be an uphill battle, there was a heady euphoria, a rising sense of hope. There was also anxiety. At one point I took him aside.

"Do you understand," I said, "that what you're doing is a hell of a lot more dangerous than climbing mountains?"

"Yes," he said quietly, "I know."

But there was no time to lose; we had a campaign to organize. The next afternoon, I flew back to Seattle. Waiting for me at the airport was Congressman Brock Adams. Check in hand, he made the first donation to the Washington State Kennedy for President campaign. We used the money to rent space for the campaign headquarters in an office between Fifth and Sixth Avenue on Union Street in Seattle, one block away from the original REI site. Volunteers poured in, and the place exploded with activity. I asked Dave Lester, an old friend with a political science degree, to run the office. He had witnessed the riots that had erupted in the nation's capital the summer before, after Martin Luther King Jr.'s assassination, and felt that Bobby was our best hope to pull the country back together again.

And that was the odd thing about Bobby: although he came from a privileged background, he appealed most to the have-nots in society. Even during the riots, he would wade into solidly black neighborhoods in major cities and just visit with folks, talking and listening. He was safe because they knew he was genuine. His record on fighting poverty and hunger in the South and his support of the civil rights movement spoke for him. Those he talked to, or who listened to what he had to say, believed him and told their friends. For the same reason, Bobby also began to gain support among young people, who had been expected to support Eugene McCarthy. With a speed that amazed me and shocked the so-called "experts," the campaign gained momentum.

I had my work cut out for me in the Washington State campaign. We opened additional offices in Tacoma and Spokane, raised money, printed issue papers, recruited volunteers, established phone lists, tried to woo older Democrats who favored Hubert Humphrey, got supporters elected to precinct committees, distributed buttons, posters, and other paraphernalia, and coordinated all this with national campaign headquarters.

Then one day Bobby's brother-in-law, Steven Smith, called and said, "Jim, we need help in Oregon. We'd like you to hit every town under five thousand population and get out their vote for Bobby." The campaign needed to win a primary in the Northwest.

I thought about being away from my family and my job managing REI and then recalled something Bobby had said: "This is a hard, hard road I am looking down. I don't know where it will lead. It will be a difficult effort. Not just for me, but for a whole lot of people, all kinds of people. Think what it will do to them. It will tear some of them apart. They have to make a choice, often a very painful choice. . . . " And so I made mine and headed for Oregon.

Using a chartered plane, I stumped for Bobby throughout rural Oregon and soon learned why the campaign staff had warned me, "In Oregon you're on another planet." In town after town, I would step into the local Grange Hall, where twenty or thirty people had assembled, introduce myself, give a short pitch for the senator, and ask for questions. The first one was always the same:

"Why is he trying to take our guns away?"

It was difficult to get to any other issue. Oregonians had little experience with, and seemed to have little understanding of, the kind of deep social and racial rifts that were tearing the country apart. I felt like a salmon swimming upstream when I tried to get them to grasp the issues on which Bobby was running. What's more, Oregon was a big union state, and the Teamsters—the union Bobby had taken on a few years earlier—was the largest union in the state. The mayor of Portland had also been indicted during those investigations (which could have explained why I always seemed to get stuck in traffic jams without police help whenever I was there). Finally, the competition was stiff; Senator McCarthy was spending a lot of time in the state. I felt Oregon slipping away.

While I was wrestling with Oregon and Washington, though, Bobby was focused on California. He knew he had to win the California primary. If he could win there, he stood a better chance of winning New York and capturing the Northeast. Though naturally shy, Bobby was a physical campaigner. He threw himself into the crowds and tried to reach as many people as possible. They responded with frightening enthusiasm.

Once in April and once again in May, I joined Rafer Johnson, the poised and graceful Olympic decathlon winner, and Rosey Grier, the 300-pound defensive lineman, who was one-quarter of the Los Angeles Rams' "fearsome foursome," to give Bobby support in California—in particular, physical support. The crowds terrified me. At rally after rally, the three of us literally had to battle to get Bobby to the speaking platform, then do it all over again to get him back to the car. Traffic would slow to a standstill as people tried to reach his convertible to touch him. There were crazies at the rallies too, waving vicious, often bizarre signs full of hate. In one crowd I saw a sign in a tree that said, "Bobby killed President Kennedy." I pointed it out to Rafer Johnson. He muscled through the crowd to the tree, jumped high, yanked it down, and tore it up.

In mid-May Ethel called: "Jim, he's getting more and more death threats, and I'm worried," she said.

With my campaign responsibilities in Washington and Oregon, not to mention my responsibilities to my family and job, I couldn't think of anything more I could do. I had to trust Rafer, Rosey, and Bobby's head of security, Bill Barry, to protect Bobby.

On the campaign trail in Portland, Oregon, 1968—Jim (second from left), Blanche, Bobby, and Ethel. Photo: Whittaker family collection

On June 4, the night of the California primary, I reserved the Presidential Suite in Seattle's Olympic Hotel for the Washington State delegates, our campaign workers, and supporters. I knew that if Bobby took California, it would really galvanize our campaign in the Northwest. I had four television sets and a loudspeaker system set up and arranged for Bobby to call us from the Ambassador Hotel in Los Angeles. We had wine and appetizers and awaited his call. It was close to eleven o'clock when the results came in. Kennedy had won. The room went wild.

The telephone rang, and it was Ethel. I shouted out my thanks and congratulations over the noise in our suite, and then she said, "Here's Bobby." Over the loudspeakers we'd set up, he thanked the delegates for being there and encouraged them to support his candidacy, and then he thanked the volunteers and all those who had supported him this far. Finally, he said, "Thanks, Jim, for helping to pull me up."

"Thanks, Bobby. We love you," I said.

He hung up and went down to the ballroom of the Ambassador Hotel to acknowledge his win and thank the people of California. I left our party and was driving home when I heard over the radio that Bobby had been shot.

I turned around and drove directly to the airport. The staff at United Airlines put me in the Red Carpet room, and then whisked me into a first-class seat on their next flight to Los Angeles. I took a cab to the hospital. The Kennedy staff had the police let me in.

In the early hours of the morning of June 5, doctors operated to remove the bullet fragments from Bobby's neck and skull, but they were not optimistic; Bobby had shown no brain activity from the moment he'd been admitted. He never really had a chance. Throughout the day, members of the family and friends arrived. We were all just numb. Alone with Ethel and Teddy in the hospital room that night, I held Bobby's hand and wept. At 1:44 A.M., as Ethel and I held him, he turned gray and cold. Ethel fainted. I gathered her up and, while Teddy held the door, carried her to a room they had reserved for her. I held her until she regained consciousness.

A day later, Bobby's coffin was loaded into a hearse to be taken to Air Force One, which President Johnson generously had dispatched for him, and we flew to New York. The funeral was held at St. Patrick's Cathedral, and Ethel asked me to be one of the eight pallbearers. As we stood by the coffin, thousands upon thousands of people filed slowly past, many sobbing uncontrollably. Outside, thousands more lined the street. During the service itself, at Ethel's request, Andy Williams sang "The Battle Hymn of the Republic." He sang it without accompaniment, his gentle, clear voice rising up through the still air. Gradually, others in the cathedral began singing too, filling the church with the song. Then the people out in the streets began singing as well.

Normally, the train trip from New York to Washington, D.C., takes four hours. But thousands of people crowded along the tracks all the way through New Jersey, Pennsylvania, Delaware, and Maryland, and the trip took eight hours. (Tragically, two people died under the wheels of an express coming the other way.) As the train passed, people held hand-lettered signs: "RFK We Love You," "God Bless You Bobby," "Robert, John, Martin," "Bobby, You Were Our Hope." And all along the way, people sang the "Battle Hymn."

On board, Ethel and Rose Kennedy, Bobby's mother, kept passing through the twenty-one cars, being gracious hostesses and encouraging us to wave back at the people lining the tracks. "Come on now," Rose would say, "these people have been standing for hours and we must show them our appreciation." It was an astonishing demonstration of strength and courage.

I wasn't that strong. I cried for Bobby. I cried for Ethel and the children, especially for the unborn baby Ethel was carrying, who would never know him. She had lost a wonderful husband. The children had lost a wonderful father. And the world had lost a leader who possessed the courage, sensitivity, and ability to improve life on the planet.

Bobby was to be buried next to his brother at Arlington Cemetery, just across the Potomac River from the capital. By the time we got there, it was ten at night, pitch black except for candles held by the crowd. We moved slowly, carrying the coffin through a sea of people. I was toward the rear of the coffin on the right-hand side. Steve Smith was in front. As we worked our way up the grassy slope, we were blinded by television camera lights, and it was impossible to see where the grave site was located.

"Can anybody see where the hell we're going?" Steve asked softly.

"No!" several of us whispered back.

We moved a bit farther, and Steve turned his head sideways again: "Bobby is up there right now saying, 'What a bunch of assholes; you guys can't even find the path to where you are supposed to bury me!'"

Pallbearers carry the coffin of Senator Robert F. Kennedy, St. Patrick's Cathedral, New York—(left to right) Dave Hackett, Steve Smith, Robert McNamara, Lord Harlech, Lem Billings, John Glenn, Jim Whittaker, Averell Harriman. Photo: Whittaker family collection

That did it. I almost strangled trying to stifle my laughter, and I could hear the others struggling too. The weight of Bobby's coffin was nothing compared to the weight of grief we had all been carrying, and now, if only for a moment, it lifted a bit. We found the grave and said goodbye to our hero and champion. He had always brought out the best in all of us—even now, at the very last.

The following months were incredibly difficult. I kept going over and over the scene in the kitchen of the Ambassador Hotel. What if I had been there? Could I have done anything? Could I have prevented it? I couldn't get over the simple, stupid way he was killed. I couldn't shake the sense of loss, of waste, of the possibilities that were so easily, suddenly, pointlessly erased.

I also ached for Ethel and the children. Every few weeks I flew back to Hickory Hill for a long weekend to do what I could. We all did, all of Bobby and Ethel's friends. But trying to fill even a little bit of the cavernous void that Bobby left behind seemed impossible.

Sometimes it was downright comical. Ethel's baby was due two months after Bobby's death. We were all nervous about the delivery, wanting to make sure nothing would go awry. Rafer and I were at Hickory Hill one day close to the due date. We had just finished a set of tennis when one of the children ran to the court:

"Mummy wants to see both of you right away!"

We sprinted to the house and found Ethel in the midst of labor pains.

Rafer and I panicked. We half-walked, half-carried her down the steps to her convertible and hurriedly stuffed her into the back seat. Rafer jumped in with her. I jumped into the front seat and took command of the wheel, fumbling around with the keys trying to start the damned car.

"What's the matter? Don't they drive cars out there in Seattle? Hurry up! HURRY UP!" Ethel commanded.

I finally got the car started, and we roared out the gate and onto the highway in what I hoped was the direction of Georgetown Hospital. Ethel was not comfortable and was letting us know it in no uncertain terms as we tore through Georgetown, a charming Washington neighborhood of eighteenth-century townhouses and not-so-charming narrow, one-way streets. I had no idea how to get through the maze. The closer we got to the hospital, the worse Ethel's labor pains grew and the more confused her directions were from the back seat. At last I found the emergency entrance of the hospital. Rafer and I jumped out and got Ethel inside. Nurses and orderlies rushed up and took her away. I was a wreck; Rafer was sweating like he had just won another decathlon.

In a few hours we were on our way back to Hickory Hill—all three of us. It had been a false alarm. Two weeks later, Rory—Ethel and Bobby's fourth daughter and eleventh child—was born.

Luckily for both of them, neither Rafer nor I were in town at the time.

Chapter Eight

ROLLER COASTER

The decade of the 1960s was for me, as it was for America as a whole, both the best of times and the worst of times.

As the decade began, business at The Co-op was booming, and although I was putting in an awful lot of hours, the work was deeply rewarding. I had two young sons I adored and who roughhoused the way Louie and I had when we were kids. Blanche and I had moved from our house on Mercer Island to a little beach cottage on the west shore of Lake Sammamish, east of Seattle and closer to the Cascades, and I set to work renovating it.

I wanted to give the cottage stronger footings and, at the same time, create a daylight basement that would give us more room. It's just my nature that when an idea for a project occurs to me, the fact that I've never done it before doesn't seem to hold me back. Consequently, I just started digging. I hauled wheelbarrow after wheelbarrow of dirt out from under the house, removing what seemed to me to be a random array of unnecessary supports while I was at it. Tom Tokareff, the head of the ski school where I taught on weekends, was a builder, and he was going to pour concrete footings for the new basement. The day he came by to check out the job, he took one look at my handiwork and yelled:

"Jesus, Jim! Get some braces up; the only thing holding this house up is the fireplace!"

Jim with Lloyd Anderson at the 11th Avenue REI store, about 1964.
Photo: Frank Denman

The house survived, and we thrived. Carl became an excellent swimmer and swam competitively in grade school. Both boys were skiing by the time they were four. Louie and Pat moved to a cottage a couple of doors down, and our older brother Barney lived close by too. I kept working on the house in my spare time. Life was good.

If I'd been a little more introspective in those days, I might have seen that my home improvement efforts were a kind of metaphor: perhaps I was trying to build stronger footings for my life—as a businessman, as a provider, as a father, and as a husband.

I've always loved both the mountains and the sea, and even though we had our cottage on the lake near the Cascades, one day in 1961 I found myself flying with Barney in a seaplane to the San Juan Islands, an hour or so north of Seattle. We landed at a sheltered bay on tiny, and practically deserted, John's Island. We had come to look at waterfront property, and we both fell in love with the place the moment we stepped off the plane's floats onto the pebble beach. I bought the very piece of land we were standing on, and Barney bought the parcel next door.

In time, Barney and I each built weekend cottages on the island. Blanche especially loved our John's Island home, and she and the boys spent summers there. I'd work in Seattle during the week and commute to John's on the weekends. On the outside, at least, we seemed to have everything.

On the inside, however, it was different. Blanche and I were not getting along. There had been tiny signs that something was not quite right between us as early as my army days in Colorado—a sense that we actually shared fewer things in common than perhaps we had thought. With my usual "cockeyed optimist" approach to life, though, I just concluded that we needed more time to get to know each other better—after all, my being away most of the week with a bunch of soldiers didn't give us much time together. After we returned to Seattle, and even as we became a family, those differences grew. I was certain, however, that the key was to try harder. What I didn't grasp then was that a good marriage takes more than determination; I would have to work to get to know and understand Blanche better, and she would have to work to get to know me too. Gradually, however, it became clear that that was hard for both of us to do.

I had come from what I was beginning to realize had been a remarkably

happy-go-lucky family. Blanche hadn't been so lucky. She'd had a more difficult childhood, and I realize now that she carried the fears and anxieties of that
childhood around on her back like a heavy knapsack. But I was so busy and so
full of hopes for us, I confess I hardly even noticed the weight she must have
been carrying.

In a sense, we were the classic 1950s all-American family. I was away from
home far too many hours running The Co-op and earning money with weekend work too, and Blanche was a homemaker raising our sons. But by now it
was the 1960s, and that formula wasn't working as well any more. In a strange
sense, the more active and busy my life was, the more passive and sedentary
Blanche became. We argued constantly, about almost everything—the children,
our increasingly different friends, how to spend our time.

The 1963 Everest expedition was, as I think back, probably a relief for both
of us. I was away in the Himalaya for more than four months, and it gave both
of us plenty of time to think. The longer I was away, the more I missed our
family and the more convinced I became that I could make things work between us. After all, I thought, if I could climb Everest, I could certainly make
our marriage work. I came back determined to do it.

I didn't anticipate the glare of public attention that came along as part of
the package of being the "First American on Everest"—I don't know how anyone could. Blanche seemed to handle it well. There were parades and parties,
awards and honors, and she was right there with me.

There were also tangible financial rewards. It certainly didn't hurt my position at The Co-op, now called REI, that the manager was the first American to
summit Everest, and business continued to grow. Even more important to my
family's financial health, I got my first big product endorsement opportunity.

In the 1950s an Italian climber named Vitale Bramani concluded that a considerable number of mountaineering accidents were caused by the Tricouni
nails on the soles of the boots that climbers wore. While good on snow, ice,
and mud, they were like wearing ball bearings on a smooth slab of rock. They
also conducted cold through the sole to the foot, increasing the incidence of
frostbite.

Bramani developed a hard rubber sole, lugged to prevent slipping, that
provided excellent friction and wore almost like iron. It also acted as an insu-
lator between the snow and ice and the boot. Combining the first few letters of

his first and last names, he named the product "Vibram," and it quickly became *the* mountaineering boot sole, replacing Tricouni nails in no time. Our co-op imported this sole from Vibram Italy in the early 1950s, and in 1954, most of the Mountain and Cold Weather Command wore combat boots with Vibram soles too. In 1963 I had stood on the highest point on earth in Vibram soles. And that was what a fellow named Ed Varnum wanted to talk to me about when he called a year or two after I climbed Everest.

Ed was the president of the Quabaug Rubber Company in North Brookfield, Massachusetts, a company that manufactured rubber soles for street shoes and leisure wear. Ed had just negotiated a contract with Vibram Italy to be the exclusive manufacturer and distributor of Vibram soles in the United States, and he wanted the use of my name and photograph to promote Vibram soles because I'd worn them to the top of Everest. In return, he offered me $200 a year plus 1 percent of the income from every pair of soles they sold. I agreed, and promptly fell into a pot of gold.

I was paid $800 the first year, $2,000 the next, and then sales just took off. Pretty soon the Vibram sole—also called the "waffle stomper" because of the patented pattern of its rubber lugs—was not only on the bottom of the best hiking and climbing boots but on leisure shoes as well. It caught on with college students cultivating a rugged image. To keep up with demand, Quabaug Rubber ran three shifts a day. As sales soared, my endorsement checks did the same. In time, my annual earnings from Quabaug exceeded my yearly salary as president and CEO of REI. The Whittakers were doing very well indeed—at least financially.

For a while, married life improved. But after Bobby Kennedy and I became friends, our lives shifted into a sort of social high gear. When I took time off from work, which was rare, we often spent it with Bobby, Ethel, their kids, and a dizzying array of celebrities—who seemed to think we were celebrities too. These were heady times: parties at Hickory Hill, skiing at Sun Valley, rafting the Colorado River, and of course, working on Bobby's presidential campaign. But they were also hard on Blanche, and most of the difficulties were my fault.

If I'd been able to stand outside our marriage and look at it from a distance, perhaps I could have seen the obvious: the more I grew and the more my life expanded after Everest, the more Blanche seemed to retreat. I suspect life in the company of the Kennedys was especially difficult for her, although I

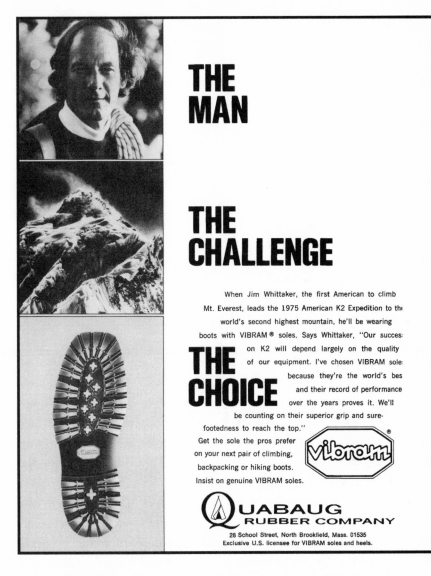

An advertisement for Vibram soles, 1975. Photo: Quabaug Rubber Company

didn't realize it at the time—in part because I was having so much fun myself. I don't think the problem necessarily was the glamour of being with that crowd as much as it was the competitiveness of all the Kennedys. The Kennedy women were an especially formidable bunch—active in a wide range of sports, quick-witted and articulate, ready to take on anything and anyone.

145

Blanche just wasn't made that way, and although she accompanied me on most of these activities, she was more and more the outsider, watching—and critiquing—from the sidelines. In a sense, between my newfound fame as a mountaineer and all the space the hyperactive Kennedys took up, there wasn't much room left over. Blanche, who had always been somewhat circumspect, withdrew further and further. We knew we had problems, and even though it was uncommon then, we sought the help of a counselor. But it didn't help much.

On August 8, 1967, Blanche and I had our third son, Bobby—named, of course, after Bobby Kennedy. It should have been a new beginning for us, but it was really the beginning of the end. Within a few years, with three growing boys, the house on Lake Sammamish had gotten crowded, and Blanche wanted to move. She particularly wanted to move back into Seattle where there would be more neighbors and she would be "closer to civilization," as she put it. I wasn't thrilled about moving away from the lake, but I could understand Blanche's point—we were somewhat isolated. Still reeling from Bobby Kennedy's assassination and its aftermath, and desperate to find a way to make Blanche happy, I agreed. In 1970, we bought an enormous old house in the Capitol Hill neighborhood, in the heart of the city.

I should have known better. The house had three floors, eight bedrooms, five bathrooms, a ballroom, and an aviary, of all things. For a while, I dreamed of creating a little piece of the natural world in the glassed-in aviary by bringing in tropical plants and colorful birds, but I never got around to it: I was too busy fixing things. Built in 1913, the house had old plumbing and wiring and constantly needed maintenance.

During the preceding few years, while I had been busy forming new friendships through REI and through Bobby Kennedy's presidential campaign, Blanche had been finding comfort in an entirely different group of friends. Somewhere along the way, she had become a "born-again Christian" and something of a spiritualist. It wasn't long before the house, which was way too big for the five of us, filled up with an assortment of her itinerant born-again friends.

I would come home from work for dinner and find—in addition to my family—a dozen or so strangers seated in our huge dining room saying a prayer for the mountains of food they were about to consume. Often as not, the doorbell would ring during dinner and there would be someone new, saying, "Is this the Whittaker house? God sent me." They would all stay up late at night, "speaking in tongues" and "laying on hands." I'd go upstairs and try to get some rest . . . and peace, only to be awakened at two in the morning by the sound of chanting voices.

It was ghastly. Bobby was just approaching four at the time, but Carl and Scott, sixteen and fourteen, respectively, were as bewildered as I was. I gradually realized both of them were smoking marijuana, and while it was part of the culture of the time, it may also have been their way of responding to the bizarre phantasmagoria their home had become. Carl in particular was staying away from home later and later each night. Things were spinning out of control, and I could neither ignore nor endure it any more.

One night in September of 1970, lying in bed listening to the chanting downstairs, I decided I'd had enough. Early the next morning I rousted everyone out of bed—the faithful typically slept until noon—and had them gather in the living room.

"I had a vision last night," I told them, "and it was of me throwing every one of you out of this house! Is that clear to all of you? Everybody out by five o'clock!"

"Peace be with you," they chorused with their usual glazed smiles. And then, as if they were being sent off on a holy pilgrimage instead of into the cold, cruel world where there were no more free lunches, dinners, or beds, they mumbled "Amen" and "Hallelujah" and began drifting out of the room.

I was sitting in the study when Blanche roared in.

"You can't do this!"

"Oh yes, I can," I said firmly.

"Then I'm going with them," she countered.

"That's fine with me," I replied.

And that was the effective end of our marriage.

Blanche phoned a week later from Los Angeles, and I told her that I was filing for divorce and that if she wanted to see her children afterward she'd better return to Seattle. She did—without her entourage.

I moved into an apartment, keeping an eye on the house lest Blanche's born-again band return, and began the long and painful process of divorce, irritated to find myself paying for both her lawyer and my own while they wrangled over the details. We were divorced in 1971. We sold the big house, and Blanche bought a house in Magnolia, another Seattle neighborhood, on a bluff overlooking the sound. She also got the John's Island property. The court gave her custody of Scott and Bobby; Carl stayed with me. The marriage was over, but I blame myself for not being able to hold it together.

It doesn't matter how crazy, destructive, or just plain miserable a marriage has become, the divorce itself is awful and hurts like hell. There's a period afterward when it feels like someone's lifted a 200-pound pack off your back and you're euphoric, but it's a bit like being a balloon: you float, but you're empty inside. I decided I didn't ever want to be married again.

I don't know which was harder on the kids, life before the divorce or after it. I didn't know much about drugs in those days, but I suspected from the glazed look in his eyes that Carl was in trouble. Scott seemed in better shape, and Bobby was too young to really understand what was going on.

Carl was a bright boy, and I decided that perhaps what he really needed was a challenging school where he would be surrounded by other bright kids and be taught by the best teachers. I enrolled him at Lakeside in North Seattle, one of the finest private high schools in the country. Within a week he was cleaning the school's shower with a toothbrush as a penalty for breaking the rules. I was at a loss. I talked with Ethel Kennedy about Carl, and she suggested that I consider sending him to Middlesex, a private boarding school in Massachusetts where Ethel's own son, David, was a student. Carl and David had become good friends, and Carl seemed interested in the idea. We flew east, checked out the school, Carl liked it, and we signed him up. I prayed that this new environment, free of the baggage he had to carry in Seattle, would be the answer.

It wasn't. He started out all right, but he broke a leg skiing in Vermont, and then his grades began to slip. The headmaster assured me that Carl was capable but needed to work a little harder. Ethel told me she was having the same problem with David. Then they were caught drinking beer on campus and were almost expelled. The next year, Carl and David were expelled—for using drugs on campus.

Carl came back to Seattle and tried other schools, but he fell in with a crowd that seemed to be more interested in taking hallucinogens than in taking the kind of outdoor physical risks that had been the testing ground of my own youth. I loved him deeply, but we didn't seem to be able to communicate, and I had run out of ideas. One day, assuring me he would be all right, Carl moved out of my apartment to make it on his own.

Meanwhile I got to visit Scott and Bobby on weekends and some week-nights. It was wrenchingly difficult to see the two boys for only a few hours and then have to return them to Magnolia Bluff and a world that I couldn't share. I missed them more than I had thought possible. Jesuit teachers have a saying, "If you give me your child until the age of seven, I will give you a Catholic for life." Scott was already fifteen years old, but Bobby was only five and, seeing him so little, I worried about what he was and was not learning. But it was beyond my control.

Scott held up well through this period and, in 1975, was accepted to Western Washington University in Bellingham and moved on campus. Meanwhile, in addition to alimony and child support, I had also been paying Blanche's way through four years of school at the University of Washington. In 1977 Blanche got a degree in sociology and abruptly moved to Hawaii. With Bobby. There was nothing I could do to stop her. In those days, the idea of true joint custody was still in the future; the law favored the mother over the father, and she took him away.

From then on I saw Bobby only when he had a vacation or holiday from school—he was a six-hour flight away, halfway across the Pacific. His visits were wonderful, but it was heartbreaking to have to hug him goodbye, trying not to cry, and watch him walk down the ramp onto the plane, alone.

I remember vividly standing on the beach in West Seattle one day and realizing that the water of Puget Sound at my feet connected with the Pacific and thus to a beach in Hawaii that Bobby could be standing on at that very minute. I squatted down, put my hand in the water, and wept for my son.

Later I learned that while swimming in Hawaii one day, Bobby had felt the same connection to me.

■

Throughout these years, both before and after Blanche and I divorced, I buried myself in work at REI, in part to avoid my unhappiness at home. Here, at least, my efforts bore fruit.

Not long after I returned from the Everest expedition in 1963, we finally closed the old second-floor walk-up store on Pike Street and moved into a wonderful old warehouse building on Capitol Hill. At last we had a street-level storefront. The interior of the warehouse perfectly suited REI's rugged image: high ceilings, massive old fir beams, concrete and brick walls, and a worn, creosote-hardened industrial wood floor. Compared to our original location, the new store was vast; even so, we soon needed the entire second floor of the building for our mail-order business.

We were growing very quickly. We set up our own testing department to ensure the reliability of the equipment we sold. We hired climber and engineer Carl Magnussen to run the department, and we tested everything, paying special attention to carabiners, slings, pitons, ropes, ascenders, and other climbing equipment. It was no exaggeration that our customers' lives depended on the quality of the gear we sold them.

We also advanced the retailing concept of "private label" goods—that is, we not only retailed things other people manufactured but we also manufactured some of our own products. For example, in the early days, I had relied on a now-famous, but then quite small, company called Eddie Bauer for our down clothing and sleeping bags. I had even used their products on Everest. When they decided to become direct retailers themselves, we decided to become manufacturers. Lloyd Anderson and I entered into an equal partnership with George Trager and John Hartsfield, whose Trager Manufacturing already produced gaiters, rucksacks, and backpacks that fit on our own aluminum pack frames. We formed a new company I called THAW (using the first letters of our last names) to produce our own down products. This not only gave us greater control over product quality but also eliminated a middleman, permitting us to capture more of the profit while still offering our customers a lower price than if we were buying from a wholesaler. THAW did very well, and eventually REI bought out Trager and Hartsfield, making both of them a lot of money in the process.

By 1965, the year I led Bobby up to the summit of Mount Kennedy, REI had its first million-dollar year; sales reached $1.3 million, and we had fifty thousand members. Between 1965 and 1968 our sales more than tripled, reaching $4 million, and membership doubled, to more than one hundred thousand. By 1970, when Blanche and I separated, REI's sales had reached $7.5 million. On New Year's Day, 1971, I became president and chief executive officer of REI (Lloyd had retired), and by the end of that year our sales had leaped to $10 million, and we had a quarter of a million members.

It was at this point that I began wondering about the cost of our success to the very thing we loved the best: the outdoors. More and more people were heeding John Muir's advice to "climb the mountains and enjoy their good tidings," but I could see from my own hikes in the Cascades and Olympics that we were loving nature to death. Trails were becoming badly overused and worn, accelerating erosion, and trash was collecting in some of the most pristine places in America. I resolved that if REI professed to love the wilderness and encouraged others to do the same, then we'd better be willing to get involved in caring for the wilderness.

Our board members agreed. Soon we were promoting the message, "If you pack it in, pack it out," through our catalogue and donating money to fledgling environmental and conservation groups. I began testifying at wilderness hearings in both Washington State and Washington, D.C. We also committed to undertaking environmental clean-up missions of our own. We started close to home.

Pratt Lake is a classic alpine lake, crystal clear and cold and surrounded by jagged peaks, in the Cascades not far from Snoqualmie Pass, an hour or so east of Seattle. Its proximity to the city was its biggest problem; mistreated for years by steadily increasing numbers of indifferent or ignorant hikers, backpackers, and hunters, the trails and lakeside had become littered with trash, and bullet-ridden beer cans were scattered all over the lake bottom. One July day, REI organized a bus convoy carrying 120 volunteers to the Pratt Lake trailhead. Our crew included both Seattle Mayor Wes Uhlman and the son of Washington Governor Dan Evans, a backpacker and outdoorsman himself. We carried empty backpacks and bags and spent the day patrolling the entire area up to and around the lake. I was a scuba diver and led a team of divers into the lake to scour the bottom as well.

At day's end, Pratt Lake was as clean, and nearly as pristine, as it had been a century earlier, and our volunteers struggled back down the trail with nearly a ton of trash. Photos in the papers the next day showing the mayor hauling out litter publicized our cause and also helped establish REI's reputation as a company committed to environmental protection, a commitment it maintains today through dozens of special programs. We became a company that "does well by doing good," and our business continued to grow robustly.

We also strove to "do good" for our customers. We'd always been committed to fair prices and knowledgeable service, and of course, we paid our members annual dividends as well. But it was our semiannual sales that got the really big publicity.

Inventory is not like wine; it does not get better as it gets older. Even with sporting goods, each new season brings new designs and styles and last year's goods lose some of their luster. What's more, excess inventory is, in effect, money that's sitting on a shelf in a warehouse not earning anything. The sooner you get rid of excess inventory, even if you make no profit on it, the sooner you can use that money again on something from which you can earn a profit.

Even with the best planners and merchandisers on your staff, you cannot predict perfectly what customers will buy or, for that matter, what will happen with the weather, which determines so much of what people do outdoors in the Northwest. Excess inventory is inevitable. To clear it out, we started to hold twice-yearly clearance sales that offered incredibly deep discounts. We also took this opportunity to replace our rental equipment with new goods by selling off the previous year's now-used equipment—ski equipment in the spring, hiking and climbing equipment in the fall—at a fraction of their real value. I don't think I fully realized the impact this sale concept would have on our members until, the night before one of our first big sales, I closed up shop, locked the doors, and turned around to find a line of tents set up along the sidewalk all the way to the end of the block and around the corner. People were actually camping there for the night to be the first to get in the doors the next morning!

When I got to work the next day, the tents were packed up and the line went on forever. A local reporter interviewed one of the customers:

"How long have you been waiting to get in?" he asked.

"All night!" the customer said with a grin—as if it were a badge of honor.

"So where are you from?" the reporter asked.

"Utah," the young man replied.

"No," the reporter said, "I mean now. Where do you live *now*?"

"Utah!" the customer said again.

The reporter was amazed. I knew that more and more of our members were from outside the Northwest, but it hadn't occurred to me that we had become a sort-of destination for people—a reason for leaving home and traveling to Seattle. It was just incredible.

When I finally opened the door, mayhem ensued; I had to jump out of the way as bargain-crazed outdoor enthusiasts dashed into the store, racing around like kids in a candy shop. It was crazy, but understandable: our customers got gear they wanted at a great price, and we got rid of gear we didn't want and made money in the bargain. And the business just kept growing. Thirty years later, REI is still holding its clearance sales; the only difference is that the line of tents the night before is much longer.

Of course, all this growth was not without its complications. In 1955 I was the company's sole employee; now I was CEO and we employed a couple of hundred people. I worked hard, however, to make sure all our employees understood the unique nature of the company they worked for and were committed to the kind of personal attention I'd emphasized from the beginning. In that sense, at least, we were still that second-floor walk-up where you could be part of a community of like-minded people, not just a customer.

As our membership grew, our board of directors grew too. In the early days, management and board meetings usually consisted of an afternoon or evening at a restaurant talking business and climbing in roughly equal proportions. But as REI grew, that easy informality disappeared. In a co-op, the members—that is, the customers—are the owners, and they elect the board from among their own membership. Sometimes these new board members had neither climbing nor skiing experience. More troubling to me, sometimes they had little or no business experience either and yet felt compelled to examine every decision management made.

As the 1970s began and the company continued its rapid growth, we had a steady stream of new board members, and I ended up having to spend more and more of my time educating and preparing reports for them—which meant less and less time with my employees and customers, where the real business of the company got done.

I suppose it's the classic entrepreneur's trap: you help create a business founded on something you love, and when it succeeds, you end up doing things you don't love. The more paperwork I did, the more obvious it became to me that about the last thing in the world I was suited for was a desk job.

But the fact is, I was too busy with another matter to worry about this nagging little problem.

Sailing on Puget Sound aboard the first Impossible, *1975—(left to right) Dianne, Bobby, Jim, C.B. Whittaker. Photo: David Alan Harvey/National Geographic Society*

Chapter Nine

NEW HEIGHTS

It was love at first sight.

I had arrived in Calgary, Alberta, late in the day for a summer 1972 meeting of the U.S. National Parks Advisory Board, to which I had been appointed five years earlier. It was an honorary position, meaning unpaid, but the honor was all mine. I served with Lady Bird Johnson, who chaired the board (I was vice chair), and among others, astronaut Wally Shirra, architect Nat Owings, wildlife biologist Sigurd Olsen, wolf expert Durwood Allen, and Marian Ochs Heiskell from the *New York Times*. Calgary, the home of the Western Regional Headquarters of Parks Canada, was to be the first stop on a trip to study how the Canadians handled private land "inholdings" in their western national parks. The former First Lady could not attend the Calgary meeting, so I was to stand in for her as chair.

When I walked into the meeting room at the Calgary Inn that evening, dinner was over and a few people were still milling around talking. Across the room, Nat and Durwood were having an animated conversation with someone who, from the back at least, appeared to be a very beautiful woman. She had lustrous auburn hair that fell nearly to her waist and shone in the soft light of the dining room. She wore a smoky blue, open-backed dress that revealed a trim, athletic figure. Nat and Durwood were mesmerized. As I walked toward them, the woman turned to face me, and I saw why.

She was simply stunning. About five-foot seven, with a lovely rounded face that positively radiated energy, intelligence, and good humor, Dianne

Roberts flashed me a dazzling smile as she introduced herself as executive assistant to the regional director of Parks Canada. She had organized our trip and would be our guide. My interest in the national parks of western Canada skyrocketed.

The next morning we boarded an air-conditioned bus to visit Banff National Park, about an hour's drive west of Calgary, and then drove northwest to Jasper National Park along the 180-mile Banff–Jasper highway—arguably the most spectacular stretch of mountain highway in the West. The sky was cloudless and the view magnificent as we sped along chatting and enjoying the jagged snow-covered peaks of the Canadian Rockies. I had warned Parks Canada that our group contained a few people who would appreciate breaks along the way, but by midmorning, high in the mountains with not a café to be seen, it didn't look like it would happen. Then in the middle of nowhere, the bus slowed and pulled over to a wayside viewpoint. There beside an emerald lake was a table covered in white linen and arrayed with silver urns of hot coffee and tea, pitchers of cream, sugar, delicate cookies, china cups and saucers, silverware, and cloth napkins. Sipping coffee with the board members, the majesty of the Rockies encircling us, I glanced over at Dianne and thought to myself, "This woman has a lot more going for her than just looks."

That evening, in Jasper National Park, we had a grand outdoor barbecue. I learned that Dianne was twenty-four years old, single, and had skipped grades in school and graduated in only three years from the University of Calgary with a degree in English and psychology. Strong-minded and independent, she had hitchhiked across Europe alone and had a passion for photography.

That night I took stock of myself and immediately wished I were younger. I had just turned forty-four. I had three sons: Carl, seventeen; Scott, fifteen; and Bobby, five. Carl was living with me. I had been divorced for a year and had sworn never to get married again. And yet here I was, head over heels in love with a woman I'd just met. It would have helped if I had known that Dianne, at that same moment, was feeling the same way. Years later she would tell me that after only a few hours together, she had vowed to herself, "I am either going to marry this guy or have one hell of an affair."

The next day we boarded a Canadian Pacific train bound for Vancouver, British Columbia. I had forgotten how pleasant it was to travel by rail—and how romantic. I thought of the Twentieth Century Limited, the Orient Express.

Members of the National Parks Advisory Board—(left to right) Peter Green,
Durward Allen, Marian Heiskell, Jim. Photo: Loretta DeLozier

Our group relaxed in the club car, having drinks, waiting for dinner. Later we
listened to the clickity-clack of the rails as moonlight washed over the landscape beyond the windows. I sat with Dianne as we crossed Canada, heading
for the coast.

Over the next few days our group toured Fort Langley National Historic
Park in Vancouver; took a ferry to Victoria, on Vancouver Island; chartered a
boat to Trial Island, a battered, windswept rock outside Victoria Harbor with
one of British Columbia's stately manned lighthouses; watched rainbows, dolphins, and Orca whales; then flew the length of Vancouver Island, admiring
the wild coast but being dismayed by how much of the virgin forests had been
clear-cut. Returning to Victoria, the board spent its final evening at the elegant,
old-world Empress Hotel on Victoria Harbor.

The next morning we went our separate ways, but I missed Dianne even
before I crossed the Canadian border. By the time I got to Seattle, I was really
in trouble. Trying to intellectualize the whole thing, I made a list of the pros
and cons—not least of which was the question of whether it was possible to
build a lasting relationship with someone almost two decades younger.

In the months that followed, it came to be rumored that I bought a florist shop and a telephone company just staying in touch with her. (At one point, Dianne's boss walked into her flower-packed office and asked, "Who died?") That fall we got together in Vancouver and sailed around English Bay. In the winter we skied at Sun Valley. I told her I couldn't give her gold and silver, but I promised that life with me would never be boring. That seemed to do the trick; we were engaged by the following spring.

Gradually, I met her friends, and she met mine. One of mine, REI board member Sid Volinn, married to the irrepressible Dr. Ilsa Volinn, warned me one day, in his heavily accented English and with a twinkle in his eye, "Jeem, life viss zeeze independent vimmen iss not all roses." Maybe, but it was clear to me that an independent woman was what I had longed for all along.

On June 9, 1973, a year after we met, Dianne and I were married on the deck of my new West Seattle home overlooking Puget Sound and the Olympic Mountains. Naturally—for Dianne, at least—she kept her last name. This was fine with me, but it wasn't fine with the U.S. Immigration Service. They closed their office and huddled with five lawyers one afternoon to determine whether they could issue a "green card" in the name Roberts to someone whose husband was named Whittaker. It seems comical today, but in 1973 it took the intervention of Washington State Senator Brock Adams to get them to revise their rules.

We were typical euphoric newlyweds. Hand in hand, we took long walks in Lincoln Park, near our house, and out to Alki Point, with its view across Elliott Bay toward the lights of the city. Perhaps not so typically, when my friend and Everest summit-mate, Nawang Gombu, visited from Nepal with his wife, we all climbed Mount Rainier together. Dianne took to serious climbing immediately. (In fact, she climbed Mount Rainier four times.) I was impressed by her physical strength as well as her determination and drive. Consequently, when at a meeting of the American Alpine Club, my friend, Seattle attorney and mountaineer Jim Wickwire, asked if I would be interested in organizing and leading an expedition to climb K2, I accepted—for both of us.

◼

K2, at 28,250 feet, is the second-highest mountain in the world. It straddles the border between China and far northern Pakistan in the Karakoram Range of the Himalaya, a rugged, inhospitable piece of geography Pakistan and India had battled over ever since Pakistan had become an independent state. The Balti people who live in this remote region, called Baltistan, have names for many of the 20,000-foot-plus peaks in this region, but K2 is so remote, and has been seen by so few human beings, that when they call it anything, they call it only Chogori, "the big one." Like "Peak XV," the world's highest mountain, later called Everest, the world's second-highest mountain was discovered by a British survey team in the mid-1800s and identified simply as "K2"—the "K" for Karakoram, the "2" because it was the second peak surveyed. Unlike Everest, it never got another name. K2 it was then, and K2 it is today, and somehow this arcane, almost mysterious name suits it. So does another, informal name given it by earlier climbers: "Savage Mountain."

It is more difficult technically to climb than Everest, and by 1973 only one expedition had succeeded in reaching K2's summit, although six men had lost their lives over the years trying. An Italian expedition led by Ardito Desio put two climbers, Achille Compagnoni and Lino Lacedelli, on the summit in 1953, but one of their expedition members died during the attempt. Over the years, beginning in 1938, four American teams had tried to reach the summit, but none had succeeded. During a 1953 attempt, my old friend and Mount McKinley ropemate, Pete Schoening, had performed one of the greatest saves in mountaineering history. Pete was descending the mountain, roped to a stretcher holding an injured team member. He was anchoring the stretcher with an ice ax belay, when the other two pairs of climbers fell and became tangled with the stretcher. In a massive display of skill, strength, and determination, Pete held his belay and saved the whole party.

As I thought about the expedition Wickwire proposed, I hoped we wouldn't have to resort to such heroics. It had been a decade since I had climbed Everest, and I was, at forty-six years old, getting a bit "long in the tooth" by conventional standards for Himalaya climbs. But I knew I was still in top physical condition, and so Dianne, Wick, and I began the long process of organizing the expedition.

Because of political turmoil and soured relations with the West, Pakistan had been closed to climbers for fifteen years. But a warming of relations, and the help of my friend Ted Kennedy, who had opened a dialogue with Pakistani Prime Minister Zulfikar Ali Bhutto, helped us obtain a permit for the spring of 1975. Then Wick and I began putting together our team.

The first person I invited was my brother Louie. I was still disappointed by his decision to abandon the 1963 Everest expedition, but he was also my most trusted climbing partner, and I wanted him to have a chance to summit a Himalaya giant. As the head of Rainier Mountaineering, Inc., Louie had led more than 120 ascents of Mount Rainier and was in excellent physical condition. What's more, with his children now nearly grown and his business well established, I knew that this time he could afford to join us.

Wickwire, our deputy leader, had summited Mount Rainier dozens of times himself and was a skilled mountaineer. Two climbing friends of his, Fred Dunham and Fred Stanley, also joined us—and would henceforth be known simply as "the Freds." Rob Schaller, a seasoned climber and pediatric surgeon, would serve as our team doctor. Leif Patterson, an even-tempered Norwegian immigrant and mathematics instructor in British Columbia who had extensive climbing experience in Peru and Alaska, also accepted our invitation, as did Galen Rowell, an expert rock climber. Finally, Wick's friend and climbing partner Steve Marts, a filmmaker, also signed on. Ten of us in all—a small but, we thought, capable group, though few had experience above 20,000 feet.

Meanwhile Dianne and I focused our attention on securing sponsors and funding and ordering clothing, equipment, food, medical supplies, radios, oxygen bottles—everything we'd need to sustain our team and a few high-altitude porters for at least three months in remote and hostile conditions.

In January 1975 we held a shakedown climb on Mount Rainier. The weather was perfect—which is to say that winds up to sixty miles per hour ripped through our camp, tore at our tents, and plastered us with snow. Despite the conditions, or maybe because of them, I came away feeling confident that we had a solid team.

In the next few weeks, Dianne, Wick, and I (along with various children) sorted and packed the expedition's gear and supplies—ten tons of it—into 50-pound porter loads. We then had it loaded onto an American President Line freighter bound for Karachi, Pakistan, where we would collect it at the beginning of the expedition.

At fifteen minutes past midnight, on April 16, 1975, our plane lifted off from Seattle, with Copenhagen as our first stop. In the air over Iceland, thinking about our team's departure, I wrote in my diary, "The hardest part of any expedition is saying goodbye to family. Leaving loved ones for months, knowing you are going to a place that has a certain amount of danger, makes the parting concentrate into an ache in the heart and throat. But this time, how different from Everest: to have my wife, my love—and my brother—to enter that majestic arena."

We spent the next night in Copenhagen and then flew on to Karachi, arriving early on the morning of the eighteenth. Then after breakfast and formalities with U.S. officials there, we piled back into another plane for the short flight to Rawalpindi, where we were met by Manzoor Hussein, a twenty-five-year-old army lieutenant who was our government-assigned liaison officer. The next day we were to fly northeast from Rawalpindi to an airstrip at Skardu, a town on the Indus River, at the gates of the Karakoram. We checked into the Flashman Hotel in Rawalpindi for the night to await the next leg of our journey. It would be the first of many, increasingly uncomfortable, nights at the Flashman.

The next morning we learned that clouds at Skardu had postponed our flight. We were to receive the same news every day, day after day, for nearly a week and a half. Almost immediately, team members came down with the usual Third-World bugs, and the longer we stayed in Rawalpindi, the sicker we became. At one point or another, nearly everyone on the team spent time camped on the toilet or throwing up.

It's amazing how quickly morale can drop when people are frustrated and sick. It didn't help that several of our more recently married team members were getting calls from their wives begging them to come home. We really needed to get the expedition on the road.

Then out of the blue, after a few days in Rawalpindi, Louie took me aside and, in hushed, confidential tones, told me that he and Wickwire were concerned that it might jeopardize the expedition if Dianne were to try to go all the way to the summit. Frankly annoyed, I told Louie that Dianne was a team player and was along to take photographs for the *National Geographic,* one of our sponsors, and do whatever she could for the good of the expedition. Louie knew as well as I did that the mountain would decide who among us would reach the summit. Debating it down here in the heat and humidity of Rawalpindi was foolish—and corrosive. I couldn't tell whether Louie felt legitimately concerned or was just jealous that I had my wife along. Louie, I remembered, could be a pain in the ass.

Meanwhile, between dashes to the bathroom, we shopped the bazaars and took pictures. I went to the bank and withdrew $30,000 in rupees to pay the porters we would be hiring, stuffed them into a nondescript old red REI duffel bag, and walked back to the hotel, trying to look nonchalant.

Finally, on April 29, our C130 transport got off the ground. We flew past Nanga Parbat, 26,600 feet, and into the region loosely called Kashmir. The farther we flew, the more the mountains bunched together and reached skyward until finally, there it was: K2, towering above the rest. "It is a true monarch," I wrote in my journal, "and its symmetry is marvelous. It seems almost too perfectly proportioned, a pyramid in fine balance."

As with Everest in 1963, we had a long walk ahead of us to reach K2. Using the records of the earlier Italian and American expeditions, I had mapped out an approach that would put us at Base Camp with enough time, supplies, and energy left to have a good shot at climbing K2.

But first we needed to get all the rest of our supplies to Skardu. Once again, flights were being delayed by cloud cover. After several more frustrating days, on May 2 we loaded what gear we had onto tractor-drawn trailers and into jeeps and headed up the Shigar River valley to the village of Dasso, where the road ended, certain that the rest of our supplies would follow the next day. There we faced a new and daunting task.

We would need more than five hundred porters to carry supplies to Base Camp, more than one hundred miles away—porters to carry not only our food and gear but also to carry food for themselves, for we would soon put the last settlement behind us and be completely on our own.

There are no Sherpa in Pakistan, and no high-altitude villages where the people are already acclimatized, as there are in Nepal. In fact, because Pakistan had been closed to expeditions for the previous fifteen years, there were no experienced porters of any kind. That didn't mean we had a shortage of candidates, however. We had arranged for someone to scout out potential porters for us a month before our arrival, and now as we approached Dasso, it was clear this had been an effective strategy. There were hundreds of people waiting for us, far more than we could ever employ. They had come from as far away as sixty miles. And no wonder: in just a few weeks, our porters would earn more than a college graduate in Karachi could earn in a year.

As we pulled into Dasso, they clamored around us. Most wore long loose pants and tunics made of a tan homespun fabric, and nearly all wore the region's characteristic Gilgit hat, a knit cap with a rolled edge. None had any portering experience, although some argued that they had good credentials because their fathers or uncles had carried loads for the Italians in 1954. Slowly, since it was clear we couldn't hire them all, we picked the ones who seemed the most fit and had what Manzoor felt was the right attitude. Unable to converse either in Urdu, Pakistan's official language, or Balti, the local dialect, we left the screening up to him. Managing the porters was his job.

As it turned out, we didn't have to hurry. Weather problems continued to

Porters loading up at Dasso for the first day of the K2 approach march.
Photo: Dianne Roberts

delay the delivery of the last of our supplies to Skardu, and it wasn't until May 7 that they had all arrived, been sorted, and distributed to the porters in Dasso. During this new delay I tried to get a feeling for how our team members were handling the trip so far. The seasoned travelers among us seemed to thrive, inhaling the spices and flavors of this exotic land where women covered their faces and men prayed five times each day, facing Mecca. But some of the team were having trouble adjusting to the different customs, milling porters, strange food, and odd smells and sounds. What we needed was action.

Finally, on May 8—twenty days after we had arrived in Pakistan and way behind schedule—our expedition began the long, hot, dusty trek into the Karakoram. In addition to our expedition team, Manzoor, and various official hangers-on, we had 588 load-bearing porters. From a distance, as we plodded up into the valley of the Braldu River, the dust from more than a thousand shuffling feet looked like a long plume of smoke, as if the trail itself were burning. And in the nearly ninety-degree heat, some days that didn't seem like an illusion at all.

We were traveling through a high desert in the rain shadow of the Karakoram. It was a barren, rocky, nearly colorless landscape of neutral tans and grays. Apart from the occasional scrubby sage bush, vegetation was sparse; the only trees we encountered were cottonwoods growing in the irrigation ditches that surrounded the occasional stone-built village. On our first day out we made a remarkable fifteen miles, arriving in a place called Chokpo bushed and footsore.

As we would be almost every day, we were up at 5:30 A.M. the next morning and out as soon as possible to avoid the heat. The porters were amazed at the size and weight of the packs we carried, especially Dianne's, which weighed about 40 pounds—not including the cameras she was also carrying. We wanted to set an example for them. The sole exception was Galen Rowell, who refused to carry loads in order to take photographs. The cohesion of any expedition depends, in part, on each member feeling that all the other members are pulling their share of the weight. Many of the team members felt Galen was not, and there was plenty of grumbling.

We were making our approach march earlier in the year than most previous expeditions; it was barely spring. In the villages along the Braldu River, the ground was freshly tilled and the first crops were being planted. At slightly higher elevations, the soil was still being worked in preparation for planting. Above these terraced plots, snow still clung to the hillsides. And above that was a world of ice and snow.

Most of the time our route followed the raging, snowmelt-swollen river, often along high terraces deeply broken by gorges, called nullahs, cut by torrents racing down to the river from the slopes above. We spent a lot of time, and energy, climbing down into the nullahs, fording the streams, and climbing back out again on the other side. Just as often, however, the terraces disappeared as the valley narrowed and the river roared through narrow passes in the mountains. These deeper valleys were terrifying. We had to pick our way across steep, unstable slopes, sometimes on rickety wooden "balconies." Beneath us, the turbulent brown river roared and rumbled as it rolled boulders as big as cars downstream. Conversation was impossible, and a slip off the narrow trail meant disaster. The gorges were often impassable defiles, so we had to climb high over the steep ridges, descending again on the other side of the ridge crest. To make matters worse, from time to time the rocks balanced on the slopes above us just seemed to let go as we approached, and it took concentration to avoid being knocked into the river like so many bowling pins.

Still, the days went by without incident, and we arrived at the village of Askole, at 9,000 feet above sea level, some eighty miles from the base of K2 and the last settlement we would encounter. We set up tents and relaxed in the shade of the willows and cottonwoods as villagers came out to stare at us. Only men appeared, talking excitedly among themselves, pointing and gesticulating. As is typical in Muslim cultures, the women remained hidden, although we did see some at a distance, working in the fields. As usual, Dianne drew the most attention. With her figure covered by baggy pants and a camera vest, her hair cut short, the men would look at her beautiful face and argue over whether she was a woman or an attractive boy. Later Dianne was able to approach and photograph several women—among the first pictures ever taken of the Balti women living in the mountainous regions of far northern Pakistan.

It was at Askole that we ran into the first serious porter problem. Manzoor informed me that the porters wanted to lay over for a day in Askole *and* be paid half-pay for the day off. He also told me they were now demanding to be paid for their return from Base Camp as well, which had never been part of the plan—or the budget. There had been a few small porter incidents earlier that Manzoor seemed unable to resolve, and I already had a slow burn going inside of me about the situation; that afternoon, I fumed to myself in my journal:

> *Only a week ago, they were fighting for the right to be porters and now they are complaining about carrying, even though their loads are no heavier than ours. The problem is there are no regulations set down by the government as to what must or must not be paid. The porters are one thing, but we also have been forced to take along—and pay—12 village chiefs and four policemen. And none of them carries his own food or supplies (nor does Manzoor), so we have to pay for porters for them too! We all feel like we're getting ripped off . . . If other expeditions are to enter this valley, the government is going to have to standardize the porterage charges and charge fair rates. I am going to make a full report on this and send it to the Prime Minister.*

It became our job to establish guidelines and negotiate them through Manzoor. But the porters knew Askole was the last village on the route and that from now on there would be no local replacements to recruit if they "walked off the job." They had us over a barrel, and Manzoor (though he carried a revolver) seemed to have little influence over them. In fact, the porters seemed to overwhelm him. He was caught in the middle between over five hundred of his countrymen and ten North American climbers. If I hadn't been so frustrated myself, I might have felt sorry for him. But all I could think about was that if they were complaining now, when the terrain was good, how would they react when the going got tough?

It didn't take long to find out. Above Askole the weather was cooler, and we encountered occasional rain and patches of snow. Though the loads they carried were 10 pounds lighter than those carried in the Everest expedition, the porters complained they were being pushed too hard. In addition, because spring was so late in coming, many had yet to till their fields, and now as the days and weeks passed, some of them wanted to abandon the march to do that. Each day several dozen porters would just up and quit and demand to be paid, and I would have to spend a couple of hours hassling with them and settling up. It was infuriating.

At least we were making progress up the valley. On May 15 we rounded a bend in the river and saw the massive Baltoro Glacier filling the valley bottom ahead. The glacier—rumpled and brownish gray with dust, rubble, and rock that rained down from the steep peaks at its sides—would be our highway to the mountain for the next thirty-five miles. On the seventeenth, we climbed up through the glacier's terminal moraine and arrived at a place called Lilliwa, just as the lowering sun spotlit the massive rock fangs of Paiju and the Trango Towers above us. The next day we arrived at Urdukas, a Balti name that means "split rock," and camped to one side of the glacier.

At Urdukas, only a third of the way up the glacier, the porters went on strike. It had snowed the previous day, and although it was now clear and warm, they simply refused to move. Many wanted to get paid and turn back. I agreed to pay off and release those who were sick or injured, but stood firm on the rest, arguing that their agreement was to carry all the way to Base Camp.

We negotiated fruitlessly for days. To make matters worse, it became clear that Manzoor had underestimated how much food the porters would need, and we were running out. A few of our porters agreed to carry loads higher, though for higher pay, and some walked out without any pay, but the majority simply refused to budge. After nearly a week of this, I'd had enough. It was time for a showdown. At one of our endless negotiating meetings with Manzoor and a group of porter leaders, I reached into my pocket, pulled out a one hundred-rupee note, and held it up.

"If we don't move immediately, this expedition is through," I told them. "No one will be paid any more money. We will burn our rupees, burn everything, and go home."

Then I took a cigarette lighter, lit the note, and watched as the flames licked down to my fingers. There was dead silence for about five seconds, then bedlam. The porters in the tent argued and exclaimed to each other in loud voices and the news quickly spread to the several hundred others gathered outside. The next day we were marching up the Baltoro Glacier again, though still with far fewer porters than we needed. We would have to carry loads to Base Camp in stages, paying more than we could afford and taking far more time than we could afford as well. But we were moving.

The head of the Baltoro Glacier is a sort of T-junction where two smaller glaciers, the Upper Baltoro and the Godwin-Austen, converge, turn ninety degrees, and then head down the valley together as the main Baltoro Glacier. Called Concordia by earlier explorers, this spot was the first chance we had to get a clear view of our objective from the ground. I recalled an earlier explorer, Sir Martin Conway, who had described

> *the majesty of K2, almost too brilliant for the eye to rest upon in its mantle of sunlit white. It was clear from base to summit, a broad and heavy mass, four-faced and four-ridged, like the Great Pyramid. Here, for me, the glory of this transcendent scenery culminated.*

And transcendent the scenery was. Concordia was like the great hall of the mountain giants. On every side, looming high above us, were 20,000-foot-plus peaks. Down the valley on the left were Biarchedi and Masherbrum, and across the valley on the right Lobsang and Muztagh Tower. At the head of the valley, the six summits of the Gasherbrum group were directly ahead of us, along with Broad Peak. Up the upper Baltoro, to the right, rose Chogolisa (also known as Bride Peak). And, of course, up the Godwin-Austen to our left was K2, at 28,250 feet, lording over all the others.

We rested at Concordia for a couple of days as loads continued to be ferried from below, and then finally, on June 5, we reached and began supplying our Base Camp at 17,600 feet. It had been forty-seven days since we had arrived in Pakistan, and we had only just reached the base of the mountain. In the pit of my stomach, I was already anxious about our chances of reaching the summit.

While we waited, yet again, for the rest of our supplies to reach Base Camp, the toll the delays and porter problems had taken on our team members began to show. Louie rode Galen constantly about not carrying his fair share of the load. A few others were quietly discouraged and homesick; Fred Stanley, taking a pee one day, said simply that he wished he could crawl through the hole he was making in the snow and emerge at home, in Ellensburg, Washington.

Meanwhile Louie continued to pick on Dianne, sometimes through me, sometimes directly. Despite the fact that it had been Dianne and I who had done almost all of the organizing for the trip, he was miffed when she expressed opinions about how the climb above Base Camp might be staged. Despite the fact that Louie had never before climbed with oxygen and Dianne and I had been discussing how and when the team would use oxygen for nearly two years, he was angry when she expressed her opinion on the subject. And despite the fact that she had thus far done at least as much work as he had and carried loads nearly as heavy, it was clear Louie did not consider Dianne a full member of the team. It seemed to me that in his eyes she was just my wife, along for the ride, and he resented it.

Thinking back on these events, some of which Louie has written about himself, I have to admit I should have been more sensitive about the effect Dianne's presence had on my brother. Even though we had drifted apart quite a bit after he decided not to go on the Everest expedition, the fact was Louie was my twin, and I think he had expectations—perfectly reasonable ones—of the two of us spending more time together than we actually were. Frankly, so had I. But I was with my new bride, and she was the person I wanted to spend most of my time with.

I also don't think Louie fully grasped the huge difference between being one of the climbers, as he was, and being the expedition leader, as I was. As a climber, he was free to focus on the journey and the upcoming ascent, while, as leader, I was bedeviled by the hundreds of nagging problems of managing the day-to-day logistics of the expedition—not least of which was that we were running out of money to pay porters and the rest of our funds had still not arrived from Skardu. By the end of the day, I didn't really want to frolic with him and the rest of the guys; I wanted the peace, comfort, and companionship of my wife. I can see now that not only Louie but all of the guys probably resented the fact that I had that option.

Through all of this, I was thankful for Leif Patterson. The consummate diplomat, Leif had an uncanny ability to find just the right words or suggestions to resolve disputes among members of the group, including Louie and me. He retained and communicated a sense of optimism, even when things were at their most difficult, and kept us all talking to each other. He was a team player through and through.

Meanwhile, though, we had a mountain to climb, and we wasted no time getting started. On June 6 Louie and Wick scouted a site for Camp I at about 19,000 feet, and the next day Dianne and I started making carries to it from Base Camp. At the same time, Louie and Wick kept pushing the route higher up the Savoia Pass, along the unclimbed northwest side of the mountain. On the tenth, they made it to the top of the pass, a tough climb up steep rocks and ice, setting fixed ropes along the way, but didn't find a good spot for Camp II before the weather forced them down.

Over the next three days I struggled to reach a site for Camp II, but I was often working in blizzard conditions, kicking steps in the fresh snow and struggling to free the ropes that Louie and Wick had installed. Finally, on the thirteenth, Galen and I managed to put up two tents at the top of the pass. The site was small, perched on a cornice overhanging China, and had a wonderful view, but it was also fiercely windy.

Two days later Fred Stanley and I had set up a winch to haul supplies up the steep slope to Camp II. Fred Dunham stayed below, feeling ill. Leif was there too, struggling with a worsening case of bronchitis. Louie, Wick, Galen, and I kept trying doggedly to push the route higher on the sixteenth, but we were forced to retreat to Camp I because the route to Camp III turned out to be more technically difficult than we had anticipated and required more hardware than we were carrying.

That afternoon, Louie, Wick, Galen, Rob, Dianne, and I were regrouping at Camp I when Fred Stanley radioed from Base Camp and launched into an angry speech claiming that Louie, Wick, and I had made a pact back in Seattle to reach the summit and use the rest of the team as porters. He was threatening to quit. Those of us at Camp I were shocked. From our point of view, Stanley was down at Base Camp because he chose to be there, while we struggled to push the route. What did seem to me to be true was that there was a widening gap of commitment to the task between "the Freds" and Rob on the one hand and the Whittakers, Wick, and, to perhaps a slightly lesser extent, Galen on the other. If anything, it seemed to me Dianne was the one who was being "the porter." Leif, who Rob had now diagnosed as having pneumonia, was as usual the peacemaker. At Base Camp trying to recover, he calmed down the two Freds and quietly suggested that I do what I could to get Fred Stanley higher.

During the next two days, relations improved, and we all worked hard to supply Camp II and get to Camp III. But the combination of technical difficulty and poor climbing conditions frustrated our advance. It had looked so doable from the air.

Meanwhile the weather had been uncooperative almost every day, with fresh snow and wind-stacked drifts. During one of these supply runs, Galen called for help from Camp II. He was having difficulty breathing, feared he had caught Leif's pneumonia or had pulmonary edema, and didn't think he could make it down alone. I started up from Camp I alone to help him. At the

Jim above Camp I. Photo: Dianne Roberts

foot of the steep slope to the pass, however, I encountered the deepest powder snow I'd ever been in. Each time I moved, it kept sloughing off the slope above, collecting at the bottom around me. As I moved forward, it came to my waist, then shoulders. I was sinking in the soft, white fluff. I wondered whether I'd sink into it completely, like quicksand, and suffocate. I took off my pack and threw it ahead of me so I could crawl up on top of it for support. More powder sloughed off, and I ended up essentially swimming forward until I made contact with the hard surface of the steep ice slope ahead, where I resumed climbing. I found Galen in his tent and helped him down to Camp I. From there, he went on to Base Camp alone on skis and found he was running a fever.

On June 19 the weather went from bad to worse and just stuck there. Unlike Everest, there is no predictable "climbing season" on K2; Karakoram weather is just too unpredictable. By the twentieth, more than a foot of new snow had fallen, and it showed no signs of slowing. Dianne and I tried to push up to Camp II, but were forced back by whiteout conditions and avalanche danger on the steep pitch. The only one moving was, of all people, Leif, who was feeling better and carrying loads from Base Camp to Camp I with a couple of our high-altitude porters.

On the twenty-first, two more feet of snow fell. The morning of the twenty-second was still stormy, but there were clear patches, so Dianne and I headed up toward the winch platform to send mail, equipment, and food up to Camp II, where Lou, Wick, Rob, and Steve Marts were stuck. But when we reached the base of the wall, we couldn't find the winch platform. We looked around and finally realized it was beneath us, buried under several feet of snow. After several hours of digging, with avalanches swooping down the face of the slope, we uncovered the winch and got the loads up to the higher camp, then retreated to Camp I.

The weather finally cleared on the twenty-fifth, but by this time everyone was sick with one malady or another except for Louie, Wick, and me. The next day the three of us made it back to Camp II and tried once again to get beyond the ridge to establish Camp III. Try as we might, however, we could not find a route beyond a range of pinnacles that blocked our way. By midafternoon yet another snowstorm blew up and pushed us back down to Camp II.

When you're snowbound, unable to move because of avalanche danger, you lie in your tent desperate to read anything. Labels on clothes take on a new significance. Directions on how to prepare food become a good read. A book you've read a mere half-dozen times is a treasure. If you have a good, unread book, you are in heaven . . . or at least on a journey to somewhere beyond the tent. We had such a book, *Mount Analogue*, written by French climber-philosopher René Daumal. Published in the 1930s, it is a whimsical parable about a mountain higher than Mount Everest and said to be the link between heaven and earth. It was undiscovered, so the story went, because it was hidden in a kind of space-time warp. However, a series of mathematical deductions had indicated that the mountain would be on an island, also hidden, somewhere in the South Pacific. A group of scientist-climbers set sail from France on a yacht named *L'Impossible* to penetrate the warp and find the magic mountain. It is a lovely book, full of pithy quotes on mountaineering and life. One passage seemed particularly apt:

So it is that the mountaineers band together for the arduous climbs and descents, the painful and inevitable falls; with guiding hands grasped and helping hands outstretched. Weaknesses, errors and misunderstandings are the warp of a hard apprenticeship. But, for those who do not lose heart, there gleams from time to time, at the bottom of a crevasse or on a vertiginous ridge, the priceless crystal, the moment of Truth.

I knew we were rapidly reaching our own moment of truth. By June 30 it had been snowing continuously for days. Each morning we would have to crawl out of our tents and shovel away hip-deep snow to keep them from collapsing altogether. The snow continued, almost nonstop, for another week. Avalanches roared down off the flanks of the mountain. Illnesses plagued us. One of our high-altitude porters became ill, and Rob had to help him down to Base Camp, where the porter began throwing up eight-inch worms. Then another high-altitude porter became sick. Stuck on the mountain for weeks longer than we had planned, our supplies were dwindling.

Finally, on July 11, I authorized the release of the following telegram:

The 1975 American K2 Expedition has failed in its attempt to reach the world's second-highest mountain. The expedition suffered serious delays reaching base camp as a result of porter strikes and bad weather. On the mountain, a very difficult route and severe weather halted the team's progress for over 20 days. Time has run out. All team members are healthy. However one high altitude porter is seriously ill and has been carried down to 15,000 feet for helicopter evacuation. The team will leave base camp on July 15 and expects to arrive in Skardu about July 28—James Whittaker, Expedition Leader.

There really was no other choice. The snow was too deep and the avalanche danger too great. What's more, it seemed impossible to push the route beyond the pinnacles to establish Camp III—and we had no idea what lay beyond that. We had simply run out of time and energy. Deeply discouraged, we cached our oxygen and equipment at Base Camp for future expeditions and began our retreat back down the Baltoro Glacier toward Skardu, and home.

The hike back was not without its great moments, however. As we descended, it became clear that spring had arrived in the Karakoram. At Urdukas we saw our first blades of grass. The green was almost blindingly vivid after so long in a world of snow, ice, and rock. The warming earth smelled like the most exotic perfume, and we luxuriated in the sunshine. At one point, Galen snapped a picture of Leif, arms lifted to the sunshine, smiling rapturously, drinking in the beauty of the moment and the luxury of simply being alive. Despite the sheer drama of the scenery through which we had passed in the previous months, that was the image I would remember best long after the expedition was over.

■

We returned to a reception that I can only describe as bizarre. Shortly after we reached home, Galen called to tell me that we were being accused of having Central Intelligence Agency (CIA) personnel on the team and of having placed a listening device on the Chinese border. I was dumbfounded.

To make matters worse, American Alpine Club President Bill Putnam told us, "Some serious charges have been made against your expedition and we're investigating them." A few days later, the Tacoma *News Tribune* ran a headline

Team members descend from Camp I with a sled full of oxygen cylinders to be cached for a later expedition. Photo: Dianne Roberts

that said: "Alpine Club Leader Claims K2 Climbers Left an Abyss of Ill Will." Below it, Putnam was quoted as saying, "People who could influence the government have given us real indications of serious unhappiness with the group led by Seattle's Jim Whittaker." The article discussed our porter problems and ended with another quote from Putnam that climbers must learn "to conduct themselves as members of the human race."

Putnam, of course, had not been on the expedition, nor had he spoken with any of us. It turned out that the source of the charges that we had mistreated the porters was a letter to a friend in the United States from none other than Manzoor—who had thoroughly botched his job of assembling, hiring, supplying, and managing our porters.

The charges had the ironic effect of drawing our team back together in solidarity. We were uniformly outraged. Despite being extorted and victimized by the unregulated porterage system, we had paid the porters a total of $85,000 for their carries—far more than had been originally agreed. In the end, we didn't begrudge them this money; we had decided at the outset to pay and treat the porters well and were glad the money had gone directly into the pockets of poor villagers, without some third party taking a cut of the proceeds. That there were disagreements and disputes arose not from mistreatment but from mismanagement by Manzoor (who, it transpired, had never been clear to the porters about what the task entailed) and the complete lack of government contracts, guidelines, or regulations for porters *and* expedition leaders. The fact that spring had been late and many of the porters still had not tilled their fields before they signed on with us didn't help any either.

Needless to say, the American Alpine Club's "investigation" never went anywhere—other than to defame those of us who had been on the expedition. (Galen's take on the matter was that Putnam "was involved in petty power struggles within the club" and was trying to discredit him and Wickwire to get them off the American Alpine Club board.) What's more, it was revealed later that the CIA nonsense had come from someone who was bitter that he hadn't been invited to join the expedition.

Still, it was a sour end to a difficult expedition.

Chapter Ten

REPRISE

"You *are* going back, aren't you?" Ethel Kennedy said to me one day. It wasn't really a question.

Dianne and I had been wrestling with the same issue ever since our return from the unsuccessful K2 expedition. Jim Wickwire was still raring to go, as if the frustrated 1975 attempt had only whet his appetite. Rob Schaller and Leif Patterson wanted to be counted in too. We had tried so hard and learned so much. K2 was unfinished business, and I knew I wouldn't be satisfied until it was finished.

But we knew we would do it differently. We would go in the summer this time, in the hope that the weather—always unpredictable in the Karakoram— would be less hostile. We would seek out a better route to the summit. We would resolve the porter problem so the approach went more smoothly. And we would put together a larger, more experienced team.

The porter problem already appeared to be resolved. After our 1975 attempt, I had written Pakistani Prime Minister Zulfikar Ali Bhutto a long letter (with a copy to Senator Ted Kennedy) describing the difficulties we had faced with our porters and providing a list of suggestions. To my delight (especially given the Putnam controversy), the minister of tourism, Shahzada Saeed-ur-Rashid Abbasi, wrote back only two months later, on February 19, 1976, that they had appreciated my suggestions and would implement them. Clearly the

Aerial view of K2. Photo: Dianne Roberts

government had begun to take seriously the economic opportunities that expeditions provided for this remote region and realized reliable porter support was critical. The climbing calendar was already packed: a Polish expedition had received permission for an attempt in 1976; a huge Japanese expedition, with fifty climbers, was planned for 1977; and another expedition, led by my friend, the famed British mountaineer Chris Bonington, had a permit for 1978.

All this was both good news and bad news. These expeditions would provide valuable experience and training for porters on the approach and, at the same time, gather valuable information about the mountain itself. On the other hand, it was making it very difficult for us to get a permit. Our 1976 application to climb in 1978 was rejected, but a direct appeal by Senator Ted Kennedy to Prime Minister Bhutto helped, and on New Year's Day, 1977, we received permission for an expedition to follow Bonington's attempt in the summer of 1978.

To finance the expedition, I hit upon a novel idea: instead of trying to find a few big sponsors, why not increase awareness of and interest in mountaineering by asking the general public to support us with small donations? The plan worked. We persuaded advertising agencies and magazines to help publicize the climb and our fund-raising campaign, and slowly but steadily, the contributions rose to meet our budget.

Meanwhile Wick, Leif, Rob, Dianne, and I (I had invited Louie, but he declined) concentrated on building the team. Convinced that one of the reasons for the failure of the 1975 expedition had been the relative inexperience of most of the team members, we decided that this time we would choose only highly motivated climbers with experience over 20,000 feet. Dianne and I also agreed she would not be the only woman. Accordingly, we invited Cherie Bech, thirty-two, a nurse who had reached 24,700 feet on Dhaulagiri in Nepal. She accepted, as did her husband, Terry, thirty-eight, an ethnomusicologist who had lived in Nepal for nine years and climbed many times above 20,000 feet. Seven other top climbers signed on as well: Craig Anderson, thirty, a zoologist who had been on the 1973 Dhaulagiri expedition; Chris Chandler, twenty-nine, a physician who had summited Everest in 1976; Skip Edmonds, thirty, another physician who also had Himalaya experience; Lou Reichardt, thirty-four, a neurobiologist who summited both Dhaulagiri and Nanda Devi in India; John Roskelley, twenty-eight, who had done the same; Rick Ridgeway, twenty-eight, a writer and filmmaker who had reached 26,200 feet on Everest in 1976; and Bill Sumner, thirty-five, a physicist who had climbed extensively in the Northwest and Nepal.

Then tragedy struck. During the 1977 Christmas holiday, six months before we were to leave for K2, Leif's wife, Marijke, called. Leif had been out climbing for the day with his twelve-year-old son, Tor, and another boy on Chancellor Peak near their home in British Columbia. When they failed to return that night, Marijke had alerted the Parks Service. The next morning Leif, his son, and his son's friend were found dead at the base of the mountain, roped together and buried in an avalanche. Our team attended a candle-lit memorial service in the log cabin Leif and Marijke had built themselves, surrounded by the Selkirk Mountains. Nearby was another partly built, Norwegian-style cabin that Leif had been building, using traditional Norwegian hand tools. We vowed to come back after the climb and finish that cabin.

It was almost impossible to imagine replacing Leif, but eventually I picked two other climbers who were both physically strong and good team players: Dusan Jagersky, thirty-seven, a Czech immigrant who had climbed widely in Europe and Alaska and guided on Mount Rainier; and Al Givler, thirty, a former REI employee who had an outstanding climbing record in the West and Alaska and who always seemed to have a twinkle in his eye.

Then it happened again. I was attending a wilderness hearing in Seattle and had just given testimony when a reporter handed me a note that said, "Urgent. Call Jim Wickwire at Glacier Bay Lodge, Alaska, immediately." I raced to a phone and reached Wick who explained, with difficulty, that he and filmmaker Steve Marts had been climbing with Al and Dusan in the Fairweather Range, near Glacier Bay. On their descent, Al and Dusan, who were roped together, fell past them down a 3,000-foot cliff. It had taken Wick and Steve two days to hike out to a phone. He doubted Al and Dusan were alive, but he needed help to find them. I called Louie, and we immediately flew up to Glacier Bay, met Wick, and had a helicopter land us in the snow at the foot of the cliff just below a cloud layer. The next morning we found their remains. They apparently had been killed instantly.

Reeling from this second tragedy, we decided that we would not try to replace them. Instead, we would climb in their honor.

Then a far smaller but still threatening event occurred. One weekend I was shaving the bark off a log for a cabin I had started to build on the Pacific Coast.

Leif had sparked my interest in traditional building crafts, and I was using a heavy, old-fashioned drawknife, pulling it with both hands. The knife slipped out of my left hand and came back down on top of it. It was a small cut, but the knife was sharp, and suddenly I couldn't lift three fingers. The tendons had been severed.

Three hours later I was in the operating room at Swedish Hospital in Seattle as an anesthetist probed above my collar bone with a long needle. I warned him that he was going to puncture my lung. "Not to worry," he said, and when he finally finished probing, my arm went numb. The surgeon sewed up the tendons and the nurses put me to bed in the hospital for the night.

In the middle of the night, I woke up breathing hard and got out of bed. As I stood there, panting, I felt my left lung doing something weird. I called for help and soon learned that as I had feared, my lung had collapsed. I couldn't believe it. Here I was, about to leave for K2, and I had one lung and only seven functioning fingers.

The next morning the doctor came in.

"Mr. Whittaker," he asked, "who is your thoracic surgeon?" as if everyone had a thoracic surgeon. I should have asked him, "Who is your lawyer?" but I didn't. He presented my options: either put a hole between my ribs and stick in a rubber tube to suck out the excess air in my thoracic cavity so the lung could expand again or do nothing and let the lung mend on its own over a period of six months to a year.

I needed advice quick. I called my friend and former Everest teammate, Dr. Tom Hornbein, who was a professor of anesthesiology at the University of Washington School of Medicine.

"If it was me, Jim, I'd go for the operation. It's quicker." Tom advised.

I had the operation.

Afterward, I lay in my hospital bed with a tube sticking out of my chest while a small pump chugged away, slowly reducing the pressure around my left lung. As the lung expanded again, it rubbed against my chest cavity and hurt like hell. Dianne was at my side when the anesthetist who had caused the crisis in the first place waltzed into the room and in a teasing sort of voice, said, "So this is the famous climber who's going to K2." I was not amused.

"Get . . . the . . . fuck . . . out . . . of . . . here . . . you . . . sonofabitch!" I gasped.

He disappeared in a flash.

In the coming weeks, the lung healed, the tendons knit together virtually as good as new, and our team knit together too, as we all slowly recovered from the losses of Leif, Al, and Dusan. After deciding not to try to replace Al and Dusan, we added a new team member after all: Dusan's widow, Diana Jagersky. A former REI employee and outdoor enthusiast, Diana had been as excited as Dusan had when we invited him to join our expedition. After a lot of thought, we asked Diana if, as a sort of homage to her husband, she would be interested in joining us to help organize Base Camp. To our delight, a week or so later she agreed, and as it turned out, she made a significant contribution to the expedition.

■

At last, on June 13, 1978, we left Seattle. The first sign that our luck was turning came in New York, at a layover at Kennedy International Airport. While we were there, Dianne told Jake and Susanne Page—friends from Washington, D.C., who had come up to see us off—that she had wanted to take along a tape of Aaron Copland's "Fanfare for the Common Man," to play at Concordia at sunrise, but she hadn't been able to find it. They promised to send it, got onto their plane back to D.C., and promptly sat down next to . . . Aaron Copland. A few weeks later the tape caught up with us in an envelope signed "K2 or bust—Aaron Copland."

By then we already felt things would be different this time. We had swept through Karachi, and after a few days making final preparations in Rawalpindi and the capital, Islamabad, we arrived in Skardu, Pakistan, on June 20, with no serious delays.

We were sorting our nearly eight tons of gear and supplies later that same evening when I learned that Chris Bonington was at the district commissioner's house, not on K2, that one of his team members had been killed, and that Chris wanted to see me. Alcohol is forbidden in devoutly Muslim Pakistan, but I grabbed a bottle of Old Hermitage whisky from our "medical supplies," rushed over to the district commissioner's home, and barged in. Chris, looking haggard, jumped off a couch, and we embraced.

"May we have two glasses?" I asked the commissioner. "It is a custom in my country and Chris's to toast the death of friends with a drink." He left the room and came back a few minutes later, not with two glasses but three. Together, we drank the whole bottle while Chris told his story.

His team had reached Base Camp smoothly, without porter strikes or delays. They had begun to ascend the lower section of the unclimbed West Ridge, rigging fixed rope as they climbed, but snowfall had been a problem and avalanches were coming off the mountain much of the time. ("Just like 1975," I thought to myself.) They had established Camp III, and Doug Scott and Nick Estcourt, roped together, were climbing up to it when the entire snow slope they were on broke under them and avalanched down. "It was an unbelievably big slab," Chris said, "Maybe eight feet thick, and when it came off it roared clear across the glacier floor." Chris said it looked like Estcourt had pulled Scott off, but apparently their rope had caught on a rock and broken, saving Scott. They never found Estcourt.

Pete Boardman, another well-known mountaineer who was a member of Chris's team, would later talk about the mountain with our team member Rick Ridgeway:

> I think we were all a bit surprised. Didn't quite expect it, you know, to be such a bloody big climb. I think we probably underestimated it a little, there just weren't enough of us, and we realized right off there was no way we could get up it. Too much hard climbing too high . . . That's quite a hill; I don't think any of us have seen anything quite like it. It's a phenomenal hill.

As I left Bonington, he wished us luck: "Somebody has got to climb K2 in style," he said, "and I think it will be your expedition."

In style. It was a peculiar turn of phrase, but I knew what Chris meant: a small team on an unclimbed route. A team like ours. And the odd thing was that instead of spooking me, the tragedy that had struck Chris's expedition left me feeling more confident, not less, about our own chances. At some level, I felt we had already paid our dues.

The next day we met our government-assigned liaison officer, Mohammed Saleem Khan. No young, inexperienced lieutenant with a sidearm this time; Saleem didn't need a revolver. Six feet tall, a stocky 200 pounds, with fiery eyes and brushy gray hair, he was a soon-to-be-retired sergeant-major in the Pakistani Army who positively exuded an authority earned through years of

The district commissioner, liason officer Saleem, and Jim do the final paperwork before the team departs, Skardu. Photo: Dianne Roberts

commanding troops. He immediately took charge of all the details of getting us started from Skardu, including the rounding up of our initial group of porters.

On June 21 our gear and supplies were loaded into trailers and hauled by more than a dozen tractors up the valley of the Shigar River. Meanwhile Saleem had our jeeps lined up neatly, ready to go. The only things left to do were to receive the formal send-off by the district commissioner and take the official photograph. Just as Saleem was arriving with the commissioner, the jeep carrying Roskelley and Wickwire pulled out and, amid much hooting and hollering, roared out of town, leaving us in a cloud of dust.

In a place like Pakistan, formalities matter, and we had just had a major breach of protocol. Saleem was furious.

"Why did you send them on?" he demanded.

"They left without permission," I said.

"Can you not control your own team?"

"Yes, I can control them. They didn't know any better. It won't happen again." I was fuming.

When we caught up with the team, I raised hell. Wickwire said Roskelley had talked their driver into going ahead.

"I warned him you were going to be pissed off," Wick said.

He was right about that. That night, in Shigar, I held a meeting and reiterated the agreement we had all made months earlier to work together, as a team,

John Roskelley and Lou Reichardt check out porter hopefuls at Dasso.
Photo: Dianne Roberts

to put somebody on the summit of K2. Though in the telling it seems like a minor incident, it had been an embarrassment for the commissioner and a major loss of face for Saleem who, as I knew from the 1975 expedition, we would need to have on our side. What's more, it raised my doubts about Roskelley's ability to be a team player. There were enough things to worry about; I didn't need a loose cannon in the group.

The next morning we piled back into the jeeps, and I put the incident behind me. On this day we would face our first major task: screening and hiring the hundreds of porters we would need for the approach. The word had been sent out that candidates should wait for us at the trailhead, in the village of Baha, at the point where the Braldu River joins the Shigar.

We arrived about noon and there they were, hundreds of them, cheering and jumping and running as we approached. While Wickwire and Roskelley prowled around the throng looking for the strongest candidates, Saleem quickly took charge, ordering them to queue up in front of him so we could review their credentials. Saleem conducted the interviews, and our three doctors—Rob Schaller, Skip Edmonds, and Chris Chandler—stood by to check the health of those to whom Saleem gave the nod. Each would receive a contract, developed by the government and specifying what would be expected of them and what they would be paid. And each porter would sign the contract with a thumbprint, sealing the agreement. Saleem questioned the candidates closely. At one point, in the middle of interrogating one of them, Saleem stopped talking, picked the man up, and sent him sailing over a rock wall to the ground. The porter scuttled away, grinning sheepishly, while the others laughed uproariously. I looked at Wickwire and gave him a thumbs-up sign. We gave Saleem a pair of K2 ski poles like the ones we hiked with, both as a token of our appreciation and a badge of authority.

The next morning, June 23, as we prepared to begin the 110-mile trek to Base Camp, we beheld a scene straight out of the movies.

Saleem stepped up to a rock high above the heads of 295 porters, carefully positioning himself so that the rising sun shone above his left shoulder. The milling crowd stopped moving, and in moments, you could have heard a pin drop. He began to speak, his voice gradually increasing in volume and passion until he sounded like a Baptist preacher exhorting his flock. He waved his ski poles and finally came to a crescendo. The silent porters suddenly roared out cheers, picked up their loads, and raced out of camp.

It was awesome.

On the trail he occasionally beat malingering porters with his ski poles, mostly just hitting their loads. The porters would grin, dodging and moving faster up the trail like it was a big joke. For several days our caravan marched across the high terraces above the milky Braldu River, descending every few miles into nullahs, some hundreds of feet deep, cut by lateral streams—a grueling landscape I remembered all too well. The only difference from the 1975 expedition was the temperature, which in these early days often exceeded 120 degrees. Each evening we camped at a riverside village—the only spot of green in an otherwise parched, sandy brown world.

At Askole we ran out of villages and headed deep into the Karakoram wilderness, steadily gaining elevation. We had learned from the returning British expedition that a crude bridge over the Dumordo River, a tributary of the Braldu above Askole, had been washed out. We'd brought equipment to rig a rope and pulley system—a Tyrolean traverse—to cross it, and Roskelley and one of the porter chiefs had gone on ahead to set it up. A bit hair-raising, it nonetheless worked brilliantly, and with only a day's delay, expedition members, porters, and gear made it across unscathed.

We were closing in on the Baltoro Glacier now, and a day after crossing the Dumordo, we rounded a bend of the Braldu and there it was, a vast tongue of dirty ice filling the valley floor ahead, with the river erupting at full flow from beneath its face. That night we camped at Urdukas. Earlier in the day the team had gotten its first glimpse of K2—that immense pyramid—before it winked out of sight behind clouds; now we were hemmed in on all sides by 20,000-foot-plus giants: the Baltoro Cathedrals, Lobsang, Masherbrum, and far away at the head of the glacier, the Gasherbrums.

The next day, at 15,000 feet and well ahead of schedule, we reached Concordia and the head of the main Baltoro Glacier. Two days later we hiked up the Godwin-Austen Glacier into Base Camp. The march that had taken us nearly a month in 1975 had taken only thirteen and a half days this time. And we'd not had a single serious porter problem.

Since many of the porters had been carrying food we'd eaten along the way, we had been gradually releasing and paying them off for days, as the food loads were used up. Now, at Base Camp, it was time to pay off most of the rest,

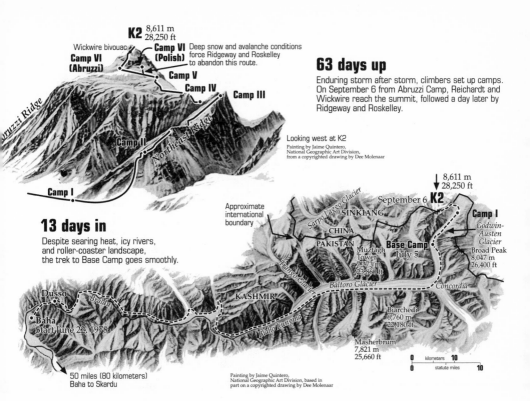

K2 8,611 m
28,250 ft

Wickwire bivouac

Camp VI (Abruzzi)

Camp VI (Polish) Deep snow and avalanche conditions force Ridgeway and Roskelley to abandon this route.

Camp V

Camp IV

Camp III

Abruzzi Ridge

Northeast Ridge

Camp II

Camp I

63 days up

Enduring storm after storm, climbers set up camps. On September 6 from Abruzzi Camp, Reichardt and Wickwire reach the summit, followed a day later by Ridgeway and Roskelley.

Looking west at K2
Painting by Jaime Quintero,
National Geographic Art Division,
from a copyrighted drawing by Dee Molenaar

13 days in

Despite searing heat, icy rivers, and roller-coaster landscape, the trek to Base Camp goes smoothly.

Approximate international boundary

Sarpo Laggo Glacier

SINKIANG

September 6 K2

8,611 m
28,250 ft

Camp I

Godwin-Austen Glacier

CHINA

PAKISTAN

Muztagh Tower 7,273 m 23,860 ft

Base Camp July 5

Broad Peak 8,047 m 26,400 ft

Dusso

Braldu

Indus Glacier

KASHMIR

Baltoro Glacier

Concordia

Baha
Start June 22, 1978

Biaho Lungma

Biarchedi 6,760 m 22,180 ft

Masherbrum 7,821 m 25,660 ft

0 kilometers 10
0 statute miles 10

50 miles (80 kilometers)
Baha to Skardu

Painting by Jaime Quintero,
National Geographic Art Division, based in
part on a copyrighted drawing by Dee Molenaar

but we were short of cash. A runner from Skardu had yet to reach us with the additional money we needed to meet our obligations. But our problem turned into an opportunity. Encouraged by Saleem, the majority of our porters elected to stay with us a bit longer to make carries from Base Camp to Advance Base Camp at 17,500 feet. The twin incentives of Vibram-soled boots, donated by the Quabaug Rubber Company, which I had given as gifts to the porters earlier, and double wages for the extra work helped, as did the extra food we found at the abandoned Bonington camp nearby. (We also retrieved the oxygen bottles we had cached carefully in 1975 and found them still in good shape.) With the funds on hand we paid off the porters who wanted to leave. First thing in the morning on July 6, Chris Chandler and Rick Ridgeway left to scout the route up, and we began organizing the carries to Advance Base that would follow behind them. What would have taken us more than a week would now be done in a day or so.

We had left the heat of the lower reaches of the valley behind, but it was beginning to look like we'd left the good weather behind as well. Misty rain closed in from time to time, sapping some of the enthusiasm of the porters and giving me the willies as I began to replay the snows of 1975 in my mind.

At Advance Base I broke out boxes of cookies and candy for the porters, and Saleem shouted a rousing oration none of us understood. Then I climbed up on his rock and delivered a speech of my own to thank them, which Saleem translated. The porters shouted back three cheers for us all. As they left, I felt a huge weight lift off my shoulders. We were safe, we were healthy (although Rob had a bronchial infection), we were well established, and we had experienced none of the labor troubles of the 1975 approach. Now, *Inshallah* (God willing), all we had to do was climb the mountain.

■

While Terry Bech and I walked back to Urdukas with the porters to intercept the runner from Skardu who had their pay, the rest of the team began the process of moving gear and supplies uphill, establishing camps, and stocking them in tedious ascents and descents. We had retained four exceptionally strong porters from the Hunza valley of Kashmir, where people are said to live regularly for more than a century, and trained them as high-altitude porters, or HAPS. They would help us as far as Camp III, but then they too would leave, and the rest of the work would be up to us. Saleem stayed at Base Camp, manning the radio; Diana would eventually make Camp I her home, although she lugged many loads higher.

I caught up with the team at Advance Base after they had established Camp I at 19,500 feet, at the foot of the Northeast Ridge. The weather had cleared again, and by July 14, Lou Reichardt and Rick Ridgeway, working with Skip Edmonds and Chris Chandler, had established Camp II up on the ridge at 20,200 feet on the same site the earlier unsuccessful Polish expedition had used.

A couple of days later Wickwire and I pushed the route above Camp II over tough terrain and steep ice about halfway to our planned site for Camp III, high atop the sloping ridge. Meanwhile the others rested or carried supplies up to Camp II. By July 19, with Lou's help, Camp III was in place at 22,300 feet. Not long after, the first high clouds appeared in the distance to the southwest.

The snow started on the twenty-second, and after several days during which the team at Camp II had to shovel drifting snow to keep their tents from collapsing, all but Chris Chandler and Cherie Bech had retreated to Camp I. We waited, debated logistics and summit routes, and watched the snow swirl.

A line of porters departs K2 Base Camp, bearing loads for Camp I; Abruzzi Ridge is the right skyline. Photo: Dianne Roberts

Rumors were swirling too. A number of the team members had noticed that Chris and Cherie were spending a lot of time together; Terry, Cherie's husband, had been laid up at Base Camp with an ankle injury. My attitude was "If her husband isn't worried, I'm not worried, unless it interferes with the climb."

Roskelley apparently felt otherwise and, as was his nature, was outspoken about it.

"If my wife ever did anything like that," he told Rick, "I'd shoot her, not to mention what I'd do to the guy."

Aside from speculation, of course, there was no evidence that Cherie—or Chris—were doing anything "like that," and the truth was John had been grumbling not just about Cherie but about women on expeditions in general for some time now. I finally confronted him about it.

"John, for God's sake, what is your problem with women on expeditions?" I asked.

"Women don't belong on expeditions," he said, practically shouting. "It's too dangerous and they aren't strong enough. I can't stand women on climbing expeditions."

"Why didn't you tell me that before?" I asked.

"You wouldn't have invited me," he said.

He was right about that. Certainly, a weak team member jeopardizes everyone's safety. But I couldn't make the jump with him that women were automatically weaker and therefore a danger. I'll admit that with my wife, Dianne, along on the climb, I was not exactly in a purely objective position, but the truth was our female team members had done—and would continue to do—yeoman work to help us reach our goal. I just didn't buy John's macho climber routine. I kept thinking that somehow John felt whatever success he might have on the climb would be diminished, at least in his eyes, if women achieved the same thing.

On July 27 the day dawned clear at last, and spirits lifted too. Gradually, breaking trail through deep snow and clearing the ropes, the team worked back up to Camp III, supplying camps as they went.

Then between July 30 and August 3, in a spectacular feat of technical mountaineering, Rick Ridgeway and John Roskelley, later joined by Jim Wickwire and Bill Sumner, negotiated what must be one of the hairiest traverses on earth, the knife-edged ridge between Camp III and Camp IV, at 22,800 feet. Inching across a sixty-five-degree ice slope of rock and ice, just beneath the unstable snow cornice of the ridgeline, the climbers installed fixed ropes, alternating leads. On one side was a drop of thousands of feet straight down into China; on the other, a similar drop into Pakistan. No room for error. With the weather deteriorating quickly, the team found a small platform for three tents: Camp IV at last. They didn't linger though, retreating instead back across the traverse to Camp III, to food and rest, as the weather closed in again.

The next day Lou and I joined them, carrying loads from Camp II. I had just begun a discussion about waiting until Camp V was established to decide who was most capable of summiting when John launched into another of his tirades. This time Dianne was the target.

"I don't want to have to go out and rescue anybody and risk my own neck," Roskelley said, "just because they shouldn't have been allowed to cross from Camp III to Camp IV in the first place. Dianne, for example, should not be allowed to go to Camp IV."

I blew up. "Look, dammit," I said, "Dianne came on this trip to help out as high as she can. She has worked as hard as anyone, deserves the chance to go, and she'll cross with me whatever you think. You don't have to risk 'your neck' in any way."

"Everybody here," Roskelley shot back, "knows the only reason she's along is because she's your wife."

I was thoroughly pissed off. It wasn't that John didn't know how capable she was, nor did I really believe he thought her presence caused any risk to him. It was a "she-hasn't-paid-her-dues" attitude. Dianne had been instrumental in putting the whole expedition together. Besides, who was John Roskelley to tell me how good my "client" was? He had little or no experience as a professional guide, and I'd been guiding on Mount Rainier since a year before he was born. My life had depended on judging my ropemates' capabilities, and I knew Dianne's very well indeed. Later, after cooling down, I thought how nice it was going to be to hear John eat his words.

"It's ironic," I told Dianne later in our tent. "These women who John thinks shouldn't be on expeditions are making it possible for him to climb for the summit of K2."

The storm between John and me turned out to be the least of our worries. The snowstorm outside continued almost without letup for days, clearing at last on August 7. On that morning John and Wick came down from Camp III to break trail for those of us coming up with more supplies. During the next two days, the team—Dianne and Cherie included—made several traverses over the knife-edge to Camp IV with supplies. But on the eleventh, the weather forced us back down—most of us to Camp I. The next day, Chris, Cherie, Skip, and Craig descended from Camp IV to Camp III.

Constantly frustrated by the weather, people's nerves were fraying. Despite my attempts to run a democratic operation that gave everyone an even

John Roskelley and Rick Ridgeway re-erect tents after a snow and wind storm at Camp III. Photo: Dianne Roberts

chance, different levels of skill and motivation were sorting us into two groups. Mediating between the two was difficult, not to mention thankless. As expedition leader, and having already summited Everest, I felt no compelling need to summit K2. The others, each in his or her own way, had been wrestling privately, and occasionally publicly, with their summit ambitions. In my heart I knew the mountain would tell us who was most fit for the final assault. Meanwhile the work of the climb itself kept focusing us, and on August 19, Rick, John, Lou, and Chris reached the site for Camp V, at 25,200 feet. It was a major victory, but we were far behind schedule.

And again, the snow began. By now the pattern was clear: a few days of clear weather followed by nearly a week of storms. This one was the worst so far. So was the interpersonal storm down at Camp I. I had announced some days earlier what seemed to me to be the obvious: the strongest, most highly motivated climbers would be in the first summit attempt, and they were Lou, John, Wick, and Rick. Some of the other team members were furious, saying it was too soon for such a decision and arguing for a dual attempt at the summit: a direct ascent above Camp V, the route the Poles had tried, and a traverse to the

Abruzzi Ridge route the Italians had taken. We agreed, but the snow kept falling, and we went nowhere. A letter Dianne wrote to our friends, the Pages, captured the mood:

> *Well, the weather has stopped us—really stopped us. I fear that summer has turned to winter, and our supplies might run out before we get the four or five days of clear weather we need to complete the climb. The team is still in good shape in most respects, but there is no question we are getting gradually weaker from such a long time at high altitude. I know I can go back to Camp III, carry loads to Camp IV and V, and maybe even to Camp VI, but if you ask me to do it twice, I'm not sure. Can we last into September if we have to? There is an old rule of thumb on Himalayan climbs: if you don't get the mountain in forty-five days, you don't get it at all. We arrived in Base Camp July 5, fifty days ago today. Psychologically I think we have some problems. A few people are homesick—not enough to keep them off the mountain, but it shows in their motivation. I think everyone still wants the summit, and will work to get someone there, but there are a few who would be just as happy to go home now without it. We have also split into two groups. I'm not sure how or why this happened, but it has to do with styles, personalities, and moralities. Jim is doing his best to keep the group together—doing a good job, I think—but he is taking a lot of flak from a lot of people. Perhaps that's the lot of the leader.*
>
> *Right now we're trying to work out logistics for two simultaneous summit attempts with slightly different routes from Camp V to the summit. Personally, I lean towards throwing all our eggs in one basket and heavily backing one summit team with a support party in a position to move up the following day. But we have so many prima donnas who think they can walk to the top of this thing. No one could agree on a summit team, and when Jim tried to name one, the others called "foul" and more or less refused to carry loads for the first team. Mo Antoine, a British climber (one of the best) whom we met on the approach march, commented (rather prophetically, as it turned out), "The reason not many of you Americans get to the top of your mountains is that you're too damn democratic." We had a good meeting this evening. A lot of mudslinging, but feelings had to come out. Jim (bless his heart) took a lot of mud in the face and tried to pull people together. Maybe it worked—we'll have to wait and see. All we really need is the weather. With a few clear days, we would have had the summit long ago, I know it.*

When a bunch of independent s.o.b's (i.e., mountain climbers) get stuck in their tents for days on end, something weird happens to their rationality. Rather than blaming their situations on fate, or the luck of the draw, or simply accepting them, people start feeling victimized. All the fine qualities that emerge when people are working hard towards a single goal somehow disappear, replaced by suspicion and vindictiveness. Sigh. I think we will have the strength and desire to climb the mountain (God knows, those of us who have worked on this thing for five years surely don't want to go home without it, unless we're beaten—which we're not yet), but it is going to be a delicate operation for Jim to keep people together. We are all still talking to each other, which is a good sign. No one has threatened to leave, though I hear rumors a couple of people wanted to a few days ago. If only we have five clear days, five days of clear, or even mostly clear, weather, five days to make a mad rush from Camp I to the summit. In whatever combinations of people, by whatever route, I would be delighted, even if someone I hated (which is, fortunately, no one on the team—yet) got to the top. In the long run we would all share in the achieve- ment, and everyone would forget the petty squabbles anyway. I hope by the time you get this letter you have read in the newspaper we made the top and are on our way home. I guess we will settle, though, for whatever the fates dish out.

And whatever happens, I have learned a lot about myself (probably even more before it's over), and I've had some good times. But, by God, I need a bath and a manicure and a pedicure and a haircut, and I'm dying to put on a beautiful, expensive dress and leaf through Vogue magazine. I need to listen to a real symphony instead of the eighty-ninth rerun of Bob Dylan's "Nashville Skyline," not to mention the sound track from Saturday Night Fever— AARGH!—on our tape machine here in camp. I need to drink some good wine, eat a salad, and lie in the grass someplace where it's warm enough to stay out in the rain with no clothes on. I need to have ten bouquets of fresh flowers in the house at the same time. I want to sleep for twenty-four hours in a bed with a mattress and cool cotton sheets. I'll be home soon, but not soon enough.

On the night of August 25, the weather cleared again. The next morning John and Rick, who had been at Camp IV throughout this period, came down to break trail almost to Camp II, then returned to Camp IV. The rest of us mo- bilized to climb back up after them from Camp I with new supplies, with Lou, as usual, leading. Lou, Wick, Craig, Dianne, and I were at Camp III, ready to move across the traverse to Camp IV early in the afternoon, carrying heavy loads of supplies. (The others were still ascending below us.)

Lou left first, at 2:15 P.M., Wick and Craig at 2:45 P.M., Dianne and I at 3:00 P.M. It was clear and calm, and we needed to get the supplies to Camp IV. Not long after we crossed to the Chinese side of the knife-edge, we realized we were in for a tough climb. The wind rose steadily to a full-scale gale, clawing at our packs. Snow blew up the face of the ridge and into our goggles, forcing us to take them off frequently to see. The footprints of those ahead of us quickly filled in and, essentially, each of us was breaking trail. It was very cold. The farther we went, the worse the conditions became. To complicate matters, it was getting dark. What normally had been a two-hour to three-hour traverse was, on this afternoon, stretching to five hours. What had started out as a straightforward supply run had turned into a climb to stay alive. Dianne later told me that as we neared the camp, she had become hypothermic and was fading fast. All she had wanted to do was sit down, and she would have, she said, had I not been urging her on. Had she done so, she probably would not have survived.

At 8:00 P.M., twenty minutes behind Wick, an hour and a half behind Lou, and in a full-blown hurricane, Dianne and I literally crawled into the tents at Camp IV, completely spent, as were the others. Dianne was shivering violently, but after some hot cocoa, she recovered quickly. She had done the whole Northeast Ridge, from Camp I to Camp IV, in a single day carrying a full load—an impressive performance by any standard. Even Roskelley grudgingly had to admit it:

"She should never have tried to come across, but I'll agree," he said, "she did a hell of a job getting through that wind. She's got a lot of drive."

The wind was still high the next day, and those of us at Camp IV were bushed and agreed to a rest day. With no room for them at Camp IV, this left the rest of our climbers stuck at Camp III. Chris, Terry, and Cherie were in one tent in Camp III, and Skip, Bill, and Diana Jagersky in the other. Frustrated and feeling like he and the others at Camp III were simply being used as porters, Terry got into a shouting match, by radio, with John up at Camp IV. Diana tried to mediate, but to no avail.

Throughout this latest blow-up, Chris had been strangely silent. A little while later, while he was changing cartridges on a stove, there was an explosion

and fire. Singed but otherwise unhurt, Chris continued to sit in the tent and finally announced he was quitting the expedition. Maybe the explosion was the last straw. Maybe he'd had enough of the temper tantrums. Maybe he'd had all he could take of Roskelley's ranting; he surely resented John making loud guesses about his relationship with Cherie Bech. He couldn't be budged from his decision; he packed his belongings and returned to Base Camp.

The following day, August 28, Craig, Dianne, and I, following Lou, Wick, John, and Rick, made a carry of food, fuel, and oxygen bottles to Camp V without using oxygen, and in so doing, Dianne set a high-altitude record (25,200 feet) for North American women. The next day Cherie joined her with that record, as she and Terry carried up more supplies. After Chris's surprise decision, they had decided to put aside the bickering and accusations of the previous weeks and support the summit teams. Leaving the four summit team members at Camp V, they returned to Camp IV, while Craig, Dianne, and I, along with Diana, who had also made a carry to Camp IV, returned to Camp III where there was more room.

The next day the summit team was back at Camp IV too. It was snowing again. There was no question we had reached the beginning of winter in the Karakoram. The temperature had been dropping as steadily as the weather had been worsening, and now temperatures were well below zero. The wind made it worse.

While they waited out this latest storm, the assault team decided to separate above Camp V. Ridgeway and Roskelley were determined to push the direct but most difficult route, one the Poles had attempted two years earlier. Wickwire and Reichardt thought the avalanche hazard on the Polish route was too high. Instead, they decided to traverse left to the Abruzzi Ridge route and try for the summit over terrain they thought would "go." I agreed; the closer we'd gotten to the summit pyramid, the more daunting the direct route looked.

Upper left: The knife ridge between Camp III and Camp IV. Camp IV is just beyond the small pyramid in the center of the photo and the route to Camp V rises above to the left. Photo: Dianne Roberts
Lower left: The knife ridge between Camp III and Camp IV, with two climbers visible at the top of the small pyramid in the center of the photo. Camp IV is just beyond the pyramid, and the route to Camp V rises above, to the left. Photo: Dianne Roberts

On September 4, when the weather cleared again, the two groups split above Camp V and headed their separate ways. Both encountered deep snow. The Abruzzi team, supported by Terry Bech, unable to continue, turned back to Camp V. Rick and John made it to their Camp VI, however, and after a lot of digging, found the supplies Lou and Wick had cached there a week before.

The next morning, in clear but extremely cold weather, they began their push toward the summit—only to be turned back by extreme avalanche conditions. On the radio, I overheard Rob Schaller, down at Camp I, relaying information to them about avalanches he'd seen from there. I heard John say, "It's just too risky."

I got on the line, trying to sound hearty: "Well, I guess that's it; you gave it a hell of a try." Rick and John retreated to their tent.

Meanwhile, on their second try, Lou, Wick, and Terry (in a great and utterly unselfish performance) were nearing the proposed site for their Camp VI and, by the end of the day, had their tent up at 25,750 feet.

Down in Camp III it was snowing when Dianne and I went to bed, but around midnight I looked out of the tent and the sky was filled with stars. I was so excited I couldn't get back to sleep. "By God," I thought, "this expedition is going to summit K2!"

As dawn lit the eastern sky, I once again saw two figures plodding slowly up the Polish route; Rick and John had almost reached the point where the Polish team had quit, when they bogged down again. I raised them on the radio.

"How's it going up there, Rick?"

"Not so good, Jim, but we're going to keep pushing it."

"I'd reconsider, Rick. That slope above you looks like white death. And besides, Wick and Lou have connected to the Abruzzi route and are heading for the summit."

They rested and thought about it. About an hour later, they broke down their Camp VI, and we saw them traverse to Lou and Wick's camp and set up their tent, where they waited for Lou and Wick to return.

From Camp III, Dianne and I watched as the silhouettes of Reichardt and Wickwire crept steadily up the skyline toward the summit. We were surprised not to see Terry with them and only learned later there had been another misunderstanding: Lou and Wick hadn't thought Terry wanted to summit, and

Terry thought they didn't want him. Terry had returned to Camp V, where Cherie was resting. It was a damn shame; Terry had worked like a horse, was still strong, and I believe he could have made it.

At about 5:15 on the afternoon of September 6, sixty-four days after establishing Base Camp, Lou Reichardt and Jim Wickwire became the first Americans to reach the summit of K2. Thanks to a faulty regulator, Lou had done it without bottled oxygen. Lou knew he could not live long at that altitude, so he snapped a couple of photographs, encouraged Wick to hurry up, and immediately began descending. Wick, apparently not thinking clearly despite using oxygen, stayed on the summit an extra forty-five minutes taking pictures and depositing a microfilm list of the four thousand people who had supported our expedition. It was a mistake.

Looking through Dianne's telephoto lens, we had seen Lou descending fast as the sun set. Much later, we saw Wick begin to descend, but then the darkness swallowed him up. Later John radioed that Lou had made it to Camp VI. Wick never arrived.

Exhausted, dehydrated, moving slowly, Wick had run out of daylight and into a nightmare. He would have to bivouac, just below the summit, at about 27,800 feet. I think in some way Wick had always assumed this, that Camp VI would be too far from the summit to reach it and return, and that a bivouac was inevitable. He had taken a half sleeping bag to Camp VI with that in mind, I think. But he had soaked the bag that morning while melting water back at High Camp and had only a thin nylon bivvy sack with him and no flashlight. The wind was moderate, the temperature falling.

We all passed a terrible night, but none more terrible than Wick. Slipping down the slope and in and out of consciousness, he struggled to stay alive, talking to himself constantly, moving his frozen fingers and toes, thinking about his wife and their children, reminding himself that his violent shivering meant he was still alive.

The next morning, a miracle. Straining to see through Dianne's camera lens, I spotted Wick descending and, just below him, John and Rick ascending. They met, appeared to talk, then continued in their separate directions. That's how I knew Wick was okay; they would never have let him descend alone if he hadn't been. A few hours later, John and Rick reached the summit too—both

Jim Wickwire and Lou Reichardt, barely visible in silhouette on the ridge, en route to the summit. Photo: Rob Schaller

without oxygen—and left early enough to return to Camp VI before darkness. It had been a splendid day for American climbers, and Dianne and I were overwhelmed by our team's success.

Meanwhile, however, trouble erupted at Camp VI. As John worked to get a second stove going to melt snow, there was an explosion and instant fire. John dove out one side of the tent, Rick the other, his hair, sleeping bag, and the tent all in flames. In the end he was fine, but now they faced a new problem. They would have to squeeze in with Lou and Wick in a single small tent and pass the night short one sleeping bag. Later they all agreed it was the most miserable night any of them had ever spent on a mountain.

During the next three days, they descended slowly, first to Camp V, then to Camp IV. Having learned that Cherie was ill, Wick was having trouble breathing, and everyone was struggling, I worried that they might not be able to make the traverse. I climbed up from Camp III, breaking trail, digging out fixed roped and carrying food, and then came back down. Before Dianne and I left Camp III to make room for Terry and Cherie, and later the summit group, we took a black felt-tip marking pen and wrote a few quotes on the yellow REI pyramid tent:

Courage is the first and foremost of all human attributes, for with that one attribute come all the others.

—*John F. Kennedy*

If you play for more than you can afford to lose, you learn the game.

—*Winston Churchill*

More storms trapped the summit team at Camp III for four more days, but on September 11, after struggling through deep snow and digging out fixed ropes, they made it safely to Camp I, where Rob Schaller examined Wick and concluded he had pneumonia. We descended to Base Camp, where Saleem and our porters gave us a tumultuous welcome. There, Rob pumped Wick full of antibiotics and intravenous fluids, but he continued to deteriorate. Soon his condition had advanced to pleurisy, and he was coughing up blood. It was clear we had to get him out of the mountains to a hospital. As quickly as we could, we began our retreat down the Baltoro Glacier, helping and sometimes carrying Wick, to a pair of waiting Pakistani Army helicopters. Rob accompanied Wick, and Lou (who had severely frostbitten feet) and John elected to fly out too. Though he would undergo lung surgery and lose the end of one big toe, Wick eventually recovered completely.

The rest of us walked the 120 miles back to civilization. But this march was utterly different than the one in 1975. As Winston Churchill once wrote: "Victory is sweetest to those who have known defeat."

■

For my part, I believe conflict is inevitable when very different, very highly motivated people undertake dangerous adventures. Our failed 1975 expedition provided experience that helped pave the way for our successful 1978 expedition. And, conflicts notwithstanding, the 1978 expedition had spectacular results: with the smallest successful team in history, we placed four climbers on the second-highest point on earth, three of them without oxygen, by a new route, with the help of three women climbers, two of whom set altitude records. And, as was the case in 1975, we all returned home safely.

We did it, as Chris Bonington had predicted, "in style."

Chapter Eleven

CUTTING LOOSE

Returning to Seattle from Pakistan, Dianne and I went through a kind of re-verse culture shock. Suddenly, things worked. You could drink water from the tap and not get sick. There were toilets everywhere, and, just as incredible, there was toilet paper. People were on time, and for the most part you could under-stand what they were saying—although, increasingly, I found myself thinking that what people said didn't make a lot of sense to me.

For example, on a business trip to the Dolomite region of the Italian Alps, Dianne and I had the privilege of meeting Achille Compagnoni and Lino Lacedelli, the climbers who had first summited K2. We were struck by the fact that they were still heroes in Italy, more than twenty years after the fact. We couldn't get over the contrast between this cultural appreciation for achieve-ment, amounting almost to reverence, and the short attention span in America, amounting almost to crassness, where the question we faced after our return from the successful 1978 K2 expedition wasn't "What was the climb like?" but "What are you going to do next?"

What I did next was go back to my job at REI. There was plenty to keep me occupied.

In 1974, a year before my first K2 expedition, with business still booming and our membership growing nationwide, REI had reached an important fork

Chuck O'Brien belays another climber during practice at Buckskin Pass, Colorado.
Photo: Dianne Roberts

in the road: we could operate out of our Seattle store and serve everyone else by mail order, like L. L. Bean in Freeport, Maine, or we could begin opening branch retail stores around the country. It was a major strategic decision.

Some of our board members worried that opening branches would destroy the unique image our funky warehouse retail store had created for the company. I appreciated and, of course, felt closely connected to that image; after all, I'd worked hard to develop it. But I was more concerned about basic business realities. We had helped build a nationwide clientele for outdoor gear and now new outdoor equipment stores were opening up around the country, threatening to take away our market share. Ultimately, the board agreed with me and we chose Berkeley, California—across the bay from San Francisco and home not only to the University of California but to several thousand of our members—for the location of our first branch store.

We found a great twenty-seven thousand square-foot space located close to the campus and recruited staff from the Seattle store and the ranks of our own membership. It had been our policy to staff our store with climbers, backpackers, and skiers chosen not just for their expertise but for their friendliness, and we stuck with that policy in staffing our first branch. We weren't interested in hotshots or prima donnas. To manage the Berkeley store, I chose a young man named Wally Smith who had worked for us for nine years and had earned a business degree from the University of Washington.

A week or so before the opening, we ran a few ads in local papers and invited the mayor. The response was amazing; the papers reported customers "lined up for blocks." We exceeded 20 percent of the new store's total annual projected sales in the first three days; by the end of the year, REI Berkeley had sales in excess of $1 million.

The board got the message. In quick succession, and using the same modus operandi, we opened stores in Portland, Los Angeles, and Anchorage, and by the end of 1975, REI's total sales reached $20 million—double what they'd been only four years earlier. While I was away on my first K2 attempt, I got word that REI had had a $2 million *month*. I thought wistfully about the old days when I used to get a percentage of our total sales as part of my compensation, but that policy had been changed a decade earlier. Still, I could not help but be proud. Clearly, we had found a viable route up the mountain of our future.

Desperate now for more space, we built an eighty-five thousand square-foot warehouse in an industrial area about a half-hour south of Seattle and moved our mail-order and administrative offices there as well, freeing up more retail space at the main store. It was a smart, efficient move. It also made me miserable. The moment I was no longer in the thick of things on the sales floor I realized that my real love was being with my customers, working with my employees, keeping my finger on the ebb and flow of the business every day. I felt cut off and anchored to my desk.

With the business growing as fast as it was, I didn't have a lot of time to agonize over the situation. There were more important things to deal with. Inventory control, for example, had become a nightmare. We ordered new point-of-sale registers linked to expensive computers that tracked sales and monitored inventory, but like many businesses in those days, we struggled with the new technology, and it took a year to get the new systems fully online. In addition, our rapid growth had caught the attention of the Teamsters Union, which sought to unionize our warehouse employees. I was delighted that when the employees finally got to vote on unionization, the union lost.

The pressure and complexity of our business continued to grow, but I kept finding talented people eager to join REI and help us meet each new challenge. In a way, that had been our secret from the very beginning: hire the best, and they'll make you the best. It was because I had such a strong and capable staff that I had been able to take time off to lead the second K2 expedition; I knew they could run the place without me.

Consequently, I was taken aback by the somewhat chilly reception I received at the first board meeting after I returned from our successful assault on K2. In the company's early days, the board members would have celebrated my success, slapping me on the back and saying "Nice going, Jim." "Hell of a job." "What was it like?" "Tell us about it." Not any more. None of my current board members climbed, and as a consequence, few seemed able to appreciate what our American team had accomplished. They seemed interested in only one thing: how much had the expedition cost REI in cold, hard cash. They wanted an itemized report, a comparison with the estimate I'd given them before I left, and they wanted it by the next executive board meeting. I could understand that they felt they had a fiduciary responsibility to examine the company's involvement. What I couldn't quite understand was how the board of perhaps the nation's leading mountaineering and outdoor equipment retailer could fail to grasp the direct and indirect benefits of having the first successful American ascent of the second-highest mountain in the world be led by their very own CEO.

Nonetheless, I was happy to oblige them. I already knew that while the expedition's total budget had been nearly a quarter of a million dollars, REI's contribution amounted to less than $50,000—all of which (with the exception of my salary) was in the form of donated equipment, not cash. I detailed all this. Then I added up the number of pages *National Geographic* magazine had set aside for our story—pages I knew would be filled with pictures of the REI logo on tents, clothing, and equipment. Finally, I checked the magazine's advertising rates and calculated that we would be receiving some $1.5 million in free advertising—all for an investment of less than $50,000. I presented my report to the board at the next meeting, and they seemed satisfied at last.

But I was not. I was tied to my desk, inside, with meetings, paperwork, and more meetings. Just sitting. In a few months I would be fifty years old, and I had spent half my life at REI. It had developed into a $46 million business with over seven hundred employees. It was well established and I could move on. My Vibram sole royalties were twice the $82,000 a year I was making as president and CEO of REI. I could afford to retire.

A few months later, at the December 1978 board meeting, I announced I would retire in the coming year and was met with shocked silence. I told them REI was a strong and unique company, with smart and dedicated employees and a capable management team—one they could rely on and be proud of. But it was time for me to move on. I promised not to leave until they had found a successor.

I also requested that no news of my decision be released until that successor was found; I still had a company to run, and I wasn't about to be a lame duck. Only two months later, however, while I was attending the National Sporting Goods Association trade show in Chicago, I received a call from a *Seattle Times* reporter trying to confirm the details of my retirement. Someone from the board had leaked my decision. I was furious—most importantly because I had wanted to tell my employees, members, and customers about my decision myself. I didn't want them to be surprised or feel betrayed. Now all I could do was return to Seattle and try to repair the damage.

Within a few months, the board hired Jerry Horn, an executive from Sears and Roebuck, as REI's new CEO. He joined the company in August, and I was free, at last, to go. I had helped build the company up from a one-room, walk-up, hole-in-the-wall business with one employee to a multi-million dollar enterprise with branches nationwide, hundreds of employees, and hundreds of thousands of members. The day I said goodbye to my employees and walked out the door, all I collected was my retirement fund, worth $52,000. In a co-op, there are no stock options. But it had been a wonderful climb, with a great team.

◾

I didn't stay "retired" for long. I had one or two other irons in the fire, not least of which was the continuing income from Quabaug Rubber Company for my Vibram sole endorsement. I also had a new expedition.

A year or so after I left REI, I got a call from Phil Bartow, an old climbing friend. Originally from the Northwest, Phil now ran a program for the physically disabled in Pennsylvania. He had an intriguing idea. The next year, 1981, had been designated the International Year of the Handicapped. Would it be possible, he wanted to know, to take a team of handicapped people—blind people, deaf people, amputees, and the like—to the summit of Mount Rainier?

I told him I was sure it was possible and that more importantly it would be immensely rewarding, not just for the handicapped climbers but for all of us. Phil had climbed Mount Rainier himself and knew what was involved, and he and I immediately began planning the expedition. Phil named the project Pelion after the mountain in Greek mythology that was the home of the legendarily strong half-man, half-horse centaurs. Phil would focus on getting his team trained during the coming year, and Dianne and I promised to plan the climb itself, arrange for sighted climbers to rope up with blind ones, and ensure that everyone had the proper equipment. I told Phil that getting his team trained in advance at altitude would be critical to the plan's success.

Thus, in mid-June 1981, two weeks before our planned ascent, Phil and his team traveled to Aspen, Colorado, to acclimatize and complete their training. Dianne and I planned to join them a week later.

We were in the car on the way to the airport to do just that when we heard a bulletin on the radio that a serious accident had occurred on Mount Rainier and a number of climbers and guides were involved. I dropped Dianne off at the airport to continue to Aspen and then turned around and sped to Mount Rainier to help Louie, who ran the guide service, Rainier Mountaineering. When

I got to the ranger station at Paradise, I learned that two of the six guides involved in the accident were John Day III, the grandson of my old friend, and Peter Whittaker, Louie's son. It was June 21, Father's Day.

The park rangers gave me the details of the accident and told me a team from the Mountain Rescue Council was on its way up the mountain. I radioed Louie, who was already at Camp Muir:

"Look for me in about two hours; I'm on my way."

The weather was miserable, a mix of blowing snow and rain. I hadn't been climbing long when I met members of the rescue team, who were descending. They had been turned back by the foul weather and approaching darkness. I pressed on alone anyway; I knew I could do this climb practically blindfolded. It was almost peaceful moving through the storm as darkness descended; I was alone with my thoughts, feeling close to the wind and the snow and the mountain I knew and loved so well, despite its dangers. I thought about the climb that earlier in the day had turned tragic.

At 3:00 that morning, Peter, John, and four other guides had left the hut at Camp Muir with twenty clients. After about an hour, they took the usual break at Ingraham Flats. At that point, three climbers said they could go no farther, and one of the guides led them back down to the hut. The rest moved quickly across the icefall zone of the Ingraham Glacier to a protected area beneath a ridge called Disappointment Cleaver. Peter, John, and another guide untied from their climbers and ascended to test the safety of the snow on the steep slope ahead. Concluding that the avalanche danger was too high to continue to the summit, they had just turned around to return to the group when they heard a thunderous CRACK! and looked up to see an immense formation of ice break loose from the mountain high above them and fall a thousand feet to the glacier floor below.

At first they felt certain there was no danger to their clients; they were all in a position well away from the icefall zone. But within moments of hitting bottom, the huge mass of collapsing ice fanned out, swept sideways, and became a three-hundred-foot-wide, thirty-foot-high wall of broken ice blocks and snow that was bearing down on the climbers and guides below at more than one hundred miles per hour.

Within a matter of seconds, it was all over. The maelstrom had raced all the way across the glacier floor to the base of the Cleaver, sweeping ten climbers and one of the guides into a deep crevasse and crushing them under the weight of tons of ice. The rest of the party had been tossed about like toys, but were otherwise unhurt. It was the worst accident in American mountaineering history.

Louie was waiting for me at the hut. Peter and John had taken the survivors back down the mountain, and Louie and I were eager to ascend to the accident site in case someone else might still be alive. The park rangers, however, had closed the route because of the danger. Louie and I sat around, saying very little, waiting for the storm to ease. Meanwhile, I thought about Peter.

The bond between guide and client develops rapidly under dangerous conditions. The client's relationship with the guide is much the same as a child's relationship with a parent. Like a parent, the guide is alert, watchful, protective. A current of trust, dependence, and respect travels the rope between them like electricity. Louie's son was a first-class guide, a real credit to the guiding profession; I knew he would be badly shaken by this tragedy, aching not just for his lost clients but for their families as well.

Finally, Louie and I could wait no longer; against the rangers' objections we roped up and took off for the glacier as fast as we could go through the storm. Even under these circumstances, it felt good to be roped up with Louie again, for the first time in years, each of us knowing the other's moves as if they were our own. Louie, in better condition than I because of his guiding, led off, breaking trail through the new snow.

We reached the accident site at first light. Before us, enormous chunks of ice bigger than cars lay scattered across the whole of the glacier floor. We picked our way through them, shouting, but the only reply was the wind and the echoes of our own calls bouncing back from Gibraltar Rock. Over the course of the next few hours, we found a pack and an ice ax but nothing—and no one—else.

When I got back down to Paradise, I phoned Dianne in Aspen and filled her in. Phil got on the line and said that his team, as might be expected, was not especially keen to climb a mountain that had just claimed eleven lives. I could hardly blame them. Phil suggested that Mount Baker, north of Mount Rainier and some 4,000 feet lower, might be safer. I disagreed and told him that after the disaster the route across the icefall was probably safer than it had been for a long time.

"And besides," I said, "after all that preparation, wouldn't climbing Mount Baker be a lot like kissing your own sister?"

Phil laughed, talked with his team, and they agreed. The Pelion Climb was a "go."

A week later, I picked up Dianne, Phil, and his climbers and immediately whisked them up to Paradise so they retained their acclimatization. They were an amazing group: seven of them were blind, two were deaf, one was epileptic, and one was a Vietnam vet who'd lost a leg in the war. They were in great physical condition, and their camaraderie was exuberantly high. Phil, himself part Native American, had invited a medicine man to perform a ceremony calling for good weather, and afterward, suitably blessed, we began our climb, establishing camp for the first night at 7,000 feet on the Nisqually Glacier.

During the next two days, in light snow and mist, Louie and some of his guides helped us train the team in mountaineering basics—crevasse rescues, self-arrests, Tyrolean traverses, glissading, rope travel, the rest step, and forced breathing—the robust suck-in/blow-out respiration of high-altitude climbers.

Next, Warren Thompson, Bud Krogh, and several other members of the Mountain Rescue Council helped us haul packs and guide blind climbers up to Camp Muir. Along the way, Dianne and I began to learn something about both the spirit and the limitations of our team members. The blind climbers, for example, had absolutely no fear of heights. A Tyrolean traverse over a bottomless crevasse? No problem; they couldn't see how far they risked falling and were impatient with those who could. Deaf climbers presented a different set of challenges; often we could communicate with them only by jerking their rope first to get their attention. Signing over distances was also difficult. And of course, communication between a deaf climber and a blind climber created challenges of a whole different magnitude.

Still, we were continually impressed by the team's determination and pluck. Their wry sense of humor about their disabilities constantly caught me off guard. At one point I warned everyone about the risk of sunburn and passed around a metal mirror so they could apply lotion evenly. Sheila Holzworth, blind since the age of ten, called to me from her tent:

"Hey, Jim, can I borrow that mirror?"

"Sure, Sheila," I said, handing it in to her.

But she was already laughing: "Jim, what would I need a mirror for?"

Another time, someone was commenting that his toes hurt from the cold, and Chuck O'Brien, whose leg had been amputated below the knee, shot back, "You people with feet are always complaining."

These folks were so at ease with their disabilities, and so accomplished at accommodating them, that you simply forgot they had any. During a climb on a steep ice slope, I noticed one of Chuck's crampons was loose. I stopped him and cinched it tight.

"That's a little too tight, Jim," he said.

I loosened it a bit and asked, "How's that?"

Chuck just grinned. "Jim, that foot is fiberglass."

I began to think that the only thing that was really disabled was my brain; these characters had no mercy.

The next day we left Camp Muir, leaving behind Dr. Judith Oehler who, both blind and diabetic, didn't feel able to continue. The rest of the team cheered her for even reaching this high in her quest. Instead of making directly for the summit, as guided climbs usually do from this point, we established an intermediary camp on the Ingraham Flats at about 11,000 feet. From here, we could look directly across the glacier floor toward Disappointment Cleaver and see the chaos of ice that had been the scene of tragedy the week before. It was spooky. Up higher, there were still a few big seracs perched ominously above the next day's route. We hit the sack early, sobered by the scene before us.

At 4:30 the next morning we were roped and ready to go. I wanted to get us all up to the summit and back before the heat of the day warmed the Ingraham Glacier, increasing the risk of new icefalls. The blocks of ice on the route would make our start difficult, and I was waiting for the predawn glow to light the way a bit. As usual, the blind climbers were impatient; it didn't matter a bit to them. Finally, with ropes coiled, each blind climber with a hand on the shoulder or backpack of the sighted climber ahead, we set off briskly across the icefall to the Cleaver and safety beyond. At the top of the Cleaver, at 13,000 feet, our oldest climber, Bud Keith, said he could go no farther, so we found him a safe spot and tucked him into a sleeping bag to await our return.

Then we were at the summit at last, and there were tears of joy all around. The medicine man's blessing had worked; the weather was magnificent. The visibility was clear all the way to Canada to the north and Oregon to the south, and the sighted climbers painted word pictures for the blind climbers to make

The Pelion team on the summit of Rainier—(front row, left to right) Dianne Roberts, Jim Whittaker, Roy Fitzgerald, Justin McDevitt; (back, left to right) Chuck O'Brien, Paul Stefurak, Fred Noessner, Kirk Adams, Alec Naiman, Sheila Holzworth, Phil Bartow, Doug Wakefield, Richard Rose. Photo: Dianne Roberts

the view visible to them. To top it all off, the ranger station called us on our radio to report that Chuck's wife had just given birth to twins, a boy and a girl. Knowing something about twins myself, I clapped him on the back and said, "Oh boy, Chuck, you're in for an interesting life." It was a grand moment.

After a quick lunch, I warned our team that we'd only done half of the climb and the hard part was still ahead of us. We started back down, picking up Bud at the Cleaver. It was tough going for everyone, but especially for our blind climbers. For them, every step downhill was an act of faith, a test of courage, and when the rope went taut, they were often jerked off their feet. In addition, the snow was soft and packed up in our crampons, preventing the points from holding. It was slow going.

Despite our best efforts, the sun was already warming the Ingraham Glacier when we reached it. I gathered everyone together and talked them through the plan for the traverse below the icefall. As we had done coming up, we would move quickly and stay close together, the blind with a hand on the shoulder of a sighted climber ahead, ropes coiled and held in the other hand. There would be no talking. Only two ropes of five climbers would cross at one time. While I laid out the plan, I could hear the glacier creaking and thumping ahead of us.

Alert to every noise of the glacier, I got the first group across without any trouble. Dianne and her group had just started across when a terrifying *CRACK!* ripped the air and a suffocating roar surrounded us. I looked up; a huge serac was crashing down the glacier toward us.

"RUN!" someone yelled. It might have been me.

The sighted climbers ran but were brought up short by the ropes that tied them to their blind colleagues who tried to run but fell over blocks of ice. Justin McDevitt, one of our blind climbers fell flat on his face and, surrounded by the roar of the icefall, said to himself simply, "I'm dead."

At that same moment, Dianne and I both realized the tumbling blocks of ice would not reach the climbers, and we began shouting:

"Its all right! It's okay! You're safe!"

We gathered everyone together again and led them to our camp at Ingraham Flats, where the climbers, some still trembling, collapsed into their tents. Dianne and I made sure they consumed lots of fluids to protect against dehydration and, after a bit of food, we called it a night.

The next morning dawned beautiful again, and the spirit of our team rose with the sun. We packed up camp, roped up, and headed home. Part way down the Muir Snowfield, I noticed a big lenticular cloud forming over the summit, a sure sign that the weather was changing for the worse. But our weather blessing had held, and more important, our team was safe.

A few weeks later, we were all together again, this time in the White House Rose Garden. President Reagan congratulated the team and spoke a while with each of us, congratulating Chuck on becoming both a mountaineer and a father of twins.

Chuck and his wife had given the twins the mountain's two names, Tahoma and Rainier, as their middle names.

Chapter Twelve

ROCK BOTTOM

I was sitting on the edge of my father's bed at Mount St. Vincent Nursing Home, when he asked me if I thought it would be alright for him to simply stop eating and let life go. He was in the hospital because of a broken hip, but he was also nearing ninety and suffering from prostate cancer.

"I'd like to sort of check out, so to speak, if it's all right with you. I've had a good life, a wonderful wife, and three wonderful sons, but I'm tired now and I'm ready to say goodbye."

"We all love you, Dad," I assured him, "and whatever you want is what we want, too." Mother and Barney agreed. Louie was in the Himalaya, leading his first attempt on Mount Everest, when Dad made his decision.

And so he simply stopped eating. The good sisters of Mount St. Vincent offered intravenous feeding and oxygen, but we honored Dad's wishes and turned them down. Only four days later, as I was holding him in my arms, Cannonball Whittaker's great and generous heart stopped beating. It was April 18, 1982, two weeks short of his ninetieth birthday.

No matter how long you have to prepare for it, the loss of a parent is wrenching, like losing a limb that you still feel after it's gone. It took me more than a year to break the habit of saying to myself, whenever something interesting happened to me, "Wait till I tell Dad about this." But Dad was right; he

The first Impossible *under spinnaker off the coast of Maui, Hawaii.*
Photo: Dianne Roberts

215

had had a wonderful life, and a long and full one too. He left it with the same grace and dignity by which he'd lived it.

Painful as it was to have him gone, my life had many other comforts. For one thing, Mother was healthy and going strong. What's more, life with Dianne was very nearly idyllic. We would get up each morning before dawn, slip into the outdoor hot tub we'd installed in our rambling waterfront home in West Seattle, and watch the running lights of the Vashon Island ferry moving silently across the Sound as the sky brightened and revealed the towering Olympic Mountains away to the west. We took long walks and never seemed to run out of things to talk about. I also had the comfort of our friends, who would gather at our house on summer afternoons and sit on the wall between our lawn and the beach while I roasted planked salmon over an alderwood fire, the way Northwest Native Americans do. At the end of the day, Dianne and I would slide back into the hot tub to watch the stars.

Finally, at long last, I also had the comfort of my youngest son, Bobby, who returned from Hawaii at age thirteen and moved in with us. Now that he was a teenager, Blanche decided it was my turn to raise him. I couldn't have been happier to be able to have the simple joy of daily life with my son, instead of the pressure, rush, and inevitable heartbreak of his occasional visits in the past. Dianne took the sudden assignment as stepmom in stride, and while the path was occasionally bumpy, we three traveled the journey of Bobby's teen years together as a team.

With Bobby around we were more of a family than a couple. (Scott was finishing college and Carl was working as a carpenter in Hawaii at this time.) Before long, Dianne and I were discussing having children of our own. To be a part of the miracle of birth is the greatest gift of our Creator, and I knew Dianne would make a great mother. I was thrilled at the prospect of being a father again, but I also wrestled with the undeniable historical fact that I was already in my fifties. I had visions of being a doddering old fogey in a wheelchair at our child's high school graduation. On the other hand, Dad had lived almost to ninety, and I was still fit and healthy; I pushed aside my worries, and we embarked on this latest project with enthusiasm.

Nothing happened. After several months, Dianne had a checkup and came back with the answer: she was fine; the problem was me. I was dumbfounded. After all, I was already the father of three sons. Was I too old? Had I spent too much time at high altitudes and low temperatures? I decided to go to the fertility clinic at the University of Washington Medical Center to get to the bottom of the problem.

I began by filling out a long questionnaire about my lifestyle—whether I smoked, whether I drank, how often and how much. There were literally pages and pages of questions, the answers to which I thought were probably none of their business. Nonetheless, I completed the form and handed it to an attractive young woman who gave me a big smile and a small paper bag with a plastic container in it. She wanted a sperm sample and told me the "photography room" down the hall with the "Do Not Enter" sign on it was reserved for that purpose.

Embarrassed beyond belief, I smiled back wanly, slunk down the corridor, and ducked into a little windowless room. The room—not much more than a closet, really—was furnished with a small couch, a coffee table, and few nondescript paintings. The "photography" consisted of a stack of *Playboy* magazines on the table. In a rush of paranoia, I looked behind the paintings for hidden cameras and then sat down to consider my predicament.

How long, I wondered, should one take to return with the paper bag, the container, and its contents? Too soon, and I'd probably be labeled an over-sexed creep; too late, and I'd win the "slowest ever" award. Either way, it was ghastly. Hoping to fall somewhere in the middle of the bell curve, I stepped out of the room about ten minutes later and, trying to look like I did this sort of thing every day, walked casually back to the desk, the paper bag in my hand.

But now, instead of one attractive young woman there were three, and they were all smiling. I smiled back weakly and choked out a "Here you are miss" to the original nurse. She cranked her smile up another hundred watts or so and told me to come back in a week to discuss the results. Adopting what I hoped would look like a relaxed attitude, I strolled to the door, certain that three pairs of beautiful eyes were boring holes into the back of my skull.

A week later I was discussing the details of my personal life with the same smiling nurse. Diagnosis? Too much time in the hot tub. Enjoying herself immensely while I squirmed in my chair in utter mortification, she lectured me about how men in ancient Rome had used scrotum cups filled with hot water as birth control devices. Apparently, the heat turned the little spermatozoa lazy. Her advice? Stay out of the hot tub for a couple of months. It wasn't a hard rule to obey; we were about to embark on a sailboat race across the Pacific to Hawaii, and there was no hot tub on our boat.

◼

Dianne and I had fallen in love with sailing not long after we'd fallen in love ourselves. We'd begun by sailing a little rented Hobie catamaran around the bay in Vancouver, British Columbia, when we were still dating. In the fall of 1975, we bought our first real sailboat, a thirty-five-foot Fuji deep-water cruising cutter, and named it *Impossible* after the boat in René Daumal's book about the search for the mythical Mount Analogue. I soon felt as comfortable on the high seas as I did on high summits. And there was one significant benefit sailing had over climbing: Base Camp was right beneath your feet—bunks, gear, supplies, food, stove, fridge just a few steps down through a hatchway. It all traveled with you.

Dianne seemed at home on the ocean as well; it reminded her, she said, of the vastness of the prairies of Alberta where she had grown up. She also possessed an attribute I would soon come to envy: a complete inability to get seasick.

The next spring, with what we hoped was sufficient mastery of nautical rudiments, we entered our first race, the legendary Swiftsure Lightship Classic. This is an overnight affair in which you sail about seventy miles seaward from Victoria, British Columbia, around the lightship at the mouth of the Strait of Juan de Fuca, and back. The Fuji wasn't designed for racing, but a friend of mine, veteran sailor Van Schilling, a member of our six-man crew, said, "Racing is a good excuse to go out sailing." Dianne and I never needed an excuse to sail; we loved it too much. But we were game for giving the race a shot.

It was a miserable trip. Almost from the outset, we were plowing through twenty-foot seas in forty-knot winds. I was so seasick I couldn't climb out of my bunk to go on watch. I found myself praying we'd go aground so the boat would stop moving. By the next morning, however, we were coasting downwind over big swells with our spinnaker flying, and I had finally gotten over my seasickness. *Impossible* finished close to last that afternoon, but seasickness notwithstanding, we were hooked on racing.

Only a few months later, on the Fourth of July, we began another race from Victoria—this time, to Maui, Hawaii. Van Schilling joined us again, as skipper, and Alan Rutherford, another sailing friend, was our navigator. Our longtime friend and climbing partner, cinematographer Steve Marts, wanted to make a sailing film, so he and Van's girlfriend, Kay Henshaw, rounded out our crew.

It was a magnificent experience. In the mountains, the wind is something you tend to try to avoid. In sailing, the wind is everything. You are utterly at its mercy. When it is fresh and brisk, you race before it, sail edges snapping, taut halyards singing, sleek hull heeled over sharply, the water hissing past the rail, the boat fairly leaping through the swells. With experience, your skin becomes able to detect slight changes in wind velocity, or a degree or two shift in direction, and you adjust course and trim sails in response. You, your boat, the sea, and the wind are all of a part, independent and yet completely integrated.

In light air, the experience is more languid and graceful. With all the sails up to harness every bit of energy the wind offers, you ghost along, surrounded

The crew of the second Impossible, *a Swan 441, after placing second in the Swiftsure race, May 1981—(front, left to right) Bill Nance, Dianne, Jim, (back, left to right) Janet Baron, Alan Rutherford, Sally-Christine Rodgers, Amy Margerum, Ari Steinberg. Photo: Dianne Roberts*

by quiet, the ocean whispering along the waterline. In such conditions, you imagine yourself a great white bird and the sea a great blue sky.

And in high wind, the sails may be reefed or furled completely, with only the hull and mast catching the gale. The boat pitches down the face of one wave and climbs the next. You wrestle the helm and ride it out, engaged in a test of will, strength, and patience you pray you'll win.

An hour out of almost any saltwater marina in the world, you are in nature as it has been almost from the dawn of creation. Albatrosses swoop low over the waves on long, narrow wings so perfectly designed for lift that they seldom have to flap. Schools of bottle-nosed dolphins course alongside the boat, "surfing" the bow wave. The sea and sky mirror each other, changing color from cobalt blue to pale blue-green to glassy gray. Night comes quickly, sometimes heralded by the "green flash," a momentary trick of light refraction that occurs on calm evenings at the very moment the last of the sun dips below the watery horizon. As darkness deepens, the boat stirs millions of luminescent diatoms in the water to life, leaving a trail of fire through the black ocean, as if the keel were a burning matchstick and the water flammable. At dawn, you patrol the deck, picking up nocturnal visitors—the occasional misguided flying fish or squid—and the cycle begins again.

More than three weeks after leaving Victoria, *Impossible* glided into Maui's Lahaina Harbor flying a banner that read, "The Impossible Takes a Little Longer." We were dead last, arriving two days later than the next to last boat. We couldn't have cared less. We won the Turtle Trophy and were greeted with a great dockside party and a huge container of mai tais.

In 1979 Dianne and I took delivery of a new boat, a Swan 441 cutter. Built in Finland to a racing/cruising design, she was a real beauty and was considered the Stradivarius of sailboats. With a dark blue hull, teak decks, and a cutter rig, she looked fast even at anchor. Below decks, she was trimmed out in hand-rubbed teak and had a brightly varnished striped floor made of teak and holly. She was a joy to behold and even more of a joy to sail.

On the Fourth of July, 1982, with loudspeakers blaring the theme song from *Chariots of Fire* and a crew of eight wearing matching T-shirts, our second *Impossible* sailed proudly out of Victoria harbor bound for Maui. This time we were determined not to be last. With my son Bobby, not quite sixteen, and my K2 expedition colleague Rick Ridgeway among our crew, we pounded west through the cold gray waters of the Strait of Juan de Fuca, then set course for the blue waters of the Pacific to the southwest, gradually shedding clothes as we reached warmer latitudes.

The days flew by, and south of latitude 35, we began to see the long line of puffy clouds on the far horizon that signals the trade winds. Now we'd really be making speed. We changed from our big, light air sails to smaller sails made to handle the trades, and *Impossible* bounded through the ocean. One day, more than fifty bottle-nosed dolphins escorted us south as we ran downwind at nine knots, pulled along by our "bulletproof" number three spinnaker. We were making good time.

We stood watch in two crews of four, taking turns at the helm. Late at night I would lie in bed marveling that my own son was at the helm, guiding us across the vast Pacific, steering by the stars and the compass, the master not only of his own destiny but of ours as well. I doubt there is any moment, save birth, that is more magical for a parent as when a child crosses that invisible line from dependence to independence, from apprenticeship to competence. I was proud of Bobby beyond measure and a bit in awe as well.

Powered only by the wind, we crossed the finish line at Lahaina only seventeen days after we'd left Victoria, more than a week faster than our previous attempt and ahead of much of the rest of the fleet. It was refreshing to be able to watch our competitors straggle in behind us for a change.

After several days of raucous parties of the sort that seem part and parcel of sailboat racing, we were ready to explore. Our plan was to sail from Maui to the Big Island and cruise around for a month before returning to Seattle in late August.

We were racing across the Alenuihaha Channel between the two islands in six-foot seas flying a double-reefed mainsail and a number three jib in a twenty-five-knot beam wind, the warm salt spray blowing in our faces, when the mast snapped. In an instant, exhilaration turned to disaster. The port side lower shroud, a stainless steel rod, had let go, and the seventy-foot aluminum mast had buckled instantly and crashed to the deck, just missing Dianne and burying her in a chaos of metal, rigging, rope, and sail.

We screamed her name and were relieved to hear her call out that she was all right. Meanwhile, however, the broken section of the mast was in the water, still tangled in rigging. With each surge of the swells in the channel it threatened to pierce the hull and sink us. While the rest of the crew worked to stabilize the boat and Dianne ran below to radio the Coast Guard, I leaped into the tangled mess on our deck and, using a hacksaw and bolt-cutters, cut away the remaining rigging. Then I watched the mast, mainsail, and jib sink in forty-two fathoms of water.

Shaking with relief that no one had been hurt, but sick with disappointment, I turned the boat around and we motored back to Lahaina and then on to Honolulu to arrange repairs. Deep-water sailing has one thing in common with mountain climbing: a very small event can trigger a very big disaster. In this case, a small ball-and-socket attachment on the rod rigging just beneath the first spreader on the mast had frozen, apparently some weeks earlier. Unable to swivel in the socket, the leeward shroud had been stressed and flexed beyond its design capacity during our race west to Maui. When we turned east toward the Big Island, the shroud, now on the windward side, finally snapped, like a paper clip that has been bent once too often. The mast, suddenly unsupported, followed—a chain of events triggered by a small flaw. In Honolulu, we learned the small flaw would cost us at least a month; the new mast would have to be shipped to us—from Wisconsin.

We also learned Dianne was pregnant. Since the risk of miscarriage is greatest in the first trimester of a pregnancy, Dianne's doctor recommended that she fly home instead of sail. In the meantime, we lolled around Hawaii waiting for the mast. When it finally arrived, we installed it, saw Dianne and three others, including Bobby, off to the airport, provisioned the boat, and in late September, four of us set sail for home.

Too late, according to the weather charts. The Pacific has a nasty habit of breeding bad storms in late September and October, but we were treated to fine weather for the first week or so. One particularly brilliant sunny day, we were cruising along in gentle five-foot seas with a steady twenty-five-knot wind off our port quarter—perfect sailing conditions. We had a single reef in the mainsail and a number two Genoa jib winged out on a spinnaker pole. I had another hour to go on my watch and was sailing along blissfully, without a care in the world.

I should have been watching the barometer. If I had been, I would certainly have taken another reef in the main and battened down the hatches. Quite suddenly, off on the horizon to my left, a black-rimmed cloudbank appeared: a storm front. It was bearing down on us with astonishing speed. One minute it was on the horizon and the next it was only five miles away. Then four . . . then three . . . two, and the angry black clouds blotted out the sun. I could see the edge of the front racing toward us. Ahead of it, the sea flattened to a white froth of foam and spray. Clipped into a lifeline, I gripped the wheel and turned us farther downwind to run with the storm.

As the front hit, *Impossible* leapt forward like a startled deer. Almost instantly, our knot meter registered our speed at fourteen knots; the anemometer pegged out at over sixty knots. We were being hurled across the surface of the Pacific by the storm's fury. The wind howled, it rained furiously, and the rain and foaming sea combined into torrents of stinging spray. I hung on to the wheel for all I was worth.

After about an hour of battle, the wind dropped to a mere thirty-eight knots, and I yielded my watch and the helm, grateful to be still afloat. Stiff winds continued, and even though we had spent a day in the doldrums of a big Pacific high-pressure area, we arrived home—intact—in only fourteen days, three days fewer than the outbound "racing" leg of the voyage.

Dianne met us at Neah Bay, a small community at the northwestern tip of the Olympic Peninsula, where we tied up for a hot shower, a good meal, and a night's sleep unbroken by three-hour watches. The next day we sailed down the Strait of Juan de Fuca toward Seattle and home, accompanied for almost an hour by three gray whales: father, mother, and baby. Dianne and I took it as a good omen.

◘

Our son Charles Roberts Whittaker was born on April 24, 1983. We'd named him after both of our fathers, but it was his nickname, Joss, the Chinese word for luck, or karma, that stuck. With Joss to care for, Dianne and I had to face up to the fact that our neighborhood in West Seattle wasn't the best place for small children. Traffic roared up and down the street above us, and one morning we discovered vandals had slashed the tires on twenty-four cars parked along the road. Dianne and I both had grown up in somewhat simpler times, amid trees and wild things (we didn't count vandals as part of the latter), and we started looking for someplace more like what we'd had as children ourselves. We wanted someplace forested, facing water and looking westward toward the sunset—and perhaps a bit sunnier than Seattle.

It was my older brother, Barney, who found it. Barney had retired from teaching, and he and his family had moved to Port Townsend, a picturesque Victorian town on the northeastern tip of the Olympic Peninsula, a half-hour ferry ride and one-hour drive from Seattle. Port Townsend had aspired to be a great seaport, like Seattle, but after a building spree that left it with some great architecture, history passed it by. A backwater for decades, in the 1960s and 1970s its inherent beauty began attracting artists and others who restored the old Victorian homes and gave the town a new lease on life through tourism. In 1982, when Barney moved there, Port Townsend had two good marinas, several restaurants, a number of art galleries, a population of about six thousand people, and the occasional deer strolling through the streets.

Not far from Barney's house, west of town, Dianne and I found just what we were looking for: a thirty-five-acre parcel of land on a bluff looking west over the Strait of Juan de Fuca. There were hundreds of wild rhododendrons growing among the trees, and deer, fox, cougar, raccoon, and otter tracks on the steep path down to the deserted beach below the bluff, where seals often sunbathed. Above, gulls soared and bald eagles rode the updraft along the edge of the bluff. It was perfect, and Dianne and I began planning a home that would permit us to coexist with the wild things that shared the site.

Ever since we'd helped finish the elegant little Norwegian cottage Leif Patterson had begun before his tragic death, Dianne and I had been in love with log homes. Leif's father had even sent me a set of hand-forged tools for log building, and they were among my most prized possessions. I was itching to use them.

Once we bought the property, Dianne and I started designing our house, building a model out of half-inch-diameter wood dowels. Then we began looking for a log home company we'd feel comfortable working with. We found it in Victor, Montana. Alpine Log Homes used only fire-killed, standing lodgepole pines unsuitable for lumber, which they removed from the forest either by horse or helicopter to minimize impact on the environment, and then hand-peeled instead of milling the logs to uniformity. We showed them our plans and our model.

Barney and Jim on the scaffolding, chinking the "Log Mahal." Photo: Dianne Roberts

"If you can do it with dowels," they said, "we can do it with logs."

It would take some time to turn our plans into reality. Unlike regular construction, log homes are fitted and assembled at the builder's lot, then disassembled, trucked to the home site, and reassembled. In the meantime, Dianne and I returned to our routine in West Seattle, including our morning and evening soaks in the hot tub. Not only was it the ultimate in relaxation, but now I knew it was also a great birth control technique. I continued to believe that right up until Dianne told me she was expecting again.

On January 11, 1985, our second son was born. We named him Leif Roberts Whittaker, after Leif Patterson. A few months later, we sold our West Seattle house and moved into a log garage/guest house we'd built with Barney's help on our Port Townsend property. That summer, we laid out, dug, and poured concrete for the footings and basement of the main house, and in September, four huge trucks, each carrying 50,000 pounds of logs, arrived at the site. Six days later, thanks to two cranes and a small army of friends, relatives, subcontractors, and a supervisor from Alpine Log Homes, the entire three-story structure, thirty-five feet from base logs to ridgepole, stood gleaming in the sun.

Of course, that was the easy part. Now we had to chain-saw holes for doors and windows; install a roof; build a massive, freestanding fireplace that rose fifty feet from basement to flue-top; chink, clean, and stain the logs; construct interior walls; install plumbing, wiring, and heating systems; and, of course, furnish the place. When it was all done, our old friend from REI and the Kennedy campaign, Dave Lester, christened our house "the Log Mahal." It was spectacular.

But even as it was being completed, there was a cloud looming above our home and our lives, one far more menacing than we could have imagined at the time.

■

Two years earlier I had received a registered letter from the Quabaug Rubber Company informing me that my Vibram sole endorsement contract was being canceled. The letter gave no reason; Ed Varnum's son Herb had taken over the business, and, presumably, he had other ideas for promoting the company. I missed the steady income, but Dianne and I really had no serious financial worries at the time. Over the years we'd made some sensible investments. We also owned a small apartment building in Seattle, a condominium in Hawaii, our boat, and our West Seattle home. More importantly, we had a substantial stake in a new and growing outdoor equipment manufacturing company: Whittaker/O'Malley, Inc.

Some years earlier, not long after I'd announced my retirement from REI, I had received a letter from a man named Jim O'Malley. O'Malley had a degree from the Wharton Business School at the University of Pennsylvania, a year of marketing at Bloomingdale's, the most successful and creative fashion retailer in New York at the time, and was in the horse-blanket manufacturing business. He wanted to move to Seattle and produce a new line of outdoor products—parkas, packs, gaiters, and the like—to sell to REI, L. L. Bean, Eddie Bauer, and other retailers who were beginning to realize that rugged outdoor clothes weren't just for mountaineers anymore.

We met, and he seemed a capable businessman, so we cofounded Whittaker/O'Malley, Inc. We found manufacturing space on the sixth floor of a warehouse near Seattle's Kingdome and hired Nick Szurich, formerly with THAW, to run the production operations. Seattle artist Ellen Ziegler and I designed a label for our line with a "Because It's There" logo on a dramatic black-and-white image of a mountain. When Jim and his family arrived, they lived with us in West Seattle until they found a place of their own, and in the meantime, I introduced him to my friends in the outdoor trade, took him up Mount Rainier, and helped him design several products. Under the terms of our agreement, O'Malley was president and CEO, and I was chairman and the company's high-profile spokesman, representing Whittaker/O'Malley products at all the major trade shows—selling instead of buying for the first time in my career. It was understood that I would not spend a lot of time in the office looking over his shoulder. I was, after all, "retired."

The business thrived. In a few years we were selling our products both to outdoor specialty stores like Eddie Bauer and to department stores

Because It's There

Whittaker/O'Malley, Inc. logo

like Nordstrom. I viewed the enterprise as a long-term investment in a field I knew well.

Just before Dianne, Joss, Leif, and I were to move to Port Townsend, I got a call from Seattle Trust and Savings Bank inviting O'Malley and me to a meeting with our bank officer. I figured it was just a routine review of Whittaker/O'Malley's accounts. But when we sat down, the bank officer informed me that there seemed to be some discrepancies in our accounts. Like most manufacturing companies, we generated our operating funds—to purchase raw materials, pay staff, cover utilities, rent, and so forth—by borrowing against the value of our accounts receivable. We were entitled to borrow up to 85 percent of the value of our invoices so that we could produce products to fulfill our next orders. Now the bank officer sat before me questioning the authenticity of the invoices O'Malley had submitted as proof of the value of our accounts receivable.

I looked at O'Malley, and to my utter horror, he broke down sobbing. With tears flowing down his cheeks, he confessed to having created or inflated accounts receivable from customers like Eddie Bauer and L. L. Bean to increase the amount of money our company could borrow.

I was flabbergasted. For nearly half a decade, Jim and I had met regularly to discuss the business, design products, map out sales strategies, and assess progress. Our families had gotten together. Over lunches we talked about kids and soccer, not just the business. We were friends. Only two months earlier, I had sold my apartment building in Seattle and given the company a $200,000 personal loan, with O'Malley's promise that it would be repaid at the end of the two-month period. The repayment of that loan, and the proceeds from the sale of our West Seattle home, were to cover the cost of our new home in Port Townsend. Now, I realized, it was probably gone forever. I also realized that the guarantee I'd signed on a $150,000 loan we'd taken out at the outset of the business, years earlier, meant I'd lose that money, too. It was a disaster.

We had raw materials in the warehouse sufficient to fill a large order from L. L. Bean, but we didn't have the $10,000 it would take to pay our employees to make the finished products. O'Malley wanted to have our workers make the goods and then just not pay them. I wouldn't hear of it, and he agreed to split the cost of their wages with me. I paid the entire amount, and O'Malley gave me a $5,000 no-interest IOU—which he's never repaid. To cover our losses,

Dianne and I took out a huge mortgage on the Port Townsend house.

But the loss of the loans I had made to him was only the beginning. A few months later I learned that the fine print on that original $150,000 business start-up loan made me liable not just for the face amount, but also "jointly and severally" for all the debts the company owed the bank—almost $1 million. Seattle Trust and Savings Bank filed suit against me, personally, to retrieve its money.

Dianne and I were in shock. After seeking legal advice we realized that years of legal wrangling would eat up whatever money we had and still leave us with this massive debt. Instead, in an attempt to settle with the bank and get on with our lives, we sold virtually every asset we had left—the condominium in Maui, our beloved *Impossible*, and twenty-five of the thirty-five total acres of our property in Port Townsend. We even briefly entertained the idea of selling shares in "the Log Mahal" to our friends to raise more money. Finally, having run out of assets and ideas, but with the debt far from paid, we sought out the help of our old friend and former REI board member Sid Volinn, who was a well-respected bankruptcy judge in Seattle.

Sid told us that if we sat down with the bank and demonstrated that we had sold all our assets in a good faith effort to pay down the debt and that all we had left was our heavily mortgaged home, the bank would probably not choose to drive us into actual bankruptcy. We did exactly that and as Sid had predicted, the bank dropped the lawsuit. There was nothing left to squeeze out of us anyway.

We were financially ruined. A federal fraud bank case was pending against O'Malley, but as time passed I wondered if justice would ever be done. After two years, I met with a young Assistant U.S. Attorney and asked about the progress of the case. To my astonishment, he blew up at me, charging that I was trying to "use my celebrity status" to influence the case. I couldn't believe it. I was the good guy, for God's sake!

It took eight years, but in 1994 Jim O'Malley was finally brought to justice, in a manner of speaking. To my dismay, the Assistant U.S. Attorney reported to the court that the defendant was basically honest and had been very cooperative with the Bureau's investigation. O'Malley was convicted of felony bank fraud, put on probation, and eventually ordered to pay restitution to the bank of $39,855.55. I couldn't believe it.

Dianne and I have spent the ensuing years trying to dig ourselves out of the crater of financial disaster that O'Malley's fraud left us in; I doubt we'll ever recover our losses in my lifetime. Even if we do, how can anyone be compensated for literally years of emotional anguish and economic hardship; how do you face your children and tell them someone has effectively walked off with their college funds and whatever financial legacy you might have been able to leave them? The answer's simple: you can't.

Looking back, I realize that although I have learned to assess carefully objective dangers like the structure and stability of a snowfield, I have spent much of my life "roped up" with people who follow a code of responsibility and honor. Time after time I have trusted my life to my ropemates, as they have trusted theirs with me, with the certainty that they would treat my life as they would their own because, in a literal sense, the two were one and the same. Once in a while, however, someone comes along who doesn't adhere to that code, who doesn't even seem to know it exists. Perhaps if I had dug deeper into O'Malley's credentials, I'd have found some clue that I couldn't rely upon him. But I doubt it; that sort of thing doesn't usually show up on résumés, and it's seldom revealed in reference checks. Perhaps if I'd been more directly involved in the day-to-day operations of the business, I'd have noticed something was wrong. But that wasn't the nature of our agreement, and I kept my side of it.

Maybe it all boils down to this: you can go through life protecting yourself at every turn from disappointment and risk and, as a result, lead a safe, if uneventful, life in which you never have to trust your fellow man. Or you can lead an "undefended life," a life on the edge in which you marvel at the general goodness of people and, occasionally, get hurt. I choose the latter course. For the great balance of my life so far, that has proven the right choice. Perhaps it's not even a choice at all.

In 1986, while I was still in the depths of despair over the O'Malley disaster, I got a call that reaffirmed my faith in both the goodness and genius of my fellow man. It was a gentleman named Ed Tuck, and he posed a simple question to me.

"When someone's knocked unconscious, what's the first thing they say when they come to?"

"Where am I?" I answered without a second thought.

"Exactly," Tuck said. What's more, he had the answer.

Ed Tuck turned out to be both a venture capitalist, who had backed a few now highly successful companies, and something of a technical wizard himself. He had formed a company to develop a device that would revolutionize the concept of space the way the clock had revolutionized the concept of time: a satellite-linked, hand-held global positioning unit that could tell sailors, climbers, hikers, hunters, and anyone else in the world who might get lost exactly where they were. Instantly.

Borrowing the name of the Portuguese sailor who first circumnavigated the globe, he called the company Magellan. He wanted me to be its president and CEO.

I turned him down. I knew intuitively that Ed's idea had the kind of boldness and genius I loved, and I really enjoyed Ed himself; he was brilliant, immensely likable, and refreshingly honest. I also knew that the CEO of this company would be a millionaire as soon as the company went public, in perhaps five years. Lord knows, we sure could have used the money.

But after Dianne and I agonized over Ed's offer for a week, we realized we had reached a milestone, a turning point in our lives; we were not willing to move to Los Angeles and invest most of our waking hours during the next five years—critical years in each of our lives and the lives of our children—in the start up of a new company. With an odd combination of sadness and exhilaration, I called Ed to tell him our decision.

To my delight, he understood completely. What's more, as if he'd already anticipated the answer, he had a back-up offer: chairman of the board. It was a paid position with stock options, and I took it. In short order we found a CEO and, right on schedule, Magellan released its first hand-held global positioning system (GPS) receiver. The rest is, as they say, American business history; Magellan has been enormously successful, and its GPS units have dropped in price from $3,000 to less than $150, making safety available to almost anyone ever likely to need a quick and reliable answer to that age-old question, "Where am I?"

What's more, Dianne and I have been friends with Ed and his wife, Jan, a talented artist and sculptor, ever since.

Peace Climb leaders release peace doves at Base Camp after the successful climb.
Photo: John Yaeger

Chapter Thirteen

THE SUMMIT ON THE SUMMIT

It started out as a wild dream. By the mid-1980s, the United States, the Soviet Union, and more recently, China, had spent trillions of dollars, rubles, and yuan to build up nuclear arsenals capable of annihilating the entire globe many times over. Tensions among the three nations were high. The Soviet Union and China maintained a state of military readiness at many places along their shared border. And while President Nixon had succeeded in opening a dialogue with the Chinese some years earlier, President Reagan had been elected, in part, by fanning fear about the Soviet Union's "evil empire" and threatening to escalate the arms race with his "Star Wars" weapons-in-space scheme.

One day in March 1986, Warren Thompson and Bud Krogh approached me with an idea they'd been thinking about for two years. Fellow lawyers, climbers, and members of the Mountain Rescue Council, they had served as porters on the Pelion Climb of Mount Rainier and had become friends. They also shared an interest in world affairs. Their idea was breathtakingly simple: why not bring together the best climbers from the United States, the Soviet Union, and China and, as a demonstration of the desire of common citizens for a safer, saner, more peaceful world, mount a joint expedition, through Tibet, to the summit of Mount Everest—in short, a "Peace Climb." They wanted me to organize and lead the expedition.

It was, I thought, a brilliant and bold idea. Also, probably impossible. How could we ever hope to get Soviet and American climbers together and then enter the forbidden territory of Tibet to join with the Chinese in an officially sanctioned, three-nation expedition? Even if we could get permission, which was unlikely, international expeditions had a long and notorious history of mis–communication and mishap. Throw in the decades of political suspicion and government-sponsored misinformation between these three particular nations, and the whole idea looked like madness. Not to mention that it would be a hugely expensive logistical nightmare.

Then I remembered something I'd read that the great German writer and scientist Goethe, had said: "Whatever you can do, or dream you can, begin it. Boldness has genius, power and magic in it."

And so we began. Almost immediately, we ran into a bit of luck. It turned out that Dr. Mike Weidman, a member of the American Alpine Club, had already obtained a rare permit from the Chinese to climb Everest—which the Chinese call Qomolangma—from the Tibetan side in the spring of 1990. Mike offered to sell me the permit for $5,000 on the condition that he would be a member of the expedition. I jumped at the offer. With a permit in hand, we'd be able to spend the next three years focusing on the question of *how* to make it happen rather than *whether* it could happen.

With access to China secured, I decided to work on persuading the Soviets to participate, assuming that the Chinese would almost have to join the expedition, if only to save face. As luck would have it, another Seattlite, Bob Walsh, was at that same time organizing the 1990 Goodwill Games—a sort of mini-Olympics between the United States and the Soviet Union. Since promoting understanding and peace were the objectives of both our projects, Bob agreed to arrange for me to meet with the members of the Soviet Union's Ministry of Sports and Physical Culture, which oversaw all sports activities, including climbing.

On January 18, 1988, Bob and I flew to Moscow. With us were two early financial supporters of the expedition, Seattlites David Sabey, a former Olympic wrestler and now successful building contractor, and restaurateur Jerry Kingen. With Sabey's physique, Kingen's expensively tailored clothes and fancy Rolex watch, and Walsh's well-earned respect among the Soviets, we looked like a class act. After clearing customs in Moscow, we rode in limousines to a quaint dacha just outside the city that had only recently been vacated by British Prime Minister Margaret Thatcher and her entourage. I was impressed.

I was also glad to be alive. Sabey, a man who always seemed to be in a hurry, had tipped our driver with a $100 bill to get us to our destination before Bob and Jerry. We careened through the city, passing on curves, even driving up on sidewalks to get around traffic—a practice that did not endear us to the locals.

The next day Bob escorted us to the ministry, where he seemed to me to be almost worshipped. (One awed Russian whispered to me that with his beard he looked "just like Jesus Christ.") We were ushered into a room so filled with smoke the air was blue. Before me, at the biggest conference table I had ever seen, were representatives of the ministry, some twenty of them. Bob had business to conduct with them as well, so I waited my turn, getting more anxious and clammy-handed by the minute. Finally, he finished and introduced me. My reputation as the first American to summit Everest had preceded me, and they leaned forward in their seats to listen. I began my presentation.

Through an interpreter, I talked about the fact that, as the Goodwill Games demonstrated, athletic achievement was a human trait that crossed political boundaries and ideologies. I talked about the common yearning of all people for peace. I talked about the symbolism of a group of climbers, roped together, trusting their lives to comrades whose governments were at odds with each other.

"On the top of the highest summit in the world," I concluded, "Soviet, Chinese, and American climbers will embrace and celebrate their common achievement. We will demonstrate to the world what can be accomplished, what odds can be overcome, through cooperation and friendship. The citizens of the world will rejoice. Our three flags will fly on the summit together."

When I was done, the chairman of the committee rose and, with a hearty laugh, said, "Thank you, Mr. Whittaker, for that excellent presentation. I only wish our old friend Mr. Walsh here was as concise as you are!" Bob turned red, and I laughed nervously.

"We are interested in your proposal and will be in contact with you." I didn't know exactly what this meant, but I took it as a good omen, as it turned out to be. They asked me back the very next day, and I found myself standing with a microphone before an even larger audience convened by the committee, making my presentation again. As soon as I finished, a huge older man grabbed my interpreter and spoke to him urgently. Then the translator told me the man was Alexsandr Ivanitesky, also known as "The Tractor," the 1964 heavyweight freestyle wrestling champion of the world. Ivanitesky told the translator his father and three brothers had been killed in World War II, along with twenty million other Soviets, and that the Soviet people longed for peace and would approve of what I had proposed. With tears in his eyes, the wrestler said to me, "It will be the most important thing you will do in your entire life."

I hugged him, crying now myself, and received a bone-crushing bear hug in return. It was a reception beyond anything I had hoped for. In the next few days, while we awaited their decision, we visited the homes and families of some of the friends Bob had made while working on the Goodwill Games. It was clear to me—amidst all the vodka-toasting—that the people of the Soviet Union were as hungry for peace as we were.

Maybe it was because Mikhail Gorbachev had just been named president of the Soviet Union and change was in the air. Maybe I was in the right place at the right time. Maybe I just gave one hell of a speech. To my amazement, however, a couple of days later the ministry approved the participation of Soviet climbers on the expedition. But there was a catch: they would participate only if the Chinese government sent them a formal invitation. I returned to the States on January 28 feeling confident we could arrange that. We'd cleared one big hurdle; now, on to China.

In April Warren Thompson and I flew to Beijing (Warren was now deputy leader of the expedition), where we met with the Chinese Mountaineering Association, the organization that makes all climbing decisions in China. It was another smoke-filled room. As tea was served, the association leadership sat before us at a long table, wearing identical Mao jackets and identically grim faces.

Once again, through a translator, I made my presentation. I kept watching the audience to judge how it was going, but they were—there's no better word for it—inscrutable. When I was done, they sat poker-faced. Finally, their leader said:

"Mr. Whittaker, the Soviets have not been allowed in our country for thirty years."

Since this didn't seem to me to be a flat-out "No," I pressed ahead.

"Yes, I understand that," I said. "But not long ago, you came to our country with Ping-Pong paddles and balls, in a gesture of goodwill that made a great impression on the American people. Now we and the Soviets would like to come to China with our ice axes and crampons to make the same gesture."

This seemed to soften them some, but they warned me that they would not invite the Soviets unless they were sure they would come. It occurred to me that this was getting to be a lot like Ping-Pong: the Soviets wouldn't come unless the Chinese invited them; the Chinese wouldn't invite them unless they knew the Soviets would come. I began to feel some sympathy for the diplomatic corps.

I reiterated what seemed to me to be the trump card: China would be the host; the Soviets would be their guests, as would we Americans. The symbolism would be lost on no one.

They nodded and suggested that Warren and I take in the sights while they discussed our proposal. Warren and I decided to visit the Great Wall for a couple of days. Then we returned to the Mountaineering Association headquarters.

"We haven't decided yet," they said. "Go visit the Forbidden City."

We visited the Forbidden City and returned the next day.

"We need one more day," they said. Warren and I stayed in town and absorbed the sights (thousands of people on bikes), sounds (truck and bus horns, bicycle bells), and smells (coal smoke, diesel fumes, hot cooking oil, exotic spices) of Beijing. Then we returned to the association.

They served tea again, this time with cookies.

"You may bring your Soviet friends to climb Qomolangma. . . . "

Warren and I looked at each other in triumph.

" . . . but we will not participate."

I looked blank-faced at the interpreter, certain that he had misunderstood. He hadn't.

"But you must participate," I implored. "You must stand with us on the summit, representing one of the three most powerful nations in the world." And then the truth came out.

"You must understand, Mr. Whittaker," the leader said. "Our people have had less opportunity to devote themselves to the sport of mountaineering, compared to the Soviets and the Americans."

So that was it. They were afraid of failing. I thought how incredibly hard it must have been for them to admit this. Then I understood how much worse a loss of face it would be if their climbers failed to reach the summit. I began to see that the secret to reaching our goal was insuring that the Chinese reached theirs.

"We will bring your climbers to the United States and train them on our Mount Rainier so they will be qualified to climb Qomolangma," I offered. "And we will promise you that no country will reach the summit alone; there will be three countries on the summit together or none. If one team begins to fail, all three will have to come down. No one will lose face."

I also promised that the United States would pay their expedition costs; they finally smiled at that. Still, we got no firm answer. Warren and I left for the States with only their promise to let us know of their decision in a few months.

Five months later we received a short but sweet telegram from the Chinese Mountaineering Association: "We are pleased to be 100 percent participants in your 1990 Peace Climb."

Now all we had to do was make it happen.

As always, the first step was to build the strongest yet smallest team needed to do the job. We decided there would be five climbers from each country, making a fifteen-person climbing team. We would have no Sherpa to stock the higher camps, and this was the minimum number we'd need to ensure a safe and well-stocked summit attempt. We would also need each country to provide a leader, deputy leader, doctor, Base Camp organizer, and interpreter. With these support personnel, our total grew to thirty—the largest expedition I had ever been on, much less organized.

I sent word that each country was to select its best high-altitude climbers but stipulated that none could have summited Everest before. I didn't want it to look like one country or team member might be leading the others. This, obviously, meant I would not be on the climbing team, but that was fine by me. By now I was sixty years old, and though still in great shape, I'd already done this mountain; I wanted to make room for others. The Soviets asked whether we would have a woman on our team. I answered that we would and encouraged both them and the Chinese to invite a woman as well.

For our United States team, all we had to do was make it known that we were looking for five climbers to join an international peace climb to the highest point on the planet and the applications poured in. We found two of our climbers close to home. Ed Viesturs, thirty, a Seattle veterinarian, and Robert Link, thirty-two, a carpenter, had both been guides for Rainier Mountaineering. (Interestingly, Link was the son of the Colonel Ed Link who had been instrumental in my assignment to the Mountain and Cold Weather Training Command

during the Korean War.) Viesturs and Link both had recently summited another Himalaya giant, 28,168-foot Kangchenjunga, the third-highest peak in
the world, without supplemental oxygen. Another climber selected, Steve Gall,
thirty-two, a climbing guide and ski instructor from Aspen, Colorado, had
guided more than a dozen parties up Mount McKinley (Denali) and knew well
what conditions at 20,000 feet were like. So did our oldest climber, Ian Wade,
forty-two, the British-born vice president of the Outward Bound organization,
who was also an experienced alpinist. In selecting our team, I leaned toward
guides, not only because they were professionals and climbed often but also
because they were trained to be team players and to watch out for others.

Finding our woman climber was more difficult. Dianne, of course, had been
to just under 26,000 feet on K2 and was certainly qualified, but going to Everest
with me meant we'd both be leaving the boys for three months and placing
ourselves in harm's way. Instead, she served as executive director of the expedition from Port Townsend. That decision turned out to be fortunate, for without her help from home at a critical point in the expedition, we might not have
climbed the mountain at all.

In the end we chose La Verne Woods, thirty-two, a tax attorney and marathon runner from Seattle who had climbed to 23,000 feet on the Soviet peak
Mount Lenin. She took two months off work before the climb to train for Everest.

Our interpreter, Keren Su, was Chinese-American and a friend of Warren's.
The expedition doctor, Kurt Papenfus, thirty-three, from Snowmass, Colorado, had treated many cold weather- and high-altitude-related injuries and
illnesses. What's more, since he already lived at 6,000 feet, he had a built-in acclimatization advantage. We chose Ray Nichols, fifty-two, a mountaineer and
manager of a boat manufacturing company in Tacoma, Washington, as our
Base Camp manager and equipment coordinator. And, finally, we chose two
women volunteers, Barbara Fromm and Patty Riley, nutritionists at Seattle's
Harborview Medical Center, to design our menus and secure our three-month
food supply.

Funding any expedition is difficult, and this one looked like it was going
to be a million-dollar effort. We had decided to try to get it funded the same
way the Olympics were, by selling exclusive publicity rights to corporate sponsors, though I wasn't entirely sure how we were going to get the ball rolling.
Shortly after my return from the Soviet Union, I was at the Outdoor Retailer

trade show in Las Vegas shooting the breeze over a soft drink with Leon Gorman, president of L. L. Bean. We were both charter inductees of the Woolrich Outdoor Hall of Fame, along with Lowell Thomas, and had known each other for some time. Fresh from Moscow, I was excitedly telling him about the Peace Climb when he reached into his sport coat, pulled out his checkbook, wrote out a check for $100,000 and handed it to me. Stunned, I gripped the check in both hands.

"Leon," I stammered, "you don't have to do this!"

"But I want to," he said simply.

I ran to the nearest phone and called Seattle: "Warren!" I bellowed down the line to my deputy leader. "We're on our way to Everest!"

Thus Leon, bless his soul, got us rolling, and thanks in part to the precedent he set, we were able to secure other sponsors, including Boeing, Seafirst Bank, and a total of 166 other, smaller companies.

As the expedition came together I realized we would be climbing Mount Everest around the twentieth anniversary of Earth Day and that gave me an idea. Over the years many expeditions—including our 1963 American Mount Everest Expedition—had left hundreds of pounds of trash on Everest. Strewn with empty oxygen bottles, tents, food cans, and other abandoned gear, the South Col on the Nepalese side had been called the highest junkyard in the world. Although we would be climbing the less-traveled Tibetan side, we knew there was garbage there too, from expeditions as early as the 1921 British attempt. With the agreement of the Chinese and Soviets, we added another goal for our expedition: we would not only climb the mountain leaving as little trace as possible but we would also try to remove garbage left there by others.

As a result, the expedition became the Mount Everest Earth Day 20 International Peace Climb 1990. Our logo had a dove on the summit, the word *peace* in three languages, and the Chinese, American, and Soviet flags at the base. The thousands of T-shirts we sold with this logo became a major source of funds for the expedition.

■

We had planned a formal shakedown climb on Mount Rainier for the summer of 1989, and in mid-June, Warren and I arrived at Seattle's airport to meet the Soviet and Chinese teams. The Soviets arrived raring to go. The Chinese didn't arrive at all. We learned they had assembled at Beijing, but because of the Tiananmen Square massacre and the martial law that followed they couldn't get a flight out. There was nothing to do but head up to Mount Rainier without them.

On the bus, I got to know some of the Soviet team members. Mistislav Gorbenko, called "Slava," a Soviet climber from the seaport town of Odessa, had a Russian/English dictionary for sailors and kept asking "Where do we drop anchor?" Ekaterina Ivanova, "Katya," the woman climber from Moscow, gravitated toward Dianne and La Verne. The smallest member of the team, at five feet, three inches, Katya proved to be very strong. We learned later that her husband was a world-class weight lifter, and we decided she must hand him the weights. The leader of the Soviet team was Vladimir Shatayev, a noted climber and high-ranking member of the Communist Party. The Soviet interpreter, Vitale Medvedev, was a climber of sorts, too. His English was excellent, peppered with American slang; we were convinced he worked for the KGB.

We set up camp on a lateral moraine of the Nisqually Glacier, at 7,000 feet. We made a neat kitchen area with ice countertops and two 70-pound restaurant-style stoves that had been pulled up from Paradise on toboggans. We surrounded the kitchen area with the tents, the way we planned to lay out our base camp in Tibet. It was a great site; even the outhouse had a view, all the way to Oregon.

To our relief, the Chinese team arrived less than a week later. As we loaded the bus, I told the team, every member of which was smoking, that smoking was prohibited on the bus. They flipped their cigarettes away and climbed aboard. Halfway to Paradise, I noticed several holding their heads and looking miserable. When I asked the interpreter what was wrong, he said they needed a smoke to relieve their headaches. We stopped the bus, bought them cigarettes, and they lit up. Immediately, they brightened. It was amazing. Not one of the American or Soviet climbers smoked, but all the Chinese did. Even in snowstorms, they would sit outside, snow drifting over them, smoking.

The Chinese leader was Losang Dawa and their climbing team consisted of three Tibetans and two Chinese, one of whom was a woman. Noting the Tibetan climbers, I thought to myself that perhaps the reason the Chinese had originally hesitated to participate in the Peace Climb was that they knew they would have to work with Tibet to find climbers. "Good," I thought. "Nothing wrong with encouraging the Chinese nationals and Tibetans to work together for world peace."

One day Shatayev commented to me, through his interpreter,

"We can easily tell the American tents from the Soviet and Chinese tents."

"How?" I asked.

"Americans throw garbage into tents; Soviets and Chinese throw garbage out of tents."

"Not any more," I said. "Now all garbage inside tents." The environmental education of our climbing team had begun.

Quite a few visitors hiked up from Paradise, including television crews. While doing a live broadcast, one interviewer asked me what Russian phrases I had learned.

"Nyet probelem," I answered.

Everyone—Soviets, Chinese, and Americans—had begun using that phrase as the stock answer to any question or request. Then the interviewer turned to Vladimir, the Soviet leader, and asked the interpreter standing next to him, "What English has he learned?" The interpreter passed the question to Vladimir, who answered, with thousands of viewers watching:

"The weather sucks."

We all broke up.

In all, we climbed Mount Rainier by five different routes and with almost every member of the expedition, including support personnel. The Tibetans on the Chinese team, wearing jeans and with their climbing boots half undone, smoked and talked right up to the summit.

"Amazing," I grumbled to Warren as I pushed my sixty-year-old body to the summit, two breaths to a step. "Living in Lhasa, up on the Tibetan plateau, they basically walked downhill to the summit of Rainier."

Even more amazing, we all got along famously. Language wasn't a problem; while we climbed we spoke the universal language of the rope, and when we needed to make a decision we communicated through our interpreters.

After two weeks of climbing and team-building we broke up camp and—in keeping with our Earth Day objectives—hauled everything off the glacier and down to Paradise. On the way, Slava walked with me and, in his broken maritime English, explained that he had an infant son, Rustem.

"Is blue baby, like ocean. Will die in Odessa. Only Americans can rescue."

Later I managed to piece together the story. Rustem had been born with a congenital heart defect that required a pair of complex surgeries to correct. The first, and simpler of the two, had been performed in the Soviet Union soon after his birth. The second, more difficult one, had to be done before age two or so. Although American surgeons typically do the procedure with a 95 percent success rate, it was still extremely risky in the Soviet Union. Without the second operation, Rustem would die.

"After Everest," I told Slava, "we'll do everything we can for Rustem."

On the way back to Seattle, Shatayev, the Soviet leader came to me with his interpreter.

"The Soviets are going to lose face," he said.

"How can that be?" I asked.

"The team will have been to America and to China but not to the Soviet Union. Now you must come to my country and climb Mount Elbrus."

"We would like to do that," I assured him, "but we don't have the money or vacation time."

"Our government will pay for everything except airfares for the Americans and Chinese," Shatayev replied. Then he added, "What is vacation?"

"All of the Americans on the team work for a living," I explained. "We don't get paid by the government to go on climbing expeditions like you do. We climb without pay, during time off from our regular work—on vacation." Shatayev couldn't quite grasp this concept and insisted that we come to his country anyway. In the end, I acquiesced, and Dianne and I raised the additional money for the airfare. In September 1989 I took our climbing team to the Soviet Union to join the Chinese and Soviets on Mount Elbrus in the Caucasus.

It was my second trip to Moscow, and once again I was struck by the Third-World condition of the airport and the shabbiness of the city as a whole. "This was the country," I thought to myself, "that was going to 'bury' us." It was clear they were only barely keeping things together themselves. We flew from Moscow south to the Caucasus Mountains, which form the northern border of Georgia, on an Aeroflot Airlines plane so primitive I didn't even have a seat belt to fasten. In contrast to drab Moscow, the countryside of Georgia was lush and green, and as we gained elevation on our drive up to the mountain, the alpine flowers and snowfields were as lovely as they are the world over.

Mount Elbrus, at 18,510 feet, is the highest peak in Europe. When we reached its base, the weather looked uncertain, so even before we were fully acclimatized we set off for the summit. Robert Link and Ed Viesturs rapidly knocked off first one, then the other of Elbrus's twin peaks. Dianne and I stopped in the saddle between the two, at 18,000 feet, and watched the Tibetans almost run to the summit.

Sometime during the weeks since we'd been together on Mount Rainier, the Chinese Mountaineering Association had replaced the Chinese nationals on the team with Tibetans. Their new woman climber, Gui Sang, had been to 26,000 feet on Qomolangma fifteen years earlier. She had been named a Master Sportsman by the government—an honor that provided her and her family a home in Lhasa and a secure income. She was now thirty-five years old and had a five-year-old child, but she was eager to summit the mountain and support our goals. The Soviets had a new, younger interpreter, Boris Valentin, another KGB type, but we were all getting along well.

Back in Moscow, I huddled for the last time with the other two leaders and our translators. Shatayev wanted to know who would be the leader of the expedition. I explained, again, there would be three leaders just as there were three leaders in our respective countries, Gorbachev, Li Peng, and Bush. He argued that if there were a crisis—something unexpected or a major disagreement— there would need to be a final authority. I held out for the triumvirate. Losang Dawa leaned toward Shatayev. After a half-hour of discussion, Shatayev slammed his fist down on the table.

"We will solve the problem democratically," he said with a big grin. I sat there amazed as a high-ranking Soviet communist and a high-ranking Chinese communist voted me, an American, the overall leader of the Peace Climb. It was a democratic election; I accepted the result.

■

On March 1, 1990, after a stop in Beijing, our American team arrived in Lhasa—at 12,300 feet one of the highest cities in the world—to join the other two teams. The Soviets had driven overland, carrying our oxygen tanks and apparatus, and after a warm welcome from both teams, we set to work sorting our fifteen tons of food and equipment and loading it into trucks. A few days later our convoy pulled out of Lhasa and followed a rugged, dusty road deep into the "Mysterious Kingdom" of Tibet.

On March 8 the trucks crawled up away from the Tibetan plateau to a 15,000-foot pass, where we stopped to stretch our legs. I climbed out of the jeep as the dust settled and walked to a spot where some poles with prayer flags had been stuck in the ground. The flags were making a soft fluttering sound, and the wind muffled all other noise. Across the brown plains, a hundred miles away, the earth leaped up into one gigantic mass of rock and snow: Qomolangma. I looked at the mountain, with that plume of ice crystals blowing off the summit I knew so well, and began to cry. It had been twenty-seven years since I had stood on its crest. Now I was back. I thought about the struggle our entire team had waged to reach our goal in 1963. I thought of those before us who had lost their lives trying to achieve that same goal. I thought especially about Jake Breitenbach, who had disappeared into the Khumbu Icefall, and about Barry C. Bishop, who, when the glacier yielded back Jake's body in 1970, returned to bury him near the monastery at Thangboche. And I remembered so clearly that defining moment when Gombu and I stood at the summit.

Honking horns broke the silence and announced that it was time to move on. I wiped the tears away to see my mountain more clearly.

"Hello, old friend," I whispered.

◾

On March 10 we arrived at the foot of the Rongbuk Glacier and set up our Base Camp at 17,500 feet.

In 1921, in the official report on the first Everest reconnaissance, George Mallory described what we now saw:

> The Rongbuk Valley is well constructed to show off the peak at its head; for about 20 miles it is extraordinarily straight and in that distance rises only 4,000 feet, the glacier, which is 10 miles long, no more steeply than the rest. In consequence of this arrangement one had only to be raised very slightly above the bed of the valley to see it as an almost flat way up to the very head of the glacier from which the cliffs at Everest spring. To the place where Everest stands one looks along rather than up. The glacier is prostrate; not a part of the mountain; not even a pediment; merely a floor footing the high walls. At the end of the valley and above the glacier, Everest rises not so much a peak as a prodigious mountain-mass. There is no complication for the eye. The highest of

the world's great mountains, it seems, has to make but a single gesture of
magnificence to be lord of all, vast in unchallenged and isolated supremacy.

With our three national flags snapping together in the wind, we began to
build our home for the next two months. We set up a fifteen-by-twenty-foot
Chinese army tent to serve as kitchen and mess hall and another to house the
Chinese team. The Soviets and Americans lived in smaller Eureka umbrella
tents and two-man tents.

Almost immediately, we ran into a crisis that threatened to cancel the entire expedition. Months earlier, in Moscow, I had discovered that the Soviets
had titanium oxygen tanks that weighed only 7 pounds—just over half the
weight of the British-made tanks we'd used on K2 in 1978. I had asked the Soviets to supply our oxygen tanks and they agreed . . . for $85,000. I told them
that was way over our budget.

"We'll just have to carry the heavier bottles," I said in my most casual
negotiator's voice. The Soviet officials discussed the matter among themselves.

"Can we barter?" they asked. We could, I replied. In the end, we traded
three IBM-compatible computers with Cyrillic alphabet keyboards (our cost
$12,000) for 150 titanium oxygen bottles and 25 masks and regulators.

But now, unpacking the bottles, we could find no oxygen masks or regulators. We called Shatayev over and, after searching through everything with
an increasingly pale face, he said they must have been left behind in Moscow.

Our satellite phone wasn't working yet, so Warren jumped into a jeep with
only a phone number that Shatayev had given him for the manufacturer in Moscow, drove all the way back to Lhasa, and called Dianne in Port Townsend.
Dianne called Senator Ted Kennedy's office, and his staff got her the name
of a Russian-speaking aide in the U.S. Embassy in Moscow. She tried to reach
Moscow, but the Soviets were in the middle of the Lithuanian crisis, and all
the telephone lines from the United States into Moscow were jammed. Unde-
terred, Dianne sent a fax to the U.S. Embassy in Beijing explaining the problem and asking them to send a telex to the aide in Moscow, bypassing the phone
lines. The aide called the phone number Shatayev had given Warren, and the
manufacturer confirmed what we already knew: the masks and regulators were
in Moscow.

But the Soviets needed an export permit to send the gear to China and told

Dianne that it would take about a month to get the permit through the bureau-cracy. After many more frantic calls, the U.S. Embassy in Moscow and the So-viet ambassador to China arrived at a "diplomatic solution": the ambassador's daughter would hand-carry the gear to Beijing herself, as personal luggage. There, uncomfortable with the idea of handing them over directly to the Chi-nese, she passed them on to a reporter with the Soviet *Tass* News Service, who took them to the U.S. Embassy from which they were transferred to the Chi-nese Mountaineering Association. Finally, they were then flown to Lhasa and brought to Base Camp by jeep. Miraculously—and thanks to several twenty-four-hour days of negotiating by Dianne—the entire complex process took only a week.

Meanwhile, at Base Camp, we sorted loads for higher camps. The great ad-vantage of the Tibetan approach to Everest is that as Mallory had described, the Rongbuk Glacier acts as a gently sloping ramp to the base of the mountain. With-out an icefall like the one on the Nepalese side, we could use yaks—eighty-two of them—to carry supplies all the way from Base Camp, through intermediary Camps I and II, to Camp III, our Advance Base Camp at 21,500 feet, just below the North Col. Short and stocky, with enormous horns, yaks are incredibly strong. Each yak carried two 55-pound cartons of gear, one carton on each side. Once the yaks were loaded, their drivers led them up the dusty gray path atop the glacier.

I was fascinated by the Tibetan yak drivers and their animals. You could hardly tell the yaks from the drivers. Like the yaks, the drivers had long shaggy hair, wore yak skin, and smelled like their animals. They slept in yak-skin tents, cooked over yak dung fires, and drank copious amounts of yak butter tea. They lived off the land, migrating with their animals to find pasturage as the seasons changed and had few possessions except for their yaks. Weather-beaten, des-perately poor by western standards, they were nonetheless a jolly group, for-ever laughing and playing tricks on one another.

With an interpreter, I crawled into one of their tents one day to get to know them better. They shared with me a cup of rancid yak butter tea, and we talked until, with smoky tears streaming down my face, I ducked out of their acrid, dung smoke–filled, yak-hide tent and gulped for fresh air. Their happiness was a source of mystery and wonder to us all.

By March 15, just five days after our arrival, thanks to the yak drivers and their animals, Camp III was well established. Now we began pushing the route higher, but the going was steep and difficult right from the start. The climbers had to establish fixed ropes and, occasionally, use jumars to ascend ice faces. Then on the twenty-first, before we were able to get Camp IV established, a blizzard slammed into the mountain dumping two feet of snow on us. The storm blew down the tents at Camp III, and we retreated back to Base Camp, stumbling down the glacier in a whiteout.

That's when the next crisis hit. I had injured my left leg on the retreat, and after a couple of days, the pain increased and my calf began to swell. I remembered Dan Doody almost dying on Everest in 1963 from "a sore calf muscle" that turned out to be a blood clot. Kurt Papenfus, our camp doctor examined me and concluded that it looked like a clot had indeed formed in my calf and that unless it could be dissolved it could kill me. There was only one safe option: a three-hundred-mile ride by jeep to the nearest hospital, which was over the Chinese border, in Kathmandu, Nepal. Ray Nichols and Barbara Fromm would accompany me, and Warren would take charge of the climb. Sick with disappointment, I choked out my goodbyes and left the expedition, not knowing whether I would be able to return. We didn't know at the time that we were beginning an adventure of an entirely different sort.

When we reached the border between China and Nepal, we left our Chinese driver behind, walked and limped across the border, and hired a Nepalese jeep and driver on the other side to take us the rest of the way. Bumping over miserable roads, I was terrified that a clot would break loose and lodge in my lungs, heart, or brain. The rough road turned out to be the least of my worries. A military barricade on the outskirts of Kathmandu was our first clue that we were in the right place but at the wrong time. The citizens had been rioting for days, demanding a return to a more democratic government after nearly thirty years of rule by the king of Nepal. The city was in chaos. With the help of our driver, who spoke a little English and with whom I could communicate, we talked our way through three more barricades manned by heavily armed guards before we reached Kathmandu's Teachers' Hospital, only to discover it was full of dead and wounded rioters.

We found the emergency room and waited with two men from the Netherlands whose companion had a spinal gunshot wound. When the doctors finally got to me, the examination was hardly encouraging; they pulled out a dog-eared English medical journal and, after pulling and poking around on my leg, agreed among themselves there was a good chance I had a blood clot. They took us to a bare room littered with bloody bandages, lay me down on a cot, and using Ray's flashlight for illumination, started me on intravenous Heparin, an anticoagulant.

I hadn't had anything to eat or drink for twelve hours, nor had Ray or Barbara, who sat on the filthy concrete floor, backs against the walls, trying to rest. After pleading for food and drink for what seemed like hours, we had received one bowl of rice and one cup of tea to split among the three of us. We were all badly dehydrated, but in my case it was life-threatening. I needed liquids fast. The king, however, had imposed a strict curfew, and we had been told the police had orders to shoot to kill. We were trapped.

We were also desperate. Ray found out from a sympathetic doctor that there was a café nearby. Despite the risk of being shot, he crawled through a hole in the hospital fence, plunged into the rainy night, and returned a short while later, exultant, with cookies and four cans of Pepsi. He and Barbara each drank one and wolfed down cookies. I drank the other two cans and could swear I felt every cell in my body rejuvenating.

Then the Heparin ran out, and the doctor told me there was no more.

The following morning we heard the sound of a jet taking off and guessed that the curfew had been lifted. Ray went out again, wading through the crowded alleys of the ancient city, and returned later with the doctor from the U.S. Embassy. The doctor had brought more Heparin, but after examining me, he said I needed to get to a hospital that was equipped to determine whether, in fact, I had thrombophlebitis.

"Unfortunately," he added, "the nearest such hospital is in Bangkok, Thailand."

The next morning I hobbled onto a plane for Thailand. Ray decided to go home, and Barbara accompanied me to Thailand. I figured my chances of returning to the expedition were pretty close to nil.

The following day, however, two doctors and two interns in Bangkok ran me through a battery of tests and X rays and diagnosed a torn calf muscle but no blood clot. I was free to return to Everest. It took six days, traveling by plane, jeep, and on foot, to get back up from sea level to our 17,500-foot Base Camp. Completely wasted and no longer acclimatized, I crawled out of the jeep and limped into the waiting arms of my teammates. My heart was pounding erratically; I couldn't just feel it, I could hear it. But when they sat me down to a sumptuous dinner, preceded by vodka and caviar, I felt like a king.

I caught up on our progress. As soon as the weather had cleared, the climbers had put in Camp IV at 23,150 feet and begun pushing to Camp V. Everyone was still healthy, but there was a conflict brewing.

Early on I had realized that this expedition would carry the aspirations not only of the climbers we had assembled but of the nations from which they had come. I was committed to ensuring the safe accomplishment of both. My plan was to have seven camps established on the way to the summit, with Camp VII—

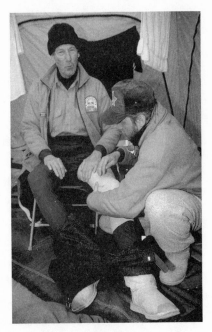

Dr. Kurt Papenfus, suspecting thrombophlebitis, examines Jim's leg at Base Camp. Photo: John Yaeger

the high camp—at about 28,000 feet. This meant, however, that the first summit assault team would have to carry Camp VII on their backs and set it up before going on to the summit the next morning. It would be higher than any camp ever established on Mount Everest and would be a very strenuous carry. My worry was that without such a camp someone might be caught out at night without shelter, and I was committed to making sure that didn't happen. There were already enough tombstones around the base of the mountain; we didn't need to add to them.

The Chinese readily agreed, but the Soviets saw things differently. Most climbers, Americans included, believe that the only way to climb safely in the Death Zone is to climb high and sleep low—that is, spend each day pushing the route higher but return to a lower camp at night in order to reduce the risks of extreme altitude.

In the Soviet Union, though, the modus operandi is to get as high as possible as fast as possible, and then stay there. No amount of medical evidence—including the collapse of one of their own team members, who went too far too fast and was down in Base Camp recovering from cerebral edema—could persuade them. They were rigid. That was the way it was done. Nyet probelem.

The American climbers were furious with the attitude of the Soviets, and for good reason. Stylistic differences aside, there were practical implications for the whole team. First, in order to climb fast at high altitude, the Soviets refused to carry full loads, making our own climbers, as well as the Chinese, feel like yaks for the Soviets. Second, because they insisted on moving high quickly, they consumed supplies and fuel they didn't carry, further complicating the process of supplying camps. Finally, they deteriorated physically much more quickly, placing the entire enterprise in jeopardy.

In my absence the problem had grown, and the Americans, in particular, were fuming; while they humped supplies to higher camps, the Soviets, carrying light packs, made snide comments about the Americans "always being last."

Finally, the Soviets and I struck a compromise: they could climb their way, but they would have to put in the high camp themselves, since the Americans and Chinese had exhausted themselves putting in the other camps.

But we still had a ways to go. What's more, Earth Day was fast approaching, and although we knew we wouldn't summit by then, we still had to get the satellite phone—which had apparently shaken apart on our approach trip—up and running. We were expecting an important phone call.

We owed the high-tech satellite phone to Bud Krogh, who, with Warren Thompson, had originally proposed the expedition years before. He had used his connections in Washington, D.C., to get the expedition recognized by the White House. Along the way, he arranged for us to have the phone. On the day before Earth Day, Warren and others had taken the phone system apart and were trying madly to put it back together. Late in the afternoon, they got it working at last, and then the generator broke down. The Soviets worked furiously on that and had it operational just before the blue hour, that magical mountain twilight that precedes the dark of night.

At 3:00 A.M., at an altitude of 17,000 feet above sea level and with the thermometer registering twenty degrees below zero, Warren and I crawled into the communications tent, lit the Coleman lantern and stove, heated up some tea water, and got ready for our call. At 4:00 A.M. sharp—4:00 P.M. on April 22, Eastern Standard Time, the telephone sitting on the black box rang, Warren turned on the tape recorder, and I picked up the receiver.

"Hello?" I said.

"Hello, Mr. Whittaker?"

"Yes."

"One moment please," the operator said. "Mr. President, I have Jim Whittaker of the Mount Everest Peace Climb. Go ahead sir."

"Hello, Jim, Can you hear me OK?" It was President of the United States George Bush, clear as a bell.

"Hello, Mr. President, I sure can."

"Listen, I wanted to simply send greetings from Earth Day to you and all the climbers from the United States, China, and the Soviet Union. And you know, reaching the top of Mount Everest in the name of peace and understanding reminds all of us on this special day that there is no task that's too great for the human spirit. So thank you for what you are doing, and I also want to congratulate your team on its very practical goal of cleaning up the debris left there by previous expeditions. That will set a great example for the whole world, especially from your unique vantage point there, so we wish you well. In a sense, I wish you were here as one of the great leaders to help celebrate Earth Day, but I think what you are doing is significant and important and will send a great signal to all of us, wherever we may be, on the blessings of a sound environment. So keep it up, and please give my best to everyone that's with you."

"Thank you, Mr. President," I said, and he was gone.

The Soviets and Chinese were amazed, even incredulous, that we had actually talked to him.

"Now," I said, "it is your turn to contact the heads of your governments."

"It's not that easy for us," they said.

"But you must try," I insisted.

Within a week, we did reach both Li Peng, who invited us to come to the Great Hall upon our return, and Mikhail Gorbachev, who honored our team and later issued to Ekaterina Ivanova the highest award a civilian can receive in the Soviet Union. These were proud moments for all of us and gave the expedition the exposure we sought with the citizens of our three countries.

Meanwhile climbers from all three countries struggled to put in Camp V,

Climbers on the route to Camp V. Photo: Steve Gall

at 25,600 feet. The weather had remained clear, but winds were ferocious and it was extremely cold. The only site available was small, with a steep drop-off on one side, and the teams had to excavate tent platforms in deep snow and ice—no easy trick in the Death Zone. Just getting there with supplies was an arduous, eight-hour trip. Returning to Camp IV one evening, one of the Soviet climbers summed it up:

"Is not difficult technical; is difficult physical. Windy. Very cold. Very difficult."

While some of our climbers pushed on from Camp V in sixty-mile-per-hour winds to establish Camp VI, we had another medical crisis. On a supply run to Camp IV, La Verne Woods found herself struggling. She'd made this carry before without difficulty, but this time something was wrong. Out of breath and feeling ill, she got on the radio and called Base Camp. After a quick consultation the doctors ordered her to grab an oxygen bottle and descend immediately, which she did, moving slowly and with great difficulty, with the help of two Soviet climbers, Slava and Alexander Tokarev. Others of us started up from the lower camps, carrying extra oxygen.

When we met them at midnight, halfway between Camps I and II, I was stunned to see how frail and weak La Verne looked. We switched her to a fresh oxygen bottle and escorted her down to Base Camp, where the doctors suspected she was suffering from pulmonary edema. We loaded her into the jeep, and she retraced my route to Kathmandu and then on to Bangkok. Doctors there found a massive blood clot in her thigh, some of which had broken off and traveled to her lungs. They said she very likely would have died within twenty-four hours if she hadn't made it to the hospital. It was a great loss to our team; thankfully, La Verne recovered and went home to the United States.

With Camp VI in place at 26,900 feet, it was time to make summit team decisions. As a group, our remaining climbers were still remarkably healthy and strong, so I decided we would send two climbers from each team to the summit on the first attempt, instead of one. Among the Americans, Ed Viesturs was almost unnaturally strong. In miserable conditions that drove others back down, he had made carry after carry to the high camps, without supplemental oxygen. But that was the problem; he wanted to summit without oxygen. I respected that and was sure he could do it, but I had decided long before that our common goal of getting climbers from all three countries to the summit together—the promise I had made to the Chinese—was our highest priority. To assure success, I required the first assault team to use oxygen. I wanted safety above all else; it wasn't a negotiable issue.

Reluctantly, but true to his promise to himself, Ed chose to wait for the second attempt—a big gamble, since there was no assurance there would be one. I chose our next two strongest climbers, Robert Link and Steve Gall.

Shatayev selected Grigory Lunjakov and Sergei Arsentjev to represent the Soviets. I checked with Shatayev to make sure they would honor the commitment to use oxygen, but the Soviet climbers were evasive. Finally, Shatayev and I got them to promise they would carry oxygen and use it if they fell behind. It was a less than ideal arrangement. The Chinese leader, Losang Dawa, chose Tibetans Gyal Bu and Da Qimi for their summit group. I knew they would use oxygen; that had always been their policy.

I got on the satellite phone and gave Dianne a progress report. "We're in position and everyone is healthy," I reported. "But it's so windy people are flying like kites on the fixed ropes. If this wind doesn't stop, we're going to have a hard time making the summit." Dianne remembered the Native American medicine man who had prayed for—and apparently delivered—good weather for our Pelion Climb on Mount Rainier a few years earlier. She called her friend Susanne Page, who had spent a lot of time among the Navajo and Hopi in New Mexico, to ask for help. Susanne called Mare Sultclah. A highly respected Navajo medicine woman, Mare said it was sheer arrogance to think of stopping the wind. But, she said, she might be able to move it.

On May 1 the first six climbers started from Base Camp and began moving up through the higher camps, fighting high winds and blowing snow. During the night of May 3, at Camp V, a new blizzard hit the mountain, dumping snow at the rate of an inch an hour, with gale-force winds. They spent the following day holed up in their tents, waiting out the storm. The next morning the weather cleared, and despite continuing high winds, they headed for Camp VI.

The next day, May 5, the six climbers left Camp VI and began to climb up to establish Camp VII on the edge of the summit ridge at 28,500 feet. High winds hammered them through the night, but at dawn the wind suddenly vanished. The sky was clear, and only a few clouds drifted slowly across the face of the mountain. I called Dianne.

Top: *The first summit climbers display the disc containing thousands of names and messages from supporters of the Peace Climb. Photo: Steve Gall*
Bottom: *Gui Sang and Ian Wade on the summit of Everest. Photo: Ian Wade*

"It's amazing," I said. "It's perfectly calm here. It's a great summit day. I guess Susanne's Navajo friend must have moved the wind."

"She sure did," she laughed.

"What do you mean?"

"Well," she said, "it's blowing about eighty-five knots here, four trees are down in the yard, and a couple of boats were capsized in Puget Sound—that's pretty unusual for this time of year."

And so on the morning of May 6, in clear and almost calm weather, the assault team headed for the summit—the Tibetans and Americans with facemasks and oxygen bottles, the Soviets without facemasks. Sometime later, Link looked closer at the Soviets and, getting Gall's attention, pointed at them. Their packs held no oxygen bottles. Determined to reach the summit without oxygen, they had violated their agreement with Shatayev and me and, in the process, placed the entire enterprise in jeopardy. Link and Gall, "totally pissed off," kept moving up with Da and Gyal, gradually pulling away from Grigory and Sergei who, despite lighter packs, were now moving slowly without the additional oxygen. (Down at Base Camp, Shatayev took me aside and said, "Don't worry, Jim. It will be taken care of when they get back to Moscow, I promise you." And from the look on his face, I was glad I wouldn't be in their climbing boots.)

The Americans and Chinese reached the top together and were forced to wait another forty-five minutes, risking hypothermia and frostbite, for the Soviets to stumble to the top. Finally, early in the afternoon, down at Base Camp the radio crackled to life. It was Link:

"Base Camp, Base Camp . . . Sergei has reached the summit of Everest. We're all on the top of the world."

The camp erupted in cheers. People were jumping up and down like kids, hugging and kissing each other. Up on the mountain, the six climbers embraced and held a pole from which the flags of their three nations flew. We had done it; it was the summit on the summit.

Over the next three days, another fourteen climbers (including some support staff) reached the top as well. Ed Viesturs did it, as promised, without oxygen. Gui Sang became only the second Tibetan woman to summit. Ekaterina Ivanova, the first Soviet woman to do so, radioed this message to Base Camp:

"I stand on top of the highest mountain on Planet Earth, for all the women in the world. Let there be no more borders, no more war; let us make a safe and clean world for our children and our children's children." I passed her message on to Dianne and within twenty-four hours it hit the papers in all three countries.

Chinese television crews arrived at Base Camp with seventy-two homing pigeons from Lhasa, to represent the doves of peace. They gave one to each of the team leaders, and on command, we tossed them into the air as the others were also being released. The birds circled overhead awhile, then headed back to Lhasa.

Within days—after burning or burying nearly two tons of accumulated trash and packing up the rest—we loaded ourselves and our gear into trucks and jeeps. As I looked back at the foot of the Rongbuk Glacier, there was no sign we had ever been there. Then we headed downhill to a world of thicker air, green plants, and living things. It had been the cleanest, safest, and most successful expedition to Everest in history.

■

We arrived in Lhasa to discover that the Chinese had lifted martial law in our honor; the citizens of the city, free for the first time in months, were overjoyed and lined the streets as our caravan nosed into town. Banners stretched across the street heralding our success, and bands and dancers were in full Tibetan costume. We stopped beneath the massive Potala monastery, which dominates the city, and walked up the long stone walkway to give thanks. Literally thousands of children lined the walk, dressed in their best, most colorful clothing, waving paper and silk flowers and playing drums and Tibetan instruments. Firecrackers exploded, and the crowd cheered and applauded us. We were in tears, overwhelmed by the warmth and affection of the people and deeply honored and humbled by their reception.

The Chinese and Tibetans threw a sumptuous dinner party for us, and during the speeches, which became less formal as the evening wore on, Losang Dawa hauled out several big boxes and handed every member of the team one of Tibet's traditional, elaborately embroidered hats with the fur ear- and forehead-flaps. Well into the party by now, we promptly put them on and wore them for the rest of the increasingly raucous evening, joking and slapping each other on the back. The anger at the Soviet climbers dissipated, and we basked in the warm camaraderie that had grown over the months and been cemented by our success.

The Chinese premier, Li Peng, had invited us all to the Great Hall in Beijing for a big recognition banquet, but although the Soviets and Chinese took him up on the offer, all the American team wanted to do was return home to our families.

■

While we were on Everest, Dianne had been busy trying to find a way to get Slava's two-year-old son, Rustem, the heart operation he needed. She had made sure to mention the boy's plight when she was interviewed about the Peace Climb and had finally been contacted by Healing the Children, a non-profit organization in Spokane, Washington, with an offer of help. They located a pediatric surgeon, Dr. Jack Leonard, and a pediatric cardiologist, Dr. Wes Allen, who were willing to donate their services. Private donations would help cover the hospital costs.

The Goodwill Games opened in Seattle in July, a few months after our climb, and the Soviet climbers were invited to the opening ceremony. We made sure there were tickets as well for Rustem and Slava's wife, Lilya. After the games, Slava returned to Odessa to look after the couple's other children, while Lilya took Rustem to Spokane for the operation. Rustem, whose skin was as "ocean blue" as his father had said, was wheeled into the operating room. Lilya, at sea herself with a foreign language and foreign customs, paced anxiously in the waiting room.

A few hours later, the doctors wheeled Rustem out of surgery. He had the rosy complexion of a healthy, normal, two-year-old boy.

And that, I thought, was exactly what our expedition had been all about.

Chapter Fourteen

LIFE WELL LIVED

It is just a little after breakfast on the morning of August 20, 1998, and I am watching pelicans from the cockpit of a fifty-four-foot steel-hulled ketch moored at a marina near Brisbane, Australia. Not far from the boat, the big, ungainly, ancient-looking birds swoop high into the air, then drop like rocks to the water, hunting for a breakfast of their own.

The ketch is called *Impossible*, the third boat so named and the biggest and most comfortable of the three. It has to be; it is our home. Dianne, Joss, Leif, and I are sailing it around the world.

We've just completed one of the more "exciting" legs of the trip so far. Ten days ago we motored away from our mooring off Noumea in the South Sea islands of New Caledonia, about halfway between Fiji and Australia, and were just approaching the one-hundred-yard wide passage through the reefs that surround the islands when the engine died. Luckily, we already had sails hoisted, and while I worked feverishly to restart the engine, Dianne and the boys sailed us safely through the pass.

With a twenty-five-knot tailwind and ten-foot seas, we decided to press on for Brisbane while working on the engine. After four days of tinkering and swearing, we gave up and sailed on toward Australia without benefit of engine power,

Joss, Dianne, Leif, and Jim in an underwater family photo, Hole-in-the-Wall, Vanua Levu, Fiji, January 1998. Photo: Whittaker family collection

becalmed on some days, buffeted by squalls and gales on others. It didn't phase us much; we were veterans. We'd already been at sea for two years.

◼

By the mid-1990s, after the success of the Peace Climb, Dianne and I had begun to climb up out of the hole in which the O'Malley disaster had left us. My families, both of them, were doing well. Carl, forty-two, was a building contractor and himself a father, having given me two grandsons, Adam and Anthony. Scott, forty, had become the outside manager of the Snoqualmie Pass ski area and had made me a grandfather a third time with the birth of his daughter, Sarah. Bobby, thirty, was traveling the world as the manager of Mudhoney, one of the original Seattle "grunge" bands. I love them dearly.

My "second family" was thriving too. By 1996, Dianne, now forty-eight, had become a marathon runner and had also earned a black belt in Tae Kwon Do. Leif, age eleven, was a straight-A student and an accomplished skier, and soccer and basketball player. Joss, thirteen, was also an expert skier and scuba diver. In addition, with an IQ that apparently is "off the charts," it sometimes seemed like he could do a better job of educating himself than his teachers could at school. Both boys had also done some roped climbing.

Although our life was good in many ways, Dianne and I realized we were spending an enormous amount of time working to meet the high mortgage payments and taxes on the Log Mahal in Port Townsend and doing so at the expense of our experience as a family. A lot of parents reach this realization at some point but decide it's part of the price they must pay to achieve "the good life." After a lot of discussion, we decided the price was too high. We sold our lovely log home, bought the third *Impossible*, pulled Leif and Joss out of school, and in October, set out to circumnavigate the globe. I suspect others thought we were crazy, but to us it seemed the only sane thing to do. This time, however, we weren't racing. We would take as long as it took, learning as much as possible about the culture and natural history of the places where we dropped anchor along the way.

For our route, we followed a simple old nautical dictum: "Go south until the butter melts, then head west." The butter melted near Puerto Vallarta on the west coast of Mexico. We stayed there for a few weeks, exploring a new culture and provisioning the boat for the long southwestward passage across the Pacific to the Marquesas Islands. Farther west, we sailed through the Tuamotu

Archipelago, the Society Islands—including Tahiti, Bora Bora, and Moorea—and American Samoa. Farther west still, we waited out the cyclone season in Fiji, where Dianne celebrated her fiftieth birthday, and we both celebrated our twenty-fifth wedding anniversary.

We've done so much scuba diving in the last two years that sometimes it seems like we've spent as much time under the water as we have sailing across it. Both boys have become experienced divers, and Joss has gone as deep as 185 feet. His passion, not surprisingly perhaps, is marine biology. Along the way, we've home-schooled the boys, although with mixed results. The places we've visited and the people we've met have been far more educational—not to mention interesting—than the textbooks we brought along.

From Fiji we sailed west again to Vanuatu and New Caledonia, finally arriving in Australia. Brisbane itself sits several miles up a river of the same name that empties into Moreton Bay. Protected from the Pacific by Moreton and North Stradbroke Islands, the bay is a vast maze of shifting sandbars and shallows roughly forty-five miles long and twenty miles wide. A dredged shipping channel follows a zigzagging course from the head of the bay on the north to the mouth of the Brisbane River and then turns upriver to the city. Our objective was Scarborough Marina, roughly halfway down the bay.

On our ninth day out of New Caledonia, we rounded Moreton Point and turned south into the shipping lane between Moreton Island and Bribie Island. Normally, we would have lowered our sails at this point and motored down the channel. But, of course, we had no engine. Instead, we had a twenty-knot headwind—which meant that to make any headway down the bay, we had to tack back and forth across the shipping lane dodging a steady stream of massive freighters and tankers that were steaming up and down the narrow channel. Watching the wind shifts, the shipping traffic, and the depth gauge simultaneously, we'd race across the channel and, when the gauge showed only nine meters, quickly come about, sails flapping furiously before snapping taut again, and then race back across the channel, shooting between freighters that loomed out of the squalls crisscrossing the bay. It was hair-raising, exhausting, and gloriously good fun.

◼

I have written this book in bursts, between watches at the helm and during our sometimes extended stays in the extraordinary places we've visited so far—

in effect, looking back through the stages of my life even as I look ahead to the next stage of the voyage. Now, as I bring the writing to a close on this brilliant and warm Australian morning, I am thinking about pelicans and yachts.

The pelicans on Moreton Bay fascinate me. They look as if they are only one step removed from dinosaurs, as if pterodactyls were their first cousins, not their distant ancestors. Their sharply angled, gray-brown wings look almost leathery; their long pointed beaks and flapping pouches seem prehistoric. A flock of pelicans can make you feel like a rank newcomer on this earth and can make the time any human being spends on it seem very short.

When I think about what a blink in time each of us is compared to the 4.5 billion-year sweep of earth's history, it seems to me that the biggest challenge we face is how to create a life of *meaning*. And that brings me to the yachts.

People work hard to achieve what they—and the advertising world—define as "the good life." But the goal itself often seems to keep advancing ahead of them, the way the horizon does as you sail toward it. Here in Scarborough Marina, *Impossible* is surrounded by the trappings of the good life. There are literally hundreds of gleaming sailing and motor yachts—millions of dollars worth of them. Most of them are seldom used. *Impossible* and its crew are the "odd men out" in this crowd; our boat is our home, our transportation, our work—our lives at this moment. Ours is a working boat, not a symbol of the good life.

As he approached death, my father had said he'd "had a good life." He wasn't being sentimental; he meant every word. He certainly didn't mean he had achieved great things or accumulated tremendous wealth. He had worked hard, loved a woman who meant the world to him, raised three children to responsible adulthood, made lasting friendships, gone fishing, and tried to take pleasure from and contribute something to the world around him. His life had meaning.

Many years ago, when our high school yearbooks were being put together, every senior was asked to say what he or she hoped to achieve. Louie wrote, "To join the Forest Service." I wrote, "To be an asset to the world." I don't think I really had any idea what I meant by that, specifically. It was more a yearning than a clear idea. As I near seventy, I'm still working on it. In a way, this memoir is a sort of progress report.

Here's what I've learned so far. First, risk is an inherent part of a life well lived. It's a prerequisite. If you stick your neck out, whether it's by climbing mountains or speaking up for something you believe in, your odds of winning are at least fifty-fifty. If you take risks with preparation and care, you can increase those odds significantly in your favor. On the other hand, if you never stick your neck out, your odds of losing—as in losing out on life's joys—are pretty close to 100 percent. This all seems obvious as I write it, except that we forget it for long periods of time—and feel unsatisfied with our lives as a result.

I think a life well lived is also inseparable from being able and willing to learn continuously. A climber who doesn't learn, almost with every foothold and handhold, is unlikely to be around long enough to have a life well lived. Learning is, in a sense, the flip side of risk. Learning is what happens when you risk a journey beyond what you know and are comfortable with, to something you don't know or aren't comfortable with. Some people my age act like they've seen it all and have nothing much else to learn. But I'm still a learner.

I'm also a bit suspicious of comfort. When people stretch out on a warm beach somewhere, cool drink in hand, or sit in their back yard with a thick steak on the grill, and say, "Ah, this is the good life," they're usually talking about comfort. I like that too, but more and more these days, I believe the key to a life well lived—as distinct from the "good life"—is discomfort. To my way of thinking, discomfort—the discomfort of stretching yourself beyond what you already know or know how to do, of struggling with adversity—is what creates the pearls in a well-lived life, just as it takes an irritant like a bit of sand inside a South Seas oyster shell to produce a real pearl.

The pain of failure has value too. I think there's a sort of hierarchy of living, not unlike the camps on a climb. If you never leave Base Camp, you never get anywhere. Maybe you get to Camp I and try for Camp II, fail on the first attempt, and give up. Live a life that way, and you never, as they say, "get off the ground." Each failure in my life has been painful to me: divorce and seeing my children struggle in its aftermath; business failure and near bankruptcy; mountains, like K2 in 1975, that despite my best efforts we failed to summit; people I have disappointed at one moment or another. What's given my life meaning is the effort to persevere in spite of these disappointments—to push the route to a higher camp. Over the years, hundreds of people have said to me, "It must have taken a lot of courage to go for the summit of Everest in a raging gale." And I think to myself today: "No, what took courage was rebuilding my heart after my divorce, starting all over again after the O'Malley fiasco, taking on K2 a second time, or climbing again after the death of a dear mountaineering colleague, of which there have been so many."

Finally, I believe that to have a well-lived life you have to give something back—to others and to this fragile planet. I feel so damn lucky to be here at all—to have had the love and support of a remarkable mother and father; the companionship of an older brother and a twin, both of whom I love dearly; the miracle of not one but two families and a wife who is my closest friend and partner in adventure; and the sheer joy of nearly seventy years of life in the outdoors. Giving back is a way of giving thanks and of sharing joy with others. I've tried to do that with the environmental policies and programs of REI, with all the courses I've taught, with my work with the National Ski Patrol and the Mountain Rescue Council, with countless speeches and motivational talks to groups ranging from several thousand Boy Scouts to a handful of corporate executives, and with this journey around the globe aboard *Impossible,* which I hope will be for Joss and Leif only one of a lifetime of mind-stretching adventures.

I find myself in sympathy with those early explorers who kept sailing toward the edge of the map, toward the edge of the known, because they simply had to learn what was there. That's what I've done all my life—as a climber, as a businessman, as a sailor, as one frail human being on this great and beautiful planet.

Here in Brisbane, we're a bit more than a quarter of the way around the globe. Soon we'll head west again and north, detouring to India. We'll leave the boat at a mooring for awhile and travel overland to Darjeeling and rendezvous with my old climbing colleague, Nawang Gombu. Then he and I, Dianne, Joss, and Leif will trek to Everest Base Camp.

I want to introduce the boys to the Goddess Mother of the Earth and say, once again:

"Hello, old friend."

INDEX

Abbasi, Shahzada Saeed-ur-
Rashid, 177
Abruzzi ridge (Himalayas), Plate
20
acclimatization, 76, 85
Adams, Brock, 133, 158
Adams, Kirk, 212, Plate 31
Adams, Mount, 70
Alaska Rescue Group, 80
Allard, William, 122, 124
Allen, Durwood, 155, 157
Allen, Wes, 259
Alpine Log Homes, 224, 226
Alpine-style racing, 76
American Alpine Club, 174-175
American-Pakistan Karakoram
Expedition, 99
Amidon, Bill, 26
Anderson, Craig
as member of 1978 American K2
Expedition, 178, 191, 195, 197
pictures of, Plates 19, 25, 29
Anderson, Lloyd, 27, 63, 67, 69, 89,
140, 150
Anderson, Mary, 63
Antoine, Mo, 193
Anvil Rock (Mount Rainier), 40
Arlington Cemetery, 137
Arsentjev, Sergei, 255, 257
Askole, 165-166; Plate 19
Auten, Al, 90, 116; Plates 4-5
avalanches
at Cowlitz Glacier (Mount
Rainier), 45
at Stevens Pass (Washington
Cascades), 53-54

Bading, Helga, 81
Baha, 185
Baig, Honar, Plate 29
Baldy, Mount (Idaho), 129
Baltoro Glacier, 166-167, 186; Plate
18
Banepa, 94
Bangkok, 249
Baron, Janet, 219
Barry, Bill, 135
Bartow, Phil, 207, 209-210, 212
Bauer, Wolf, 31-32, 36, 47
Bech, Cherie
as member of 1978 American K2
Expedition, 178, 188-191, 195,
197, 199-200
picture of, Plate 29

Bech, Terry
as member of 1978 American K2
Expedition, 178, 188-189, 195,
197-200
picture of, Plate 29
Beckey, Fred, 33
Benson, Henry, 50
bergschrund, 38
Bhutto, Zulfikar Ali, 160, 177-178
Billings, Lem, 138
Bishop, Barry C., 90, 105-106, 115,
245
Blue Glacier (Olympic National
Park), 71
Boardman, Pete, 182
Boeing Aircraft Company, 25-26
Bonington, Chris, 178, 181-182
Boone and Crockett Club, 72
Boston Museum of Science, 121
Bourdillon, Tom, 109
Boy Scouts. See scouting
Bramani, Vitale, 143
Breitenbach, Jake, 90, 100-103, 118,
245
Bremerton Naval Shipyard, 26
Brightman, Coach, 53-54
British Survey of India, 87
Brokaw, Tom, 131
Bu, Gyal, 255
Buchwald, Art, 130
Burns, Robert, 27
Bush, George, 252

Calcutta, 92-93
Calgary Inn, 155
Calvin, Warren, 50
Camp Hale (Colorado), 57-58
Camp Muir (Mount Rainier), 40-
41, 90
Campbell, Tom, 19-20, 27
Cannonball Alarm Company, 23
Carbon River (Washington), 36
Casson, Russ, 24, 50
Cave, the (Seattle University), 53
Central Intelligence Agency (CIA),
174-175
cerebral edema, 76
Chair Peak (Washington
Cascades), 37
Chandler, Otis, 130
Chandler, Chris
as member of 1978 American K2
Expedition, 178, 185, 188-189,
191-192, 195, 197
picture of, Plate 29
Cheyenne Canyon (Colorado), 60

Chinese Mountaineering
Association, 236, 244
Chogori. See K2
Chomolungma. See Everest,
Mount
Churchill, Winston, 201
CIA. See Central Intelligence
Agency
Co-op, The, 63-69, 141. See also REI
Compagnoni, Achille, 159, 203
Concordia, 167-168
Conway, Martin, 168
Copland, Aaron, 181
Corbet, Barry
on first American expedition to
Mount Everest, 90, 103, 105,
116-118
pictures of, Plates 4-5
Cowlitz Glacier (Mount Rainier),
42, 44-45
Craig, James, 122, 124
Crews, Paul, 76, 79-81

Daiber, Ome, 31-32, 36, 46-47
Dasso, 162-164
Daumal, Rene, 172
Dawa, Ang, 99, 101, 106-107, 112-
113
Dawa, Losang, 241, 244, 255, 258
Day, John, 62, 70-85
Day, John III, 208-209
Day, John Jr., 80
Death Zone, 100, 250, 254
Denali (mountain). See Mount
McKinley
Denali Pass, 76, 78
Desio, Ardito, 159
Diebold, 23
Dingman, Dave, 90, 105, 118; Plate 4
Disappointment Cleaver (Mount
Rainier), 208-209, 211
Doody, Dan, 90, 92, 102, 106, 248
Dorje, Girmi, 118
Dudh Kosi, 97
Dumordo River, 186
Dunaway, Bil, 38-39
Dunham, Fred, 160, 170; Plate 14
Dyhrenfurth, Günther, 88
Dyhrenfurth, Norman
on first American expedition to
Mount Everest, 87-90, 92-93,
98-99, 103, 106-108, 112-113
pictures of, Plates 4-5

Earth Day, 251-252
Ebert, Ed, 25

Eckenburg, Max, 32
Eddie Bauer, 150
edema, 76
Edmonds, Skip
  as member of 1978 American K2
    Expedition, 178, 185, 188, 191,
    195
  pictures of, Plates 19, 29
Eisenhower, Dwight, 80
Elbrus, Mount, 243-244
Emerson, Dick, 90, 102; Plates 4-5
epistemology classes at Seattle
  University, 53
Eskanazi, Sam, 29
Esquires basketball team, 50
Estcourt, Nick, 182
Evans, Charles, 109
Evans, Dan, 151
Everest, George, 87
Everest, Mount
  first American expedition to
    summit of, 87-119; Plates 3-4
  map of camps and geographical
    features of, Plate 1
  Peace Climb on, 233-258; Plates
    33-40
Explorer Post, 27

Fairchild, Bill, 71
Fauntleroy Congregational
  Church, 51
Fenton, Bill, 51
Fitzgerald, Roy, 212
Flashman Hotel (Skardu), 161
flood at The Co-op (REI)
  warehouse, 68-69
Fort Carson, 60
Fort Lewis, 56
Fromm, Barbara, 239, 248
Fuqua, Ray, 24

Gall, Steve, 239, 255, 257; Plates 34, 38
Gant, Hortense Elizabeth. See
  Whittaker, Hortense Elizabeth
Garden of the Gods, 60
Garhwal Himalaya Expedition, 99
Gasherbrum IV (Himalayas), Plate
  13
Gibraltar Rock (Mount Rainier),
  42-43
Givier, Al, 179
Glenn, Annie, 129
Glenn, John, 129, 131, 138; Plate 9
glissading, 28
global positioning system (GPS),
  231
Goethe, 234
Gombu, Nawang
  on first American expedition to
    Mount Everest, 98-99, 103-116,
    119, 158
  pictures of, 114; Plates 3-6
Goodwill Games, 234-236, 259
Gorbachev, Mikhail, 236, 252
Gorbenko, Lilya, 259

Gorbenko, Mistislav "Slava", 241-
  248, 254
Gorbenko, Rustem, 242-243, 259
Gorman, Leon, 240
GPS. See global positioning system
Grand Hotel (Calcutta), 92-93
Green Apple Pie Restaurant, 64-65
Green, Peter, 157
Grier, Rosey, 135
Grosvenor, Mel, Plate 5
Guye Peak (Washington
  Cascades), 28

Hackett, Dave, 138
Harlech, Lord, 138
Harriman, Averell, 138
Hartsfield, John, 150
Haskell, Mike, 50
Hatch, Don, 130
Hatch River Expeditions, 130
Hatch, Ted, 130
Head, Howard, 61
Head Skis, 61
Healing the Children, 259
Heiskell, Marian Ochs, 155, 157
Henshaw, Kay, 219; Plate 32
Hickory Hill (Bobby Kennedy's
  estate), 128-129, 131-133, 138-139
Hillary, Edmund, 87, 94, 109
Hillary Step, 109
Himalaya Makalu Expedition, 99
histology classes at Seattle
  University, 52
Holzworth, Sheila, 210-212
Horn, Jerry, 207
Hornbein, Tom
  gives medical advice to Jim, 180
  on first American expedition to
    Mount Everest, 90, 105, 115-
    116, 118-119
  pictures of, Plates 4-5
Hotel Royal (Kathmandu), 93-94
Hubbard Medal presentation,
  Plate 5
Humphrey, Hubert, 132-133
Hussein, Manzoor, 161, 163-167,
  175

Impossible
  as Whittakers' home, 264
  competes in races, 218-223
  pictures of, 154, 214, 219; Plates
    31, 41
  Whittakers sail around world in,
    261-262
Index, Mount (North Cascades,
  Washington), 33-36
Ingraham Glacier (Mount Rainier),
  211, 213, Plate 30
International Year of the
  Handicapped, 207
Irvine, Andrew, 110
Ivanitesky, Alexsandr, 235
Ivanova, Ekaterina "Katya", 241,
  252, 257

Jagersky, Diana, 181, 195, Plate 29
Jagersky, Dusan, 179
Jasper National Park, 156
Jerstad, Lute
  on first American expedition to
    Mount Everest, 89, 98, 102-105,
    112, 114-118
  pictures of, 114, 117; Plates 4-5
Jesset, Art, 46, 48-49
John's Island (Washington), Plate 11
Johnson, Lady Bird, 155
Johnson, Lyndon, 132, 136
Johnson, Rafer, 135, 139
Josie (deer), Plate 11

K2 expeditions
  in 1975, 158-176
  in 1978, 177-202
  pictures of, 163, 171, 176, 183-
    184, 189, 192, 196, 200, Plates
    12-29
Kahiltna Glacier (Mount
  McKinley), 75
Karakoram, 164, 177
kata, 110
Kathmandu, 93-94, 248
Kathmandu Teachers' Hospital, 248
Keith, Bud, 211-212
Kendall Peak (Washington
  Cascades), 28
Kennedy, Ethel, 128-129, 135-139,
  144
Kennedy, Jackie, 129
Kennedy, Joan, 129
Kennedy, Joe, 129
Kennedy, John F., 115, 119, 127,
  201; Plate 5
Kennedy, Mount, 121-127
Kennedy, Robert "Bobby", 120-
  139, 144; Plates 7-9
Kennedy, Rory, 139
Kennedy, Rose, 137
Kennedy, Teddy, 122, 129, 159, 178;
  Plate 9
Khan, Mohammed Saleem
  as member of 1978 American K2
    Expedition, 182-185, 187-188,
    201
  pictures of, 183; Plate 29
Khan, Sajeran, Plate 29
Khumbu Icefall (Mount Everest),
  86, 98, 100-104, 113
King, Martin Luther Jr., 132
Kingen, Jerry, 234
Korean War, 56
Krogh, Bud, 210, 233, 251; Plate 38

La Chapelle, Ed, 71
Lacedelli, Lino, 159, 203
Lake Serene (North Cascades,
  Washington), 34
Lasher, Jeanette, 66-68
Lester, Dave, 133, 226
Lester, Jim, 90; Plate 4
Life, 123, 126

Link, Ed, 57, 238, 244
Link, Robert, 238, 255, 257; Plate 34
L.L. Bean, 228
Log Mahal (Jim's and Dianne's house in Port Townsend), 224-226, 262
Luckett, Link, 82-83
Lunjakov, Grigory, 255, 257

Magellan, 231
Magnussen, Carl, 150
Mallory, George, 110, 245, 247
Mancini, Henry, 129
Margaret, Mount (Washington Cascades), 28
Margerum, Amy, 219
Marts, Steve
  as filmmaker on American K2 Expeditions, 160, 172, 179
  joins *Impossible* racing crew, 219
  pictures of, Plates 14, 32
Mayer, Adam, 64
McCarthy, Eugene, 132-134
McDevitt, Justin, 212-213
McKee, Theresa, 53
McKinley, Mount, 74-85
McNamara, Robert, 131, 138
Medvedev, Vitale, 241
Meyers, Ray, 25
Milky River, 97
Miller, Maynard, 90; Plate 4
Ministry of Sports and Physical Culture, 234
Molenaar, Dee, 84, 122-124
Monitor Rock (West Seattle), 19
Morse, Ray, 69
Mount Analogue, 172
Mountain and Cold Weather Training Command, 57-61, 144
Mountain Rescue Council, 31-32, 36, 46-47, 80, 210
Mountain, The. *See* Rainier, Mount
Mountaineering Club of Alaska, 76
Mountaineers Club, The, 27-28, 30, 37, 64, 68
Muir, John, 151
Mullin, Terry, 50

Naiman, Alec, 212
Namche Bazaar, 97, 118
Nance, Bill, 219
National Geographic, 127-128, 161, 206
National Geographic Society
  co-sponsors Mount Kennedy surveying expedition, 121-122
  sponsors first American expedition to Mount Everest, 89
  presents Hubbard Medal to Mount Everest climbers, Plate 5
National Parks Advisory Board, U.S., 155, 157
National Ski Patrol, 36, 54
Nepal, 96. *See also* Everest, Mount

News Tribune (Tacoma, Washington), 174
Nichols, Ray, 239, 248-249
Nixon, Richard, 233
Noessner, Fred, 212
Norgay, Tensing, 87, 94, 99, 109

objective dangers, 34
O'Brien, Chuck, 202, 211-213
O'Brien, Rainier, 213
O'Brien, Tahoma, 213
Oehler, Judith, 211
Olson, Sigurd, 155
Olympic National Park, Blue Glacier, 71
Olympic Peninsula, 30
Olympus, Mount (Olympic Range, Washington), 30
O'Malley, Jim, 227-230
Osborn, Scott, 54, 57, 61, 64
Osborn and Ulland, Inc., 54, 61, 64
Owings, Nat, 155

Page, Jake, 181
Page, Susanne, 181, 255
Paiju Peak (Himalays), Plate 17
Papenfus, Kurt, 239, 248, 250
parade at Lhasa, Plate 41
Parks Canada, 156
Patterson, Blanche. *See* Whittaker, Blanche
Patterson, Leif
  as member of 1975 American K2 Expedition, 160, 169-170, 172, 174
  death of, 179
  joins 1978 American K2 Expedition, 177-178
  pictures of, Plates 14-15
Patterson, Marijke, 179
Patterson, Tor, 179
Payne, Mel, Plate 5
Peace Climb, 232-258; Plates 33-40
Peak XV. *See* Everest, Mount
Pearl Harbor bombing, 25
Pelion Climb, 207, 210-213; Plates 30-31
Pema, Ang, 100-101
Peng, Li, 252, 259
Peters Glacier (Mount McKinley), 78
philosophy classes at Seattle University, 52
Plimpton, George, 130
Polish Route (Himalayas), Plate 20
Port Townsend, 224
porter strike at Urdukas, 167; Plate 12
poster for Peace Climb, Plate 35
Potala, Plate 40
Pownall, Dick
  on first American expedition to Mount Everest, 90, 100-101, 105, 113
  pictures of, Plates 4-5

Prater, William "Bill", 122-124; Plates 4-5, 7
Prather, Barry, 90, 104, 120, 122, 124
Pratt Lake, 151
prusik rope slings, 48
pulmonary edema, 76
Purple Merit Star, 54
Putnam, Bill, 174-175

Qimi, Da, 255
Qomolangma. *See* Everest, Mount
Quabaug Rubber Company, 144-145, 187, 226

racing Alpine-style, 76
Rainier, Mount
  climbing accident at Disappointment Cleaver, 208-209
  Pelion Climb on, 207, 210-213; Plates 30-31
  speed-climbing records set on, 72-73
  as training site
    for first American Mount Everest expedition, 89-90
    for first K2 attempt, 160
    for Peace Climb, 241-243
  view of from West Seattle, 23
  Whittaker twins as guides on, 38-39, 61-62
  Whittaker twins' rescue assignments on, 36-38
Rainier Mountaineering, Inc., 38, 160
Rawalpindi, 161
Reagan, Ronald, 213, 233
Recreational Equipment, Inc. *See* Co-Op, The; REI
Red Mountain (Washington Cascades), 28
REI, 89, 140, 149-155, 203-204. *See also* Co-op, The
Reichart, Lou
  as member of 1978 American K2 Expedition, 178, 184-185, 188, 190, 194-195, 197-201
  pictures of, 184, 200; Plates 21, 29
rest step, 28
Ridgeway, Rick
  as member of 1978 American K2 expedition, 178, 182, 188-189, 190, 192, 194, 197-200
  joins *Impossible* racing crew, 220
  pictures of, 192; Plates 14, 19, 24, 28, 29
Riley, Patty, 239
Roberts, Dianne (Jim's second wife)
  as director of Peace Climb, 239, 246-247
  as member of 1975 American K2 expedition, 158-176
  as member of 1978 American K2 expedition, 177-202
  birth of children, 223, 226
  climbs Mount Elbrus, 244

courtship and marriage to Jim, 155-157
designs Log Mahal, 224, 226
helps with Pelion Climb, 207, 210-213
pictures of
  aboard *Impossible*, 154, 219; Plate 41
  at K2 Base Camp, Plate 29
  diving at Hole-in-the-Wall, Fiji, 261
  with 1975 K2 team, Plate 14
  with Pelion team, 212
  races in *Impossible*, 218-222
  sails around the world, 261-263
Roberts, Gil, 90, 100-102, 104; Plates 4-5
Roberts, James Owen M. "Jimmy," 93, 105; Plate 4
Rodgers, Sally-Christine, 219
Rongbuk Glacier, 247
Rongbuk Valley, 245
Rose, Richard, 212
Roskelley, John
  as member of 1978 American K2 Expedition, 178, 184-185, 189-192, 194-195, 197-201
  pictures of, 184, 192; Plate 24, 29
Roundhouse (Sun Valley, Idaho), Plate 9
Rowell, Galen
  as member of 1975 American K2 Expedition, 160, 164, 170-171, 174-175
  pictures of, Plate 14
Rutherford, Alan, 218, 219; Plate 32

Sabey, David, 234
Sagarmantha. *See* Everest, Mount
Sang, Gui, 244, 256-257
Savage Mountain. *See* K2
Schaeffler, Willi, Plate 9
Schaller, Rob
  as member of 1975 American K2 expedition, 160, 170, 172-173
  as member of 1978 American K2 expedition, , 177-178, 185, 188, 198, 201
  pictures of, Plates 14, 29
Schilling, Van, 218
Schmid, Father, 51-52
Schmitt, Carl, 37
Schoening, Pete, 74-85, 159
Scott, Doug, 182
scouting, 23-25, 27
Seattle Times, 206
Seattle Trust and Savings Bank, 228-229
Seattle University, 51-52
Seattle Water Department, 69
Senner, George, 122-124; Plate 7
Shah, Gohar, Plate 29
Shah, Tajiran, Plate 29
Shakespeare, 41

Shatayev, Vladimir, 241-244, 246, 255, 257
Sheldon, Don, 75, 81, 84-85
Sherpa, 94, 96-99, 102-106, 116-119, 123
Shirra, Wally, 155
Siri, Will, 90, 98-99; Plate 4
Skardu, 161-162
Ski Patrol (Stevens Pass, Washington), 53
Smith, Stephen "Steve", 134, 137-138
Smith, Wally, 204
Snoqualmie Mountain (Washington Cascades), 28
Snoqualmie Pass Ski Patrol, 29
Snoqualmie Pass (Washington Cascades), 28
Solbakken, Knut, Plate 4
Solu Khumbu, 97
South Col team, 105, 115
speed-climbing records on Washington's major peaks, 70-74
Sports Illustrated, 129
St. Helens, Mount, 46-49, 70
St. Louis, Lyle, 31
St. Peter's Basilica, Plate 33
Stanley, Fred, 160, 170; Plate 14
Stefurak, Paul, 212
Steinberg, Ari, 219
Sterno, 66
Stevens Pass (Washington Cascades), 53-54
strike by porters at Urdukas, 167; Plate 12
Su, Keren, 239
subjective risks, 34
Sultclah, Mare, 255
Sumner, Bill, 178, 190, 195; Plates 19, 29
Sun Valley (Idaho), 129; Plate 9
Swiftsure Lightship Classic, 218
Szurich, Nick, 227

Teachers' Hospital, 248
Teamsters Union, 134
Temba, Pasang, 98
Tennessee Pass (Colorado), 59
Tenth Mountain Division, 54, 57
Tenzing, Nima, 98, 102
Thangboche, 97; Plate 4
THAW, 150
theology classes at Seattle University, 52
Thomas, Lowell, 240
Thompson, Warren
  helps with Pelion climb, 210
  roles of in Peace Climb, 233, 236-238, 246, 248, 251-252
Tokareff, Tom, 141
Tokarev, Alexander, 254
Tooth, The (Washington Cascades), 19-21
Trager, George, 150
Trango towers (Himalayas), Plate 16
Troop, 25, 272

Trott, Otto, 36, 46-47, 84
Tsering, Ila, 101
Tuck, Ed, 230-231
Tuck, Jan, 231

Uhlman, Wes, 151
Ulland, Olaf, 54, 60, 64
Ullman, Jim, 90
University of Washington Medical Center, 217
Unsoeld, Willi
  on first American Mount Everest expedition, 89, 98, 101-105, 115-119
  pictures of, 117; Plate 4
Urdukas, 167; Plate 12
U.S. Army Signal Corps, 57

Valentin, Boris, 244
Varnum, Ed, 144
Varnum, Herb, 226
Vibram soles, 144-145, 187
Viesturs, Ed
  as member of Peace Climb, 238-239, 244, 254-255, 257
  pictures of, Plate 34
Vietnam War, 132
Volinn, Ilsa, 158

Wade, Ian, 239, 256
waffle stomper. *See* Vibram soles
Wakefield, Doug, 212
Wales, Pat. *See* Whittaker, Pat
Walsh, Bob, 234-236
Washburn, Bradford "Brad," 121-122, 124; Plate 10
Wegeman, Keith, 59-60
Weidman, Mike, 234
West Buttress (Mount McKinley), 74-85
West Ridge team, 105-106, 115
West Seattle, 22
Western Cwm, 104; Plate 2
Whittaker, Adam (Jim's grandson), 262
Whittaker, Anthony (Jim's grandson), 262
Whittaker, Barney (Jim's brother), 18-22, 24, 26, 30, 225-226
Whittaker, Blanche (Jim's first wife)
  birth of children, 61, 67, 144
  divorce from Jim, 142-149
  hosts visit from Ethel Kennedy and children, 129
  marries Jim, 57-58
  pictures of, 135; Plate 10
  relationship with Pat, 59-60
Whittaker, Bobby (Jim's son), 146-149, 154, 215, 220-222, 262
Whittaker, Carl Bernard (Jim's son), 61, 142, 147-149, 156, 216, 262; Plate 10
Whittaker, Charles Bernard "C.B." or "Cannonball" (Jim's father), 22-23, 154, 215-216; Plate 10

Whittaker, Charles Roberts "Joss"
(Jim's son), 223, 261-262; Plate 41
Whittaker, Hortense Elizabeth
(Jim's mother), 22-23; Plate 10
Whittaker, James Scott (Jim's son),
67, 147-149, 216, 262; Plate 10
Whittaker, Jim
    attends Seattle University, 51-56
    birth of children
        with Blanche, 61, 67, 146
        with Dianne, 223, 226
    career of
        as guide on Mount Rainier, 38-
            46, 61
        at Osborn and Ulland, Inc., 54, 61
        at The Co-op (REI), 63, 203-207
        becomes Magellan's chairman
            of the board, 231
        coordinates Peace Climb, 233-
            258
        faces financial disaster from
            Whittaker/O'Malley fraud,
            227-230
        founds THAW, 150
        helps with Pelion Climb, 207,
            210-213
        in military, 56-61
        in Mountain Rescue Council,
            31-32, 36, 46
        joins Snoqualmie Pass Ski
            Patrol, 29
        receives first product
            endorsement, 143-145
        with Ski Patrol (Stevens Pass,
            Washington), 53
    childhood of, 21-32
    designs Log Mahal, 224, 226
    divorces Blanche, 142-149
    engagement to Theresa McKee, 53
    joins The Mountaineers Club,
        27-28
    marriages of
        to Blanche Patterson, 57-58
        to Dianne Roberts, 155-157
    mountain climbing pursuits of
        1975 American K2 expedition,
            158-176
        1978 American K2 expedition,
            177-202
        first American to reach Mount
            Everest summit, 87-119
        first climbs, 19-21
        first practice climbs, 28-29
        on Mount Elbrus, 243-244
        on Mount Index, 33-36
        on Mount Kennedy, 121-127
        on Mount McKinley, 75-85
        on Mount Olympus, 30
        speed-climbing records on
            Washington's major peaks,
            70-74
    pictures of
        aboard Impossible, 154, 219;
            Plates 32, 41

above Camp 1 on first K2
    attempt, 171
as Boy Scout, 24
as Camp Hale ski trooper, 59
as child, 18, 21, 24
as guide on Mount Rainier, 39
at cabin on John's Island,
    Washington, Plate 11
at Camp III (K2), Plate 22
at helicopter evacuation from
    above Thangboche, Plate 4
at K2 Base Camp, Plate 29
at Mount Kennedy, Plates 7-8
at presentation of Hubbard
    Medal, Plate 5
at REI store on 11th Avenue, 140
at Roundhouse (Sun Valley,
    Idaho), Plate 9
breathing oxygen after
    descending Mount Everest
    summit, 114
diving at Hole-in-the-Wall,
    Fiji, 261
during leg examination at
    Mount Everest Base Camp,
    250
finishing paperwork in
    Skardu, 183
hugging Gombu, Plate 6
on Esquires basketball team, 50
on Mount McKinley, 74, 77-78
on summit of Mount Everest, 8
preparing to leave Camp II for
    Mount Everest summit,
    Plate 3
returning from Mount
    Kennedy, Plate 10
walking on First Avenue in
    downtown Seattle, 55
with 1975 K2 team, Plate 14
with Mountain Rescue team, 32
with National Parks Advisory
    Board, 157
with Pelion team, 212
races in Impossible, 218-223
receives Purple Merit Star, 54
sails around the world, 261-263
shares lessons learned in life,
    264-266
spiritual beliefs of, 55-56
Whittaker, Leif Roberts (Jim's son),
    226, 261-262; Plate 41
Whittaker, Louie (Jim's twin brother)
    career of
        as guide on Mount Rainier, 38-
            46, 61
        at Osborn and Ulland, Inc., 54
        founds Rainier Mountaineer-
            ing, Inc., 38
        in military, 56-61
        in Mountain Rescue Council,
            31-32, 36, 46
        joins Snoqualmie Pass Ski
            Patrol, 29

with Ski Patrol (Stevens Pass,
    Washington), 53
childhood of, 21-32
joins The Mountaineers Club,
    27-28
marriage of, 58
mountain climbing pursuits of
    first climbs, 19-21
    first practice climbs, 28-29
    on Mount Index, 33-36
    on Mount McKinley, 75-85
    on Mount Olympus, 30
    1975 K2 American Expedition,
        160-162, 168-170, 172
    speed-climbing records on
        Washington's major peaks,
        70-74
pictures of
    as Boy Scout, 24
    as Camp Hale ski trooper, 59
    as child, 18, 21, 24
    as guide on Mount Rainier, 39,
        62
    on Esquires basketball team, 50
    on Mount McKinley, 74, 77-78
    walking on First Avenue in
        downtown Seattle, 55
    with 1975 K2 team, Plate 14
    with Mountain Rescue team, 32
    trains Pelion team, 210
Whittaker, Pat (Louie's wife), 58-61
Whittaker, Peter (Louie's son), 208-
    209
Whittaker, Sarah (Jim's
    granddaughter), 262
Whittaker/O'Malley, Inc., 227
Whittaker's Chalet, 91
Wickwire, Jim
    as member of 1975 American K2
        expedition, 158-161, 169-170,
        172, 175
    as member of 1978 American K2
        expedition, 177-179, 184-185,
        188, 190-192, 195, 197-201
    pictures of, 200; Plates 14, 25, 29
Williams, Andy, 129-130, 137
Williams, Claudine, 129
Wilson, Rod, 83
Windy Corner (Mount McKinley),
    84-85
Woods, La Verne, 239, 254

Yellow Band, 116

Ziegler, Ellen, 227

ABOUT THE AUTHOR

For most people, reaching the summit of the highest mountain on earth—indeed, being the first American ever to do so—would be life's zenith. For JIM WHITTAKER, one of the twentieth century's great adventurers, climbing Mount Everest was just the beginning.

Whittaker was a confidant of Bobby Kennedy and the CEO of the nation's largest member-owned cooperative, the outdoor gear powerhouse REI. He also led the first successful American expedition to the summit of K2, the world's second-highest but most dangerous mountain, and was organizer and leader of the extraordinary 1990 Mount Everest International Peace Climb, which brought the Soviet Union, China, and the United States together in common cause. Whittaker remains a sailor and explorer who, at age 70, circumnavigated the globe with his family aboard their sailboat *Impossible*. Jim Whittaker has lived a life of high adventure and rare achievement.

ABOUT THE MOUNTAINEERS

Founded in 1906, THE MOUNTAINEERS is a Seattle-based nonprofit outdoor activity and conservation club, whose mission is "to explore, study, preserve, and enjoy the natural beauty of the outdoors. . . . " The club is now the third-largest such organization in the United States, with 15,000 members and five branches throughout Washington state.

The Mountaineers sponsors many classes and year-round outdoor activities in the Pacific Northwest and supports environmental causes by sponsoring legislation and presenting educational programs. If you would like to participate in these organized outdoor activities or the club's programs, consider a membership in The Mountaineers. For information and an application, write or call The Mountaineers, Club Headquarters, 300 Third Avenue West, Seattle, Washington 98119; (206) 284-6310.

The Mountaineers Books, an active nonprofit publishing program of the club, supports the club's mission by publishing travel and natural history guides, instructional texts, and works on conservation and history.

Send or call for our catalog of more than 300 outdoor titles:

The Mountaineers Books
1001 SW Klickitat Way, Suite 201
Seattle, WA 98134
800-553-4453
mbooks@mountaineersbooks.org
www.mountaineersbooks.org